Race and Class in Latin America

Institute of Latin American Studies
Columbia University

Race and Class
in Latin America

Magnus Mörner
Editor

Columbia University Press
New York and London   1970

The Institute of Latin American Studies of Columbia University was established in 1961 in response to a national, public, and educational need for a better understanding of the nations of Latin America and a more knowledgeable basis for inter-American relations. The major objectives of the Institute are to prepare a limited number of North Americans for scholarly and professorial careers in the field of Latin American studies, to advance our knowledge of Latin America through an active program of research by faculty, by graduate students, and by visiting scholars, and to improve public knowledge through publication of a series of books on Latin America. Some of these studies are the result of research by the faculty, by graduate students, and by visiting scholars. It was also decided to include in this series translations from Portuguese and Spanish of important contemporary books in the social sciences and humanities.

This volume is a product of a joint collaboration between Columbia and Cornell Universities. Under the direction of Dr. Magnus Mörner, a conference on race and class in Latin America was held at Columbia University in December 1965. The various contributions, edited by Dr. Mörner, represent a broad diversity of area and emphasis within the general topic of race and class relations. At a time when much critical thought and action is focused on racial matters in Anglo-America, it is particularly interesting and enlightening to observe just how the many diverse racial threads of Latin America became interwoven and juxtaposed.

The publication program of the Institute of Latin American Studies is made possible by the financial assistance of the Ford Foundation.

[v]

Acknowledgments

The funds required for the preparation of the manuscript of the present volume and the holding of the Conference on Race and Class in Latin America during the National Period held in New York City on 16–18 December, 1965, were provided by the Latin American Studies Program of Cornell University and by the Institute of Latin American Studies of Columbia University. As Editor I am very much obliged to the directors of these two centers, Professors Tom E. Davis and Charles Wagley, for good advice and cooperation. The staff members of the two centers have been most helpful. I am also deeply obliged to Mr. Richard V. Moore, executive director of the Center for International Studies of Cornell University, for his invaluable assistance during the final stage of preparation of this book. The Columbia University Press offered excellent cooperation. Besides the assistant editor, Mr. Arnold Clayton, and the copy-editor, Mrs. Mary Freeman, various persons have assisted in the preparation of the manuscript as translators and typists. To all these collaborators, my sincere thanks.

The authors of the reports and papers presented at the meeting have shown much understanding and patience in the lengthy process of preparing this volume. Some of them revised their manuscripts to meet the purposes of the publication. The authors of papers in Spanish or Portuguese have carefully checked the translations of their papers. Special mention should be made of Dr. Harry Hoetink, who submitted his paper for publication despite having been unable, because of illness, to attend the meeting. The cooperative attitude on the part of the authors has greatly facilitated Mr. Clayton's and my task in editing this volume.

Magnus Mörner

Contents

CONTENTS

Race and Class in Latin America

Abbreviations

AGN   Archivo General de la Nación, Mexico City

AGNM Archivo General de la Nación, Montevideo

HAHR The Hispanic American Historical Review, Durham, N. C.

RIHGB Revista do Instituto Histórico e Geográfico Brasileiro, Rio de Janeiro

Introduction

Magnus Mörner

Few topics are more timely today than race and class. The rising political power of previously neglected social groups has thrust these issues to the forefront both in public life and in the university. In the United States and in Latin America marked social changes have occurred that impel the inter-American scholarly community toward a reexamination of old assumptions and a careful search for new empirical data.

Since 1492 the fusion of three racial stocks (Caucasoid, Mongoloid, and Negroid) on a scale elsewhere unparalleled has formed the substructure of Latin America's evolution. In turn, miscegenation has given rise to an increasingly complex pattern of social differentiation in which racial appearance (phenotype) and origin were originally major factors. It is not surprising that the variety of race relations within Latin America itself and the contrast that these relations present to conditions in some other parts of the world have excited considerable interest among scholars. Yet, although much has already been written about race and society in Latin America, current generalizations often are based more on outmoded theories and prejudices than on acquaintance with basic scholarly works. There is, indeed, an urgent need to bridge the gap between scholarly research and "common knowledge" in this field.

Moreover, this is a problem to which many disciplines may fruitfully devote attention, and there is much to be gained by pooling their various insights and points of view. The study of race relations today properly falls within the purview of anthropology and sociology, but the importance of the past is such that when it has not been studied by historians, the sociologists and anthropologists have

[1]

been forced to do it themselves. Other disciplines, such as art history and social psychology, also have important roles to play in the investigation of this infinitely vast and complex subject.

It is with these purposes in mind that the present book has been prepared. It is interdisciplinary in approach, its authors are drawn from many countries, and they are all concerned with the issue of race and class in Latin America, especially in Mexico and Brazil. The original impetus for its preparation was a conference held in 1965 under the joint sponsorship of Cornell University's Latin American Studies Program and Columbia University's Institute of Latin American Studies. The conference drew some of its inspiration from the previous conference on "Mestizaje in the History of Ibero-America" organized in 1960 by the Library and Institute of Ibero-American Studies in Stockholm, Sweden, of which I was at that time head.[1]

During 1964–1965 the present writer suggested and was asked to organize a conference on the topic of race and class as part of the Cornell Latin American Year. Columbia University agreed to co-sponsor the project and to share the financial responsibilities. The meetings were held on the New York City campus of Columbia University on December 16–18, 1965. The discussions were intensive and animated and included participation from the floor. Tapes of the sessions are in the possession of the Latin American Studies Program of Cornell University.

A standard procedure has guided the preparation for publication of the material presented at the Conference: (1) papers and reports in Spanish and Portuguese have been translated into English; (2) except for the few instances which appear as footnotes, the discussion at the meetings has been excluded; (3) the material has been rearranged into an order more suited to the format of a book; (4) footnotes have been reworked for the sake of uniformity; (5) the texts

---

[1] *El mestizaje en la historia de Ibero-América* (Comisión de Historia del Instituto Panamericano de Geografía e Historia, Mexico City, 1961). Also in *Revista de Historia de América,* Nos. 53/54, 127–218. In 1964 in connection with the Twenty-Sixth International Congress of Americanists, the distinguished Madrid journal, *Revista de Indias,* devoted a special issue to different aspects of the study of "Mestizaje," and in August, 1965, a conference on the same topic was held by the Peruvian Academy of History.

have been revised slightly and in one case abbreviated in order to facilitate reading by the general public. All translations and revisions of any importance have been approved by the authors, who, therefore, remain responsible for the texts.

I regret that, for reasons of space, it has not been possible to include in this collection the interesting papers by Fernando Cámara Barbachano, Juan Comas, Marvin Harris, George A. Kubler, Seymour Menton, and D. F. Solá.

No attempt has here been made to impose upon the authors specific definitions of the two basic concepts in the title. In view of the fact that even scholars belonging to the same discipline—not to mention those who do not—differ widely in definition and usage of these concepts, such an effort would have been presumptuous rather than realistic. One valuable by-product of bringing these contributions together is precisely to highlight the complexity of defining such terms.

With regard to "race" all the present authors naturally suggest, explicitly or implicitly, that during the national period "racial" distinctions no longer necessarily reflected the genetic composition of individuals; rather, they were based on a combination of cultural, social, and somatic considerations. The term "ethnic" often has been used in the literature to convey this connotation. In 1958, Professor Charles Wagley suggested that the term "social race" be adopted instead.[2]

It is even more difficult to arrive at a common definition of "class" despite the extreme frequency with which it is used by social scientists. Functionalists and nonfunctionalists, Marxists and non-Marxists offer widely divergent interpretations; whereas some scholars stress the difference between social class and status, others use the terms almost synonymously.[3] The political scientist Charles An-

---

[2] Charles Wagley, "On the Concept of Social Race in the Americas," *Actas del XXXIII° Congreso Internacional de Americanistas*, I (San José de Costa Rica, 1959), 403–17.

[3] Note how involved the definitions of "class" given in works of reference turn out to be: *The Social Sciences in Historical Study* (Social Science Research Council, New York, 1954: Bulletin 64), p. 48, defines social classes "as aggregates of individuals, often without specific inherent differentiating

derson suggests in this volume that the concept of social roles affords an analytical tool better suited to the infinite complexities of the Latin American situation. In any case, the arguments over definition only serve once again to underline the numerous intricacies of the issue.

Other complex problems surround the use of "caste" and "caste society." Sometimes caste system is defined simply as a structure of social differentiation or stratification in which vertical social mobility is virtually nil. At other times, defined in more detail, it coincides with the Hindu prototype. In either of these cases, strict application of the concept to Latin American conditions will encounter great difficulties. Even within the rigorously hierarchical, multiracial social system of the colonial period a certain degree of vertical social mobility was by no means excluded. Indeed, for certain individuals socioracial "passing" has always been feasible in the Latin American environment. Perhaps some scholars who use the term "caste" and "caste society" when analyzing Latin American colonial society have not escaped being unduly influenced by the fact that the people of the colonial era used the word "casta" to designate individuals of mixed blood. Properly, however, "casta" is a medieval, Iberian word designating any kind of human or animal group.[4] When the Portuguese arrived in India they applied "casta" to the peculiar Hindu system that they found there. It is chiefly from this use of the word that the scholarly term is derived; that the Iberians also used the word "casta" in the New World does not imply per se any similarity or relationship between the "sociedad de castas" and the Hindu type of stratification. Some students have used the phrase "caste society" to describe what might otherwise be called a hierarchical, corporate society with fixed estates. In Marxist terms such a society would form a contrast to a capitalist one composed of

characteristics, who enter into and maintain relations with one another on a basis of equality, in contrast to other members of the community from whom they are distinguished (for the moment at least) by socially recognized standards of inferiority and superiority." See also, for example, Sugiyama Iutaka, "Social Stratification Research in Latin America," *Latin American Research Review*, I (Austin, Tex., 1965), 8.

[4] J. Corominas, *Diccionario crítico etimológico de la lengua castellana*, I (Madrid, 1954), 722–24.

INTRODUCTION

"classes" defined according to the relationship of its members to the means of production.

The word "Indian" constitutes another point of confusion. Although Amerindian is, strictly speaking, the scholarly term for the first settlers of the New World, the more common designation "Indian," used in almost all the chapters here, has been retained since there could be no confusion with the inhabitants of India. Some of the contributors have used "indígena" to convey the socioracial connotation that has been gradually acquired by the concept of "Indian." Other contributors have used the terms more or less synonymously.

Finally, the increasingly common use of the term "mestizaje" requires some comment. Derived from "mestizo" (mixed blood), *mestizaje* means miscegenation, that is, biological fusion. But in Latin America, *mestizaje* has also been used increasingly to refer to cultural and social fusion rather than to miscegenation. As the term *mestizaje* has come into greater use, its meaning has become more and more diffuse. The Mexican anthropologist Juan Comas[5] has long warned about the confusion bound to arise from using the term *mestizaje* in a social and cultural context. The natural solution would be that of making a clear and systematic distinction between *mestizaje* (miscegenation) connoting biological fusion and acculturation (and ultimately assimilation) which refers instead to the process of cultural mixture. In any case, it is clear that the problem of definition will continue to plague students of race and class for some time to come.

The first of two principal aims of this book is to focus attention on topics that until now have been largely neglected or ignored and to encourage reinterpretation and reassessment on a more solid basis of information than has hitherto been available. The second aim is to survey the present state of knowledge regarding race and class. I believe that these purposes have been fulfilled to a large degree. Further, it is to be hoped that this volume will provoke thoughtful reactions and open up new leads for future research.

The juxtaposition of the two concepts "race" and "class" is espe-

[5] *El mestizaje en la historia de Ibero-América* (Comisión de Historia del Instituto Panamericano de Geografía e Historia, Mexico City, 1961), 96.

cially appropriate when dealing with Latin America since the two concepts are there so closely linked. The structural alterations of society which have characterized that area's history since independence have worked profound changes upon the relationship between the races. Both Richard Graham and Florestan Fernandes suggest that basic economic and social changes, such as urbanization, lay at the root of the movement toward abolition in Brazil. Professor Fernandes goes further and suggests that the European immigrant took the place of the slave in the emerging class society, thus marginalizing the Negro elements. Referring to Mexico, Gonzalo Aguirre Beltrán shows that there the Negro, on the other hand, was much more easily assimilated within the new society of economic classes than was the highland Indian. Carlos M. Rama comes to the same conclusion with respect to the Negro ex-slaves as compared to the mestizo-gauchos.

The growth of urban centers impelled by the burgeoning export economy is similarly described by François Chevalier for Peru, where it contributed to the expression of a new ideology regarding the place of the Indian community and its relationship to society as a whole.

The powerful effect of economic and political change upon social relations appears as a theme in almost all the chapters below. Whether this change may be considered beneficent or not naturally depends upon one's point of view, the group being examined, and the particular country affected. Thus, Manning Nash sees the economic change that swept over Middle America in the nineteenth century as a devastating one for the Indian communities, whereas Moisés González Navarro speaks of it as impelling the process of "mestizaje" or acculturation: the difference is not in substantive content but in tone.

The research of Florestan Fernandes, Octavio Ianni, and some other Brazilian and American scholars has tended to diminish the contrast that was supposed to have existed between race relations in Latin and Anglo-America. Prejudice and discrimination are universal phenomena. Nevertheless, differences between the pattern of race relations in different parts of the Americas and of the world are certainly significant enough to present fascinating problems. The

Caribbean, heterogeneous culturally as well as racially, is an especially rewarding field for research oriented in this direction. Harry Hoetink's paper on race relations, immigration, and social stratification in the Dominican Republic during the nineteenth century must be considered a pioneering study. As Dr. Hoetink sees it, comparative analysis should pay more attention to the status of the mulatto than hitherto has been the case. He believes that the mulattoes are accepted more readily in the Iberian societies of the Caribbean and elsewhere than in the Anglo-Saxon ones because the Iberian or Mediterranean definition of whiteness (somatic norm image) allows for a darker shade. At another level, Mario Vázquez compares the assimilation of Negroes into Peruvian society with that of European and Asiatic immigrants there, and concludes that the former were more successful because they did not preserve any nationalist feeling toward what was originally their homeland.

In Part IV the authors consider the present state of research in their respective disciplines or suggest the interdisciplinary possibilities which studies of race and class open up. To begin with, a historian, a political scientist, and a sociologist point out the major trends within their fields of study. At first sight, it appears that there is a rather large body of literature devoted to the topic. On closer inspection, however, it becomes clear that a great deal of research remains to be done and that work of high quality is limited to a few seminal monographs. Charles Anderson suggests, in fact, that the entire theoretical structure regarding the relationship between race and class on the one hand and politics on the other has to be rethought. Octavio Ianni emphasizes the degree to which the extant literature in Brazil has been directed at perpetuating myths that serve the interests of dominant groups. The present writer points to several specific and immediate research needs, including the history of the idea of race from the independence movements to the present, the numerical aspects of ethnic group relationships during the entire National Period, and Asiatic and European migration to the region, all of which have so far been inadequately treated.

The disciplinary variety of the papers offered in this volume will no doubt cause some difficulties for the reader. Sociologists, historians, anthropologists, economists, and geographers do not speak in exactly the same language. But the additional effort required of both authors and readers is highly worthwhile because, as Hilgard O'Reilly Sternberg puts it in his chapter on geographical research regarding race and class, "the study of man, culture, and environment forms a continuum."

At the same time, there is no doubt that the contributions contained in this volume present only a very fragmentary picture of the evolution of society and socioracial relationships in the immensely vast and heterogenous region of Latin America. It is to be hoped that future efforts will be able to fill in more and more of the canvas. Indeed, although each author is responsible for his own opinions, and these need not necessarily coincide with mine, the choice of topics reflects our firm belief that each is worthy of scholarly attention and suggests rewarding roads for further research and interpretation.

PART I

The Abolition of Slavery
and Its Aftermath

CHAPTER 1

The Integration

of the Negro into the

National Society of Mexico

Gonzalo Aguirre Beltrán

Gonzalo Aguirre Beltrán, Director of the Inter-American Indian Institute in Mexico City, here points out several factors that enabled the Negro ex-slave to become integrated into the class society of Mexico during the nineteenth century, factors that were lacking in the case of the Indian. These factors, he says, can be best examined at the end of the colonial period, when the slave-based economic system was declining because of internal contradictions within that system itself. When the "caste" system was deprived of its legal sanction at the time of independence the process of integration of the African elements became almost complete. This accounts for the paucity of documentary material on the Negro during the nineteenth century.

Students of Mexican social history know that there is an abundance of documents in the *Archivo General de la Nación* on various aspects of the colonial period, from the Conquest to the War of Independence. Documents can also be found quite easily concerning the history of the so-called Indian kingdoms and empires which existed before the arrival of the Europeans. Paradoxically, the researcher confronts the most difficult problem when he attempts to round out his knowledge of the pre-Columbian and colonial worlds with a study of the formative stage of the national period, which had as its background the convulsive landscape of the nineteenth century. There is a lack of pertinent documents and those which do exist are not readily available.

At first glance, the integration of the Negro population into Mexican society appears to have started during the formation of the national society or soon after. It is generally acknowledged that the slaves who contributed to Mexico's genetic make-up became so completely integrated into the process of *mestizaje* that it is now very difficult for the layman to distinguish the Negroid features of the present population as a whole. Although this implies that the integration of the Negro has been achieved during a certain historical period, there is another very different interpretation which is not dependent on the availability of facts for the national era.

The integration of the Negro population into the national society is, in fact, a process which began with the transfer of Negroes to the European colonies in America. This process continued during the three centuries of foreign domination and the first century of the national era, and today it is in its final stages. It took place in those countries where Negroes were an important segment of the total population and in certain other countries, such as Mexico, where miscegenation has blurred the original differences but where a few isolated nuclei of Negroes can still be identified by their racial characteristics.

If we consider integration as a continuing process and not as a completed phenomenon, the study of the problem requires an interdisciplinary focus made up of historical, ethnographic, and ethnohistorical components.[1] History will give us a knowledge of the past; ethnography will permit us to understand the present; and ethnohistory will help us interpret the process in its global context and give it, through the interplay of history and ethnography, a more exact interpretation. Ethnographic studies of the Negro in Mexico and, in particular, of interethnic relations between the national populations and the Negroes and between the Negro and Indian populations will provides us with a knowledge of those integrative mechanisms which encourage unity and those seigneurial mechanisms which oppose it. The comparison of present-day mechanisms with

[1] Gonzalo Aguirre Beltrán, *La población negra de México, 1519–1810. Estudio etnohistórico* (Mexico City, 1946).

those which have operated in the past is a methodological exercise which has always yielded fruitful results.

The historical study of the Negro, on the other hand, reveals that his integration into the national society was accomplished legally at the time of independence when the Constitution, the ideological charter of the Republic, abolished slavery and the "caste" structure. Upon closer inspection, this legislation was but the confirmation of a socially sanctioned situation, which was the inevitable result of the contradictions of the colonial system. Political independence and structural social change were interrelated phenomena which emerged from the colonial experience in which they had been gestated.

The fact that the leaders under whom independence was achieved originally had opposed the movement sometimes obscures the truly revolutionary nature of the War of Independence. By upsetting the colonial social structure of castes developed for purposes of exploitation, the War of Independence created the conditions necessary for the emergence of a society divided into classes. The transition from caste to class was perhaps the most transcendental result of the wars of emancipation. The effects of this structural change were not felt immediately because the political and social changes were more rapid than the economic ones.

It appears then that a historical analysis which places the end of Negro integration during the initial years of independence would explain the absence of documentation of the process of integration during the nineteenth century. Since integration had been achieved legally with the abolition of slavery and the destruction of that social structure which had been based on biologically defined strata, the Negroes and mixed-bloods had ceased to be classified as "castas." In democratically conceived postrevolutionary society, all citizens, regardless of race or ethnic affiliation, were to have equal rights, loyalties, and obligations. Consequently, neither the statistical registers, the fiscal records, nor other official documents make the distinctions which were characteristic of the "caste" system that had been replaced now by a more liberal approach.

The fact that slavery, the caste system, and colonial exploitation were abolished legally did not, of course, mean that the colonial structure disappeared simply because a constitutional system was adopted. Today, in those regions where the Indians have found refuge, it is possible to discern remnants of the colonial environment. The Indians, incorporated into communities, and the *Ladinos*, who, though members of the national society, constitute a backward sector within the rural areas, live in interethnic conflict of the supersubordination type characteristic of relationships in a colonial environment. Their existence reveals that there are still large groups in the population which are not yet integrated into the national society, despite the legal suppression of the caste system.

The case of the Negro and part-Negro population is very different. In some Pacific coastal areas, especially Costa Chica, there are still Negro communities which are easily distinguished from their neighbors by a certain remnant of colonial culture and by the somatic characteristics of their inhabitants. Nevertheless, the relations between these communities and the principal city of the region differ greatly from the seigneurial relations among Indians.[2] The Negro-*Ladino* relationship is as egalitarian as is possible between persons of different classes. What is important is that the Negro, unlike the Indian, does not view the *Ladino* as his superior and, when the communications media break his secular isolation, he integrates himself spontaneously and without compulsion into the national society.

The confrontation between the past and the present revealed by ethnohistorical method permits the student to investigate the phenomenon of integration as a process which should be studied from its origins in the colonial era. The paucity of documentation for the national period thus can be overcome by the ethnohistorical method. If the origins and development of integration can be found and studied in the colonial era, and if the mechanisms for and against integration can be observed through ethnographic investigation, it is possible to assume that the beginnings of the process of integration can be studied through historical investigations of the colonial epoch. The final stages of the process can then be studied through ethnographic investigations of the present situation, which is nothing more than a continuation of the development started during the nineteenth century. It is therefore possible to investigate the integra-

---

[2] Gonzalo Aguirre Beltrán, *Cuijla; Esbozo etnográfico de un pueblo negro* (Mexico City, 1958).

tion of the Negro population into the national society by studying the process during colonial times, especially toward the end, and obviously transitional part, of that era.

In order to escape the status in which he found himself, either by birth or by capture in a "just war," the Negro had to obtain his liberty. Then he would cease to be a member of a caste dishonored by servitude to become part of another caste composed of men who were called free. He could obtain his freedom by enfranchisement or by flight. Enfranchisement, however, did not mean that the Negro was completely free for, although it exempted him from the duties of a slave, it did not grant him full rights. The juridical position of the enfranchised or liberated Negro was an intermediate status between slave and vassal. His entire life was conditioned by the stigma of having been a slave. With none of the rights but all of the duties of those born free, the status of the former slave in society was that of a marginal individual.

The slave could purchase his freedom by paying the master his original market price. If he had acquired a trade that increased his value, a third party would set the fee to be received by the master. Although it might be expected that few slaves could obtain their freedom in this way, by the end of the colonial era manumission was not infrequent among urban slaves. Such was not the case in the mines, *ingenios*, and certain plantations, where the inventories of slaves frequently listed runaways but not manumissions. Most of the Negroes who managed to change status were young or of low value. There were, however, Negroes who paid for their freedom in installments by agreeing to serve their masters for a given period of time.[3]

Occasionally a slave obtained a small cash loan from some usurer and was thus free to change masters, although under different legal conditions.[4] Some strange situations resulted from the Negroes' efforts to attain freedom. For example, if the owner refused to accept money from his slave, the latter might buy another slave with his savings and exchange him for his freedom.[5] Clauses in the master's

[3] Archivo General de la Nación, Mexico City (hereinafter abbreviated as AGN), Ramo Civil, tomo 918, expediente 4; Civil, 918, 4.

[4] AGN, Historia, 408–48.

[5] AGN, General de Partes, 5.302.

will often granted freedom to domestic slaves, usually the females, as a reward for good service.[6] In such cases, the manumission might be motivated by religious fervor: The owner, about to be judged by God, sought to bribe the celestial judges who were to assess his actions on earth. But there were some cases of voluntary manumission by a master during his lifetime,[7] such as the freeing of female slaves who produced many offspring. Their children, of course, remained slaves.[8]

During the early years of the colonial era, consideration was given to the freeing of certain Negroes to avoid rebellions and mutinies. The metropolitan authorities believed that liberating slaves after a period of servitude would encourage them to settle peacefully on the land.[9] These ideas reflected the influence of the *Siete Partidas* by which a slave was granted liberty if he married a free woman, became a priest, had served for thirty years, or bought his own freedom. But the circumstances which gave rise to the liberal slave codes of Spain were not present in her colonies. The colonists obtained the revocation of manumission for marriage to a free woman and, from the Mexican *Concilios* of the sixteenth century, they obtained a prohibition against Negroes entering the clergy. If they never tried to obtain a repeal of the clause by which slaves were liberated after thirty years of good service, it was because the life expectancy of a Negro worker was not that long.

The slave situation continued until the middle of the eighteenth century, when colonial policy was transformed by the enlightened despotism of the Bourbons. This change coincided with a trend in New Spain toward manumission, which was rooted in the decline of the slave-based economic system. As a result many ex-slaves were thrown onto the free labor market. During the second half of the eighteenth century, it was decreed that runaway slaves from neighboring countries (but not from the dominions of Spain itself) who reached New Spain should be freed on the premise that they had fled from Protestant colonies in order to embrace Catholicism.[10]

[6] AGN, Reales Cédulas Duplicados, 18.81.
[7] AGN, Civil, 922–23.
[8] AGN, Hospital de Jesús, 146.439; AGN, Reales Cédulas, 148.47.
[9] Vasco de Puga, Cedulario (Mexico City: 1878), p. 33.
[10] AGN, Reales Cédulas, 70.25, 142.216.

In 1806, however, when slaves with revolutionary ideas which threatened Spain's control of her own colonies fled from Santo Domingo, this decree was forgotten.[11]

The enfranchised Negro had to register with the *Caja de Negros* for the payment of the tribute.[12] As long as he remained a slave he was exempt from this tax, but with freedom, like the Indian, he became subject to a poll tax. The same tax was levied against Negro mixed bloods, even if they held military posts, and it was not until the end of the colonial period that they were exempted from what Fray Antonio de San Miguel called an "odious tax." [13]

Military service was another obligation of the freed Negro and mulatto. During the initial years of Spanish dominion, the colonial government's only source of military strength were armed colonists whose chief interest was the conquest and discovery of new lands. Although these men remained ready to defend their positions and *repartimientos,* in time the fear of an Indian uprising disappeared, and except for settlers on the frontier who were subject to attack from unassimilated Indians, the colonists enjoyed relative security. After the organization of the colonial system, the metropolitan government left defense of the colony to its vassals and when the need arose, the colonists gave up their normal pursuits to enlist in the militia. Service in the militia was in fact the duty of all free male citizens, but the country was vast and the number of Spaniards small. Having become accustomed to the soft peacetime life, the colonists sought to evade the hardships of military service which their ancestors had undertaken so courageously. The scarcity of militiamen was especially noticeable in some of the more strategic but less hospitable outposts of the colony. Since they were used to harshness of climate, the Negroes were stationed in regions considered unfit for Spaniards. Thus, companies of *"Pardos"* and *"Morenos,"* commanded by white officers, were founded and saw service

---

[11] *Ibid.,* 197.105.

[12] *Recopilación de Leyes de los Reinos de las Indias,* 4 vols. (Madrid: 1756), VI.5.8; VII.5.2; AGN. General de Partes: 1.140, 7.340; AGN. Reales Cédulas Duplicados: 3.14, 3.186; AGN. Reales Cédulas: 5.169, 11.113, 122.55, 138.2; AGN. Ordenanzas: 2.223.

[13] Alexander von Humboldt, *Ensayo Político sobre el Reino de Nueva España,* transl., 4 vols. (Paris, 1822), I, 202.

throughout the colony. By the eighteenth century, there were colored troops in most of the important cities of the colony.

The application of certain militia regulations to the Negroes and mulattoes was problematical because of their anomalous social status.[14] They did not enjoy the rights and privileges of free men and, consequently, they should not have had the obligations of citizenship. For example, militiamen were permitted certain privileges, such as exemption from tribute and the use of special uniforms, arms, and decorations. Nevertheless, although Negroes and mulattoes were forced into service because of the colony's military needs, they were prohibited by law from using firearms, or wearing the silk or expensive decorations to which they were entitled as militiamen.[15] This contradiction was resolved in favor of the Negroes and mixed bloods in 1765, when a regular army was created. The Negroes and mulattoes then became professional soldiers, despite doubts about their loyalty caused by their frequent desertions.[16] The important point here is that their inclusion in the army as free men implied a weakening of the caste system.

Those sixteenth-century Spaniards who became artisans or small merchants in the cities had organized themselves into feudal-type guilds. In order to maintain their privileged position, they established regulations which prohibited colored persons, slaves or freedmen, from entering the principal trades.[17] Thus they avoided competition from groups whose greater numbers and needs might have challenged their position.[18] In practice, the guilds prevented colored people from obtaining honest jobs. This encouraged vagrancy and other antisocial activities (theft, prostitution, delinquency) which only further emphasized the Negro's marginal status.

[14] *Recopilación de Leyes*, VII.5.10.

[15] *Colección de documentos inéditos relativos al descubrimiento, conquista y organización de las antiguas posesiones de ultramar* 13 vols. (Madrid, 1885–1900), X, 274; AGN, Ordenanzas, 1.79, 1.86, 1.102, 2.105, 2.5, 4.26; AGN, Reales Cédulas Duplicados, 1.124, 3.82, 3.116, 3.137, 5.355, 5.305, 5.511, 8.62, 8.35.

[16] Rómulo Velasco Ceballos, *La administración de don Frey Antonio Maria de Bucareli y Ursúa*, 2 vols. (Mexico City, 1936), II, 59.

[17] Francisco del Barrio Lorenzot, *Ordenanzas de Gremio de la Nueva España* (Mexico City, 1920), p. 31.

[18] *Actas del Cabildo de la Ciudad de México (1524–1623)*, (Mexico City, 1889–1906), V.275; AGN, Ordenanzas, 1.51, 1.36.

Similar restrictions applied to bureaucratic jobs and the liberal professions.[19] The Roman Catholic Church prevented the Negro from entering the religious orders, a discriminatory practice maintained for centuries. As late as 1739, Pope Clement XII reiterated the prohibition, holding that the mestizos and mulattoes were "individuals generally despised by society, unworthy of holding public office and of directing the spiritual life of others." [20]

As long as colonial exploitation remained profitable, the demand for slaves was so great that barely enough could be supplied to the developing economy. Unable to compete with the Spaniards as skilled laborers, the Negroes and mulattoes were forced to compete with the slaves for unskilled jobs. Of course, the free laborer had to work harder and longer in order to earn a salary than the slave whose labor involved no such expense. As long as the free Negroes and mulattoes did not represent an important part of the labor market, their salaries varied according to the fluctuations in the supply and demand of slaves.[21] When free labor was available and cheap, as was the case during the last years of the seventeenth century and the early eighteenth century, the slave system collapsed because slave labor was more expensive than free. By the end of colonial times, the mines of New Spain were worked exclusively by free mulattoes and only in emergencies (such as strikes or mutinies) were slaves employed.[22]

The substitution of free labor for slave suggests that large numbers of free men without permanent jobs were available in the unskilled labor market. The colonial authorities considered these unemployed men vagabonds and sought to resolve the problem by repression.[23] Capitán Don Félix Calleja, "Subdelegado" of Aguasca-

[19] *Recopilación de Leyes,* V.8.40; AGN, Reales Cédulas Duplicados, 2.48.

[20] Mariano Galván Rivera, *Concilio III Provincial Mexicano* (Mexico City, 1859), p. 42; Francisco Antonio Lorenzana, *Concilios Provinciales* (Mexico City, 1769), p. 104; Nicolas León, *Las castas del México Colonial* (Mexico City, 1924), p. 6.

[21] AGN, Ordenanzas, 2.223.

[22] AGN, Padrones, 3.1; Velasco Ceballos, *La administración de don Frey Antonio Maria de Bucareli y Ursúa.*

[23] *Actas del Cabildo,* IV, 228.273; *Cartas de Indias* (Madrid, 1877), 263, AGN, Reales Cédulas Duplicados, 3.7, 3.181, 4.43, *Recopilación de Leyes,* VI, 4.2; VII, 5.4.

lientes during the last decade of the eighteenth century, left a full description of the geographical and occupational mobility of the free laborers who went from the mines in the Center to the haciendas in the North and South, hiring themselves out for meager wages at a time when overproduction of cereals, coupled with shrinking internal demand, revealed the contradictions of the colonial economic system.[24]

The slaves who were unable to obtain their freedom by other means often ran away, although escape was discouraged by threats of punishment and imprisonment.[25] The urban slaves could find refuge in the larger cities where they could pass as freedmen. The rural slave, who had fewer opportunities to obtain his freedom, went into the mountains, where he founded *palenques* and enjoyed a freedom which constantly had to be defended. Such Negroes were called *cimarrones*. The viceregal police were always ready to fight them, since their very existence defied the colonial order. They were not only a bad example for other slaves, but also a threat to the peace of the countryside where, organized into groups, they attacked the poorly defended farms and ranches and even assaulted guarded packs of mules or horses. Yet the cimarrones lived not from what they stole but rather from what they grew. They settled and planted their *milpas* on lands usurped from the slave haciendas.

Unlike the Indian, whose rights to community property were recognized, and the Spaniard, who received private lands as a settler or in recognition of his conquests, the Negro and mulatto, even free, could not own land. By squatting on a hacienda, he broke the established order and for this reason, during the early years of the colonial era, the rural aristocracy sought to destroy such settlements. The struggle between Spanish colonists and cimarrones was marked by a series of skirmishes in which neither side was able to destroy the enemy completely.[26] On several occasions the colonial government sought to sign treaties with the cimarrones. The most

---

[24] AGN, Padrones, 5.1.
[25] AGN, Ordenanzas, 1.34, 2.13; AGN, Reales Cédulas Duplicados, 3.130.
[26] AGN, Mercedes, 6.208, 5.230; AGN, General de Partes, 4.94, 6.137, 6.211, 5.65; AGN, Inquisición, 102.3; AGN, Reales Cédulas Duplicados, 5.134, 5.803.

notable efforts occurred in 1608 when San Lorenzo Cerralvo was founded [27] and in 1768 when the Pueblo Nuevo de la Real Corona was established on the banks of the Tonto River.[28] In both cases the cimarrones obtained rights to the land and to municipal self-government along the lines of the Indian republics.[29] The cimarrones, unlike the Indians, never formed corporate groups; had this been possible, they would have gone from the slave caste to the Indian caste, instead of remaining in a middle position between the two castes.

Other Negroes, settled in palenques without permission from the colonial authorities, also organized themselves according to the model of a republic (which the Spaniards had conceived for the Indian population), especially on the Pacific coast where these fugitives could defend themselves well against expeditions of armed colonists. With the consolidation of enlightened despotism in Mexico, the marginal position of the Negro republics was respected and from them came the recruits for the militias of Pardos and Morenos.

Freedom for the Negro, achieved either by enfranchisement or flight, was a factor which undermined the colonial order. Spain's recognition of the Indians' right to hold land and have a share in the means of production was important because it gave them a position (no matter how low) within the colonial order. The free Negro, on the other hand, went from the slave caste to an intermediate position between slave and freeman. Thus, he was relegated to the marginal position of middle caste, of an "outcast"; in other words, he was denied a position in the colonial order. Unable to compete with the Spaniards who were organized into guilds, these outcasts formed groups of vagrants, *léperos* in the cities, vagabonds in the rural areas.

By obtaining land rights, either by treaty or tacit agreement, the cimarrones also undermined the biological stratification that underlay the caste system. Both enfranchised and runaway Negroes were marginal men, without a definite caste. Consequently, they were the segment of the colonial population which, along with the Indian-

[27] AGN, Historia, 31.48; AGN, Inquisición, 283.26, 284.77.
[28] AGN, Historia, 359.3.
[29] AGN, Civil, 1670.4.

Spanish mestizo group, became integrated most readily into the national society that could offer them an identity (as a Mexican) and a status (citizen). At last, they had won a definite position in the social structure.

If one part of the population is to remain separate from the national society as an ethnic minority, two types of complementary conditions must develop simultaneously: one, the minority must acquire a set of differentiating characteristics that give it cohesion: and two, it must confront a set of obstacles which compels it to remain separate.[30] At the end of the colonial era, these conditions prevailed among the Indians but not among the Negroes or mixed bloods.

Racial differences, which constitute one of the most important differentiating characteristics, undoubtedly were visible among newly arrived Negroes. They were so few in number at the close of the colonial period, however, that Baron von Humboldt assumed that the number of imported Negroes in New Spain always had been small. The absence of Negroes was especially noticeable in the cities and mines of the central region. This was not the case, however, in the *ingenios* and plantations of the tropical area. But the leading nonwhite group in these places was not pure. Rather, it was a mixed blooded population of Negro-Indian and Negro-white whom the Spaniards called "castas." Although some of these "castas" were identifiable somatically, others were not and passed for Spanish.

The weakening of the "casta" system and the corruption of the colonial administration, exacerbated in the final moments of the colonial era, permitted the mixed bloods to buy their way into a better "caste" by bribing priests (who registered births) or officials of the Real Hacienda (who took the tax census). On the other hand, priests and royal officials often had to accept as Spaniards some individuals whose dark complexion might have excluded them from the best caste. Toward the end of the colonial regime, *mestizaje* between castes was so great that there were few "pure" individuals, except for those who had recently arrived from Europe and

[30] Marvin Harris, "Caste, Class and Minority," *Social Forces*, 37 (1959).

the isolated Indians. In the eighteenth century, marriages between mulattoes and Spaniards, especially Criollos, were not uncommon. The desire to rise to a better caste, which was characteristic of the mixed blood population, is an important objective proof that that segment of the population never sought to constitute a true caste, isolated from the rest by endogamy and social immobility. Consequently, racial differences were not a sufficiently strong factor to give cohesion and a sense of identity to an ethnic minority made up of Negroes and mulattoes.

Cultural differences were far more important than racial distinctions as mechanisms which prevented the integration of ethnic groups into the national society. An examination of the more significant cultural differences shows their crucial importance for the Negro and mulatto. First, there was the language barrier. The Spaniards attempted to consolidate the colonial structure by imposing Castilian as the official language. To the missionaries and clerics fell the task of spreading the faith and diffusing the Spanish tongue, which acquired much prestige as the language of the conquerors. In the final years of Spanish domination, the teaching of Castilian was required in city as well as rural schools run by parish priests. Indian languages were held in low esteem; over the years, they diminished in number until only about one hundred survived as the media of communication of an equal number of unassimilated ethnic groups. The Negroes brought to New Spain came from different regions, each with its own language. Upon arrival, they were dispersed often as a deliberate means to prevent contact among speakers from the same linguistic group. Occasionally, the African languages were used to conjure spirits in curative rites, but it is not known whether they also were used esoterically in religious ceremonies or for everyday communication. The Negroes in New Spain were forced to learn Spanish as the only means of communication with Spaniards, other Negroes, or mulattoes. In order to speak to an Indian, however, a Negro would have to learn his language. The mulattoes' mother tongue was usually Castilian. In the tropics, where the Negro displaced the Indian, the influence of African speech on Spanish was evident in changes of syntax and intonation, but these modifications produced nothing more than a rustic dialect which was not an obstacle to general communication. The imposition of an official language gave the Negro and mulatto an instrument of integration which facilitated their accommodation into the national society.

Since it was so readily visible, distinctive dress was one of the differentiating features of an ethnic group separate from the national society. For religious reasons, the missionaries forced the Indian to cover his nakedness with European clothes; these, in combination with the native costumes, gave rise to a distinctive dress for each indigenous group. Even today there are tribes which have maintained their colonial dress with but minor modifications as an outward manifestation of their membership in the community. The Negro and mulatto also were obliged to cover the naked parts of their bodies with European clothes, but only in a few cases have they maintained their particular dress. Examples are the *jarocha* or *china poblana* which identified the Negro-Indian mixed-blood. In general, the Negroes and mulattoes dressed in the Spanish style, changing their wardrobes according to the dictates of fashion. There were laws, often violated, which forbade the Negro to wear jewelry or other decorations, carry arms, or use other status symbols reserved for the *hidalgo*. These prohibitions, however, did not produce a distinctive costume which would identify the Negro as a member of a given ethnic group. This situation favored the Negro's integration into the national society.

A third differentiating factor was housing. In some rural areas, a few Negro groups introduced the round African hut, which has remained a symbol of foreign origin and lack of integration into national society. The urban Negro lived in the same housing as other citizens. What differences existed were largely a reflection of divergence in income level.

Of great importance to the Indian but of little significance to the Negro were differences in diet. Specifically, there were foods which were considered Indian because of the ingredients or the way in which they were prepared. This was not the case with Negroes and mulattoes; the rural slave's diet was rich in animal proteins, and colonial decrees ordered that the nutrition of the urban slave be sufficient and balanced. The diet of the free Negroes and mulattoes —léperos and vagabonds—was poor but not distinctive.

Unlike the Indian—who was generally involved in a self-contained and self-sufficient subsistence agricultural economy directed toward the conspicuous consumption of goods which only rarely emanated from the external market—the Negro and mulatto, whether slave or free, were engaged in the colonial capitalist economy aimed at supplying the mother country. Their functional roles included primary occupation on the plantations and in mining, secondary occupation in the *obrajes*, and tertiary occupation as domestic servants. This diversity of activity and participation in the capitalist economy facilitated the Negroes' entry into the economic structure of the national society.

The view of the world held by the Negro and the mulatto at the close of the colonial period was not very different from the criollo's. To be sure, between the two extremes, represented by an educated elite and ignorant peasants, there were differences in the level of knowledge and the degree of reliance on rational thought or magic. Yet these differences were not as radically divergent from each other as they were from the concepts of the Indians who preserved a set of ideas derived directly from ancient Meso-American thought and barely modified by acculturation. Basically, the conditions for the integration of the Negro and mulatto were as favorable as they were unfavorable for the Indian.

The cultural aspects of Negro and mulatto life were not sufficiently distinct to serve as instruments of ethnic identification. Racial characteristics were visible and undesirable in a small percentage of the total population; in the majority of cases, Negroid features were overlooked and the individual could be included in a higher caste. Since by the end of the colonial epoch racial characteristics were blurred, the association between those features and certain legal restrictions was largely inconsistent. Those restrictions were never enough to cause individuals to establish themselves in separate, segregated groups.

Racial segregation, which had been strict during the consolidation of the exploitative colonial system, became less rigid and, in time, permitted movement from one caste to another. Residential segregation was the rule for Indians but not for Negroes and mulattoes who lived among the Spaniards and were classified as *gente de razón*. As such, they were subject to civil and ecclesiastic laws, the application of which varied according to the dictates of privilege, but which were substantively the same for the Spaniards. Social segregation, which at first had determined all relations between Negroes and Spaniards, in time became more flexible. In the churches, market places, schools, cities, and rural areas, separation gave way to open contact between blacks and whites.

The Negroes and mulattoes, unlike the Indians, were not considered a separate caste. The Indians maintained and defended the colonial structure which had organized them in corporate communities that were endogamous and subordinate in the social hierarchy, and which relegated them to primary occupations in the economy. On the local level, the Indians had reconstructed agrarian or agrarian-artisan communities very similar in structure and cultural content to the pre-Columbian social organization dislocated during the conquest. They accepted certain modifications which permitted their adjustment to the colonial order as separate and differentiated entities.

The case of the Negroes was very different. Since they entered New Spain under adverse conditions, they were unable to reproduce their African social structure and culture. In those instances where the colonial authorities recognized the Negroes' rights to land and to municipal government, they built their communities according to the Indo-colonial models and adopted the culture of New Spain.

The nature of ethnic relations during the colonial era has been a subject of much discussion. To some, these relations were nothing more than a colonial variation of class relationships. They assert that the caste structure is limited to Hindu society and that to speak of "castes" out of that context is confusing. Further, it diverts our attention from the heart of the matter, which is the conflict of classes, to secondary aspects of the problem.[31] I must disagree

[31] Melvin Tumin, "Cultura, Casta y Clase en Guatemala," *Integración Social en Guatemala* (Guatemala, 1956), pp. 163–91; Charles Wagley and Marvin

with this revolutionary interpretation first enunciated at the *Primer Congreso Indigenista Interamericano* held in Pátzcuaro and still defended passionately by some. Colonial social stratification was based on a graduated series of positions, openly called castes by colonial officials, which were determined by racial, economic, and social differences. These social strata functioned rigidly during the consolidation of the colonial system and gave rise, from the very beginning, to a series of contradictions which finally destroyed it.

Within this system of "castas," the Indian was forced into a subordinate position which he later defended with even more tenacity than those who had conceived it originally. This became an effective mechanism for assuring the continuity and survival of Meso-American culture, the patrimony of the Indian caste. With independence and the abolition of the system of "castas," the Indians, who were the largest group within the colonial population, were unable to integrate themselves into a national society based on class rather than caste. They remained in separate ethnic groups because various parts of the country offered them places of refuge where they could maintain the caste structure. These still exist today and impede complete integration.

The Negroes, mestizos, and mulattoes, enfranchised or runaways, constituted the second largest group of the population at the close of the colonial epoch. The definitive destruction of the caste system resulted from its inability to contain the growing numbers of these marginal men without a distinct position in the structure, which consequently came to lack an adequate base of support. The integration of the Negro into the national society was the inevitable result of his untenable position, of his marginal place within colonial society, an undesirable situation which was resolved by the abolition of the caste system itself.

Harris, *Minorities in the New World* (New York, 1958); Oliver C. Cox, *Caste, Class and Race: A Study in Social Dynamics* (New York, 1959); Benjamin N. Colby and Pierre I. van der Berghe, "Ethnic Relations in Southeastern Mexico," *American Anthropologist,* LXIII (1961), 772–92; Rodolfo Stavenhagen, *Essai comparatif sur les classes sociales rurales et la stratification dans quelques pays sous-developpés* (diss., mimeo, Paris, 1964); Julio de la Fuente, *Relaciones inter-étnicas,* (INI, Mexico City, 1965).

CHAPTER 2

The Passing of the
Afro-Uruguayans From Caste
Society into Class Society[1]
Carlos M. Rama

The breakdown of the corporately and hierarchically organized Spanish colonial society and the creation of a capitalistic class society, in which social mobility became progressively easier, forms an interpretive framework for many studies of Latin America's past. In this study of Afro-Uruguayans, Carlos M. Rama, a historian and sociologist at the University of Montevideo, places the end of the slave system within this conceptual matrix. Not only was the "caste society" much weaker in Uruguay than it was in other parts of the colonial Spanish Empire, but its breakdown was also being impelled at the end of the colonial period by the rapid absorption of that area into the international economy. By the same token, slavery was there primarily an urban phenomenon, although the proportion of slaves in the total population was larger than often assumed. The wars of independence against Spain and Argentina as well as Portugal and its successor, the Brazilian empire, not only lasted for two decades but also often took on the quality of a civil war, thus rending the fabric of society and opening up the way for rapid social change. So the Negro slave was not only freed but also divested of his fixed status and this fact enabled him to participate in the class society more fully than either the few Indians or the mixed-race gauchos of the interior.

Although the socioeconomic structure of Latin America devel-

[1] The paper is an abbreviated translation by the Assistant Editor of the author's 39-page manuscript (Ed. remark).

oped after the rise of capitalism and its open society of classes, the pattern of stratification that took root there, and that survives today in certain areas, more nearly resembles a caste system. Within Indo-America, anthropologists and sociologists have shown this to be the case in Guatemala, Peru, and Bolivia, where the caste systems only recently have entered their ultimate "crises." As the well-studied example of Brazil proves, the transition from castes to open economic classes is also a recent phenomenon in the zones of heavy Afro-American population.[2]

This article will attempt to show that the crisis of the caste system in Uruguay began around the turn of the nineteenth century and entered its critical phase during the era of revolution between 1810 and 1830. Thanks to the presence of lower caste elements in the patriot armies and the collapse of the colonial regime, a new society could begin to evolve. As freedmen and later, slaves, took up arms, learned trades, and became aware of their civil rights, they effectively joined the new social order. This development is reflected both in the appeal of liberal-democratic ideology and the enactment of abolitionist legislation. Thus, the caste system, which had never become firmly entrenched in Uruguay, was replaced by an incipient, indeed premature, capitalist society of open classes. Thus political revolution carried within it the seeds of social revolution.[3] That Uruguay was probably the first country in the New World to undergo such a transformation has had profound sociological implications which help explain the uniqueness of its modern institutions.[4]

Development of the Slave Caste in Uruguay, 1726–1810

The beginning of the slave caste can be traced to the establish-

[2] See, for example, R. Bastide and F. Fernandes, *Brancos e negros em São Paulo*, 2nd ed. (São Paulo, 1959); F. Fernandes, *A integracão do negro à sociedade de classes* (São Paulo, 1965).

[3] This implies the rejection of the opinion expressed by Charles C. Griffin, *Los temas sociales y económicos en la época de la Emancipación* (Caracas, 1962), as far as Rio de la Plata is concerned.

[4] See C. Rama, *Ensayo de sociología uruguaya* (Montevideo, 1956); *Las clases sociales en el Uruguay* (Montevideo, 1960); *Sociología del Uruguay* (Buenos Aires, 1965).

[29]

ment of the first cities in the Banda Oriental. Colonia do Sacramento, founded by the Portuguese in 1680, was an important center of the slave trade for a century. Although Montevideo was established in 1721 by 131 free Spaniards who had neither serfs nor slaves, by 1738 the Cabildo was requesting the importation of slaves to remedy the labor shortage. By 1743 the trade was a systematic operation increasingly dominated by the Portuguese, who re-exported Negroes to Uruguay from Brazil. Since only a minority came directly from Africa, most slaves reaching Montevideo were *ladinos,* already baptized and trained, rather than "savage" heathen *bozales.*[5]

It is almost impossible to estimate correctly the number of slaves brought to Uruguay because of lacunae in the archives, complications in the colonial tallying system, the prevalence of smuggling, and the use of Montevideo as the port of entry and place of quarantine for slaves en route to other parts of La Plata and Chile.[6] Of more direct interest is the percentage of Negro slaves, freedmen, and mulattoes in the general population.

As Table I indicates, people of African origin never constituted more than 26 per cent of Uruguay's population, a proportion significantly lower than that in the neighboring colonies. For example, in Rio Grande do Sul in 1819, 30.7 per cent of the populace was enslaved, and Buenos Aires remained approximately one-third Negro until the 1850s.[7] In the Andean colonies the scarcity of Negroes was counterbalanced by the abundant supply of Indian serfs; in the

[5] Even after the English *asiento,* 1713–1750, the English were behind the trade (I. Pereda Valdés, *Negros esclavos y negros libres* [Buenos Aires and Montevideo, 1941], p. 39). For imports in 1743 see R. Schiaffino, *Historia de la medicina en el Uruguay,* II (Montevideo, n.d.) 157. On the role of the Portuguese see Elena F. Scheuss de Studer, *La trata de negros en el Río de la Plata durante el siglo XVIII* (Buenos Aires, 1958).

[6] Rolando Mellafe, *La introducción de la esclavitud negra en Chile,* (Santiago, 1959), part III, ch. 3. The statistics presented by Paulo de Carvalho Neto, *El Negro uruguayo hasta la abolición* (Quito, 1965), pp. 26–40, are not reliable.

[7] For Rio Grande, see A. Ramos in *Estudios de historia de América* (Mexico City, 1948), p. 159; cf. Jovellino M. De Camargo in *Estudos afrobrasileiros* (Rio de Janeiro, 1935), p. 162; for Buenos Aires see José Ingenieros, *Sociología argentina* (Buenos Aires, n.d.); for Chile cf. Mellafe, *La introduccion de la esclavitud negra en Chile,* p. 252.

THE PASSING OF THE AFRO-URUGUAYANS

TABLE I

A. *Population of Montevideo 1726–1843*

Year	Whites	Slaves	%	Freed-men	%	Indians	%	Total
1726	131							131
1756[a]	798	141	15					939
1760[a]	1,739	350	11					2,089
1778[b]	2,902	700	16	594	8	73	22	4,260
1803[c]	3,033	899	18	141	4	603	13	4,676
1813[d]								13,937
1829[d]								14,000
1843[e]	25,000			6,000	19			31,000

B. *Population of Banda Oriental 1778–1793*

Year	Whites	Negro Slaves and Freedmen	%	Indians	Total
1778[f]	6,695	2,486	26.1	117	9,358
1780[g]	7,272	2,653	26.2	228	10,153
1793[h]					30,685

[a] Francisco Bauzá, *Historia de la dominación española en el Uruguay* (Montevideo, 1929), 3rd ed., III, 150.

[b] Census. Distinction made between *pardos libres* (212) and *negros libres* (382). Isidoro De María, *Compendio de la historia de la R. O. del Uruguay* (Montevideo, 1901), p. 152.

[c] B. Fernández y Medina and Juan León Bengoa, *El Uruguay en su primer centenario* (Madrid 1912), pp. 12–13. The 603 "Indians" probably include both mestizos and *negros libertos* whereas the 141 freedmen are only *mulatos libertos*.

[d] Estimate by I. Pereda Valdés.

[e] Estimate based on the census taken by the chief of police in Montevideo, Dr. Andrés Lamas, at the time of abolition.

[f] Homero Martínez Montero, "La esclavitud en el Uruguay. Contribución a su estudio histórico-social," *Revista Nacional* (Montevideo, 1940–1942), nos. 32, 41, 45, 57.

[g] "Documentos para la historia argentina," XII (Buenos Aires), 388.

[h] F. de Azara, *Descripción e historia del Paraguay*, I, 344.

Banda Oriental no more than 2 per cent of the population was Indian.[8] Thus, the great majority of Uruguayans were free whites and mestizos.

[8] Sedentary Indians to whom a few nomads, such as the Charrúas, should be added.

Table I also shows that the proportion of slaves in Uruguay never exceeded 18 per cent, a high which soon began to decline. In Buenos Aires and Rio Grande do Sul, the percentage was twice as high and in Chile it was triple. The small number of slaves in Uruguay was a consequence of the colonial economy of the country which was not based on either plantations or mines to be exploited by large gangs of ignorant serfs or slaves. On the contrary, its mainstay, the pastoral industry, required the labor of skilled, mobile *gauchos* armed with knives and capable of individual initiative, characteristics which are incompatible with slavery.[9] Consequently, most of the slaves were domestic servants, urban construction workers, or field hands on truck farms.[10] It was also common for middle strata families to hire out their slaves as artisans or laborers. Since the only stimulus for the expansion of slavery was the enrichment of the white bourgeoisie, between 1750 and 1812 the slave population remained small, largely urban, and unconcentrated. Few families owned more than five Negroes, and the average fluctuated between two and three. The contrast of these conditions to circumstances in other slaveholding areas in America is indeed striking.[11]

Another point of difference is the absence in Uruguay of certain phenomena of acculturation which occurred, for example, in Brazil, Cuba, and Haiti.[12] Except for a few fiestas and dances, the Negro contributed little of his African heritage to Uruguayan culture, into which he was assimilated most rapidly.

Socially and legally, the African belonged to the lowest caste within a rigorously stratified society. Although his status was more nearly that of a "thing" than of a man, in practice he enjoyed cer-

[9] For our interpretation of the gaucho as "ejemplo de proletario libre," see *El mestizaje en la historia de Ibero-América* (Mexico City, 1961), pp. 94–95.

[10] See, for example, Horacio Arredondo, *Civilización del Uruguay*, I (Montevideo, 1951), 82; the *cofradía de albañiles* was recognized as a Negro association by the Cabildo of Montevideo on May 13, 1760.

[11] Archivo General de la Nación, Montevideo (hereinafter abbreviated as AGNM). Documentation analyzed by I. Pereda Valdés in unpublished MS (especially p. 83) intended as 2nd ed. of *Negros esclavos*. In São Paulo 95 per cent of the slaves were rural in 1806. Bastide and Fernandes, *Brancos e negros en São Paulo,* p. 41.

[12] See, for example, the excellent work by Roger Bastide, *Les religions africaines* (Paris, 1960).

tain privileges both by local custom and by imperial legislation. For example, he had the right to change masters if ill-treated, to claim freedom by right of asylum, and to accumulate his "peculium" for the purchase of liberty. In spite of these rights, the attainment of freedom was relatively rare; generations of servitude was the usual case.

Relations between master and slave, and conditions in general, were better and less violent in Uruguay than elsewhere thanks to the small number of Negroes, their residence as domestics within the master's home, their high degree of urbanization, and their rapid acculturation.[13] Nevertheless, the slaves were never allowed to forget their inferior status which public opinion sanctioned. This is not surprising since it was the higher classes that profited most from slavery. Some patricians, such as the well-known philanthropist Francisco Antonio Maciel, bred slaves for the market or engaged in the human traffic with Africa.[14]

Justice and punishment were meted out on different scales according to one's status as a slave, freedman, or free subject. The sentences imposed on Negroes often were determined less by the merits of the particular case than by the need to frighten or to appease the caste at that given moment. Like all groups, the slaves benefited from the humanization of the penal system that occurred at the end of the eighteenth century.[15]

After 1800 neither public punishment nor the traditional paternalism of his master was enough to keep the Negro slave passive. Despite an express prohibition of seditious speeches to slaves or freedmen, evidently inspired by the French Revolution and the Haitian rebellion, unrest became widespread. There was an increase in the number of runaways; some fugitives sought refuge among the Indians, others joined gaucho groups or formed bands of cimarrones. The most important act of insubordination occurred in 1803 when twenty slaves and freedmen fled from Montevideo to establish their

[13] See, for example, Pereda Valdés, MS, p. 8.

[14] AGNM, doc. 4, carpeta 6, caja 273; doc. 15, carpeta 3, caja 336.

[15] Eugenio Petit Muñoz et al., La condición jurídica, social, económica y política de los negros en la Banda Oriental (Montevideo, 1948), p. 202. See also Carlos Ferrés, La administración de justicia de Montevideo, Epoca colonial (Montevideo, n.d.).

own free community on the islands of the River Yi which was beyond the jurisdiction of the city authorities. Although the Cabildo secured permission from the Audiencia of Buenos Aires to capture and punish the fugitives, penalties never in fact were imposed, which indicates that the fugitives negotiated their own return in accord with the Spanish legal procedure known as "pacificación." [16] The opinions of some authors notwithstanding, this incident cannot be dismissed as an isolated event. Rather, it seems directly related to the crisis of colonial society that culminated in the revolution of 1810. In fact, the Cabildo asserted that the participating freedmen had absorbed revolutionary doctrines from Negro sailors aboard French ships calling at Montevideo.[17] Whatever the facts of this case, it is clear that after 1800 the Negroes began to act like an oppressed caste in rebellion. The British invasions in 1807 hastened the process of social maturation and precipitated the ultimate crisis of the caste system, which was expressed in the wars of independence. These Negro groups were ready to play a part not unlike that of the contemporaneous Indian serfs in Mexico.

The Caste of Libertos (Freedmen)

Slaves who acquired liberty, and their descendants, did not join the free white group community; they entered the intermediate caste of freedmen, a condition best described as half slave and half free. Legally, the freedman was restricted on the grounds that a person who originally had been considered property necessarily retained some attributes of this original status.[18] Once having entered this caste, the color of the freedman's skin made it juridically impossible for him to leave it, at least until 1795, when the system of *cédulas de gracias al sacar* created a legal means of individual escape.

[16] De María, *Compendio de la historia de la R. O. del Uruguay*, II, 8; AGNM, doc. 24, carpeta 2, caja 272; according to *Recopilación de las Leyes de los Reinos de las Indias* (Madrid, 1681), VII-V-34, pardon should be conceded the first time a slave deserted.

[17] In 1807 the Cabildo also prohibited "los bailes de negros . . . que son por todos motivos muy perjudiciales," *Revista del Archivo General Administrativo*, VI (Montevideo, n.d.), 372–75.

[18] Petit Muñoz, *La condición juridica* . . . , p. 317.

This system attained little importance in the Plata region and, in practice, the liberation of the freedman began only in 1801 when he was allowed to enter the military service.

Among the freedmen, there were many more mulattoes than among the slave population. Miscegenation was widespread in Uruguay; indeed, the rural population was the product of white, Indian, and Negro intermixture. It was usual for Spaniards and Criollos to have sexual relations with colored women. Moreover, the law granted freedom to the slave woman who married her master, became his concubine, or bore him children that he recognized. Such situations arose relatively frequently, giving rise to the Cabildo's official distinction between "free Negroes" and "free pardos" after 1778. Slaves, on the other hand, were all considered Negro. After a while "pardo" or "mulatto" became synonymous with "freedman." The mixing of races gained momentum toward the end of the colonial period, as the evolution of Spanish legislation clearly shows. Whereas the law of the sixteenth century forbade intermarriage, a more tolerant policy was followed after 1778 with respect to both legitimate and illegitimate unions.

Although he enjoyed personal liberty, the freedman was reduced to an inferior status in four basic ways:

1) There were certain legal restrictions on his freedom. Although by 1811 many of these had lapsed through obsolescence, freedmen were still prohibited from bearing arms, becoming priests or public servants, inheriting land, or employing Indians. The rule against holding office gave rise to several noteworthy "purity of lineage" suits during the eighteenth century.[19]

2) The economic activities of the freedman were confined to the jobs held by his Negro ancestors, who at best had been artisans. Indeed, by 1760 the guilds of tailors and shoemakers were entirely mulatto.[20] Not only did the freedman usually continue to work in his former occupation, but often he also remained with his ex-master as a free servant after manumission.

3) Socially, the freedman was forced to remain close to the slave

---

[19] The exclusion of mulattoes from municipal offices had been introduced in 1729 (*Ibid.,* I) 232–33.

[20] *Ibid.,* III, 150.

caste. In this group he found his mate, his social diversions, and an audience for his political aspirations. These restrictions were less rigid for some free mulattoes whose African origins were more distant.

4) There were few educational opportunities for the ex-slave, until the nineteenth century when several parish schools were opened to him. The freedmen who received even such rudimentary training came to be regarded as mentors by the slaves.

By 1803 the Cabildo of Montevideo was grumbling about the pride, insubordination, and disorderly conduct of the freedmen.

The Lower Castes and the Revolutionary War, 1801–1830.

From the beginning, the Banda Oriental was a frontier territory, a military zone where the Spanish Empire faced the incursions of the Portuguese, hostile Indians, pirates, and even invasions from Europe. The border war with Portuguese Brazil was fought almost continuously from the founding of Colonia do Sacramento in 1680 until the end of the eighteenth century. It is not surprising, then, that the cities which were to form the basis of Uruguayan society, Montevideo, Maldonado, and the fortresses of Santa Teresa and San Miguel in the interior, were all established for military reasons. The further strain placed on the already limited supply of manpower by defense needs led first to the importation of Negro slaves and later to their entrance into the armed forces. For escaped slaves and the freedmen, military service was perhaps the only possibility for social advancement; it was a risky route from bondage to freedom.[21]

Although "free morenos" were accepted in the Spanish Army as early as 1623, they were admitted to the colonial militia in the Banda Oriental only in 1801, when one company of free pardos (mulattoes) and one of free morenos (Negro freedmen) were organized.[22] The stimulus in Uruguay, as in Córdoba and Paraguay where similar units were formed, was the war against Portugal and

[21] Martínez Montero, "La esclavitud en el Uruguay. Contribución a su estudio histórico-social," *Revista Nacional* (Table I in the text), no. 45, p. 14; Carvalho Neto, *El Negro uruguayo*, p. 146.

[22] AGNM, doc. 108, carpeta 11, caja 250.

the increasing menace posed by Great Britain. Within these companies, the Negroes could not become officers, but otherwise they lived by the same regulations as their white comrades-in-arms. In 1806 the companies of pardos and morenos were merged and their 159 members incorporated as a unit into the Regiment of Infantry Volunteers which was organized to oppose the British invasion of Montevideo.[23] They saw action in the Battle of Cardal, after which Viceroy Sobremonte ordered the registration of all slaves capable of bearing arms. Although the fall of Montevideo prevented the realization of this project, it paved the way for the enlistment of slaves in the army in later years.

The occupation of Montevideo by the British provided many slaves with an opportunity to escape. Faced with mass insubordination, the owners had to adopt new attitudes. In February, 1807, the Cabildo Mayor of Montevideo warned the slaves that political events had not changed their status and that they would be liable to capital punishment in the event of attempted escape or disobedience.[24] Five months later, the Cabildo appealed to the British commander-in-chief to return any slaves seeking refuge with the Royal Navy.

It was during the long wars of independence, 1811–1828, that the great Negro military contribution was made. The first stage of the fighting, a struggle between Spaniards and "patriots," was ended by the Portuguese invasion of 1817. With the expulsion of the Spaniards, civil war broke out between the Orientales and Buenos Aires, followed by a second Portuguese invasion in 1820. After ruling five years, the Brazilians were expelled by force from the United Provinces of Rio de la Plata. Finally, through the mediation of Great Britain, negotiations were begun that led to peace in 1828 and to the establishment of the Uruguayan Republic, which adopted a constitution in 1830.

The real importance of these wars lies in their nature as a truly popular revolution. Using guerrilla and scorched earth tactics, the

[23] Bauzá, II, 389, confused this unit with that of "Patricios Criollos." See AGNM, Archivo administrativo, libro 167 and libro 837.

[24] Martínez Montero, "La esclavitud en el Uruguay. Contribución a su estudio histórico social," *Revista Nacional,* no. 45, p. 403.

armies lived from the land, seizing the peasants' animals and wealth. With much of the population involved in the fighting, the devastation of war left few people untouched.[25] Artigas's retreat before the first Portuguese invasion (the famous "Exodus of the Orientales") involved not only his soldiers but also their families and virtually the entire rural population, some 12,000 people.[26]

It is understandable that under such circumstances the old colonial caste society was broken down to an extent unknown elsewhere in Spanish America. In the process, the social status of the Negroes was bound to change.

The participation of colored troops in the fighting was of great importance to both the patriot cause and the Negroes' social advance. By welcoming to its ranks deserters from the pardo-moreno companies and runaway slaves alike, the patriot army tacitly recognized the freedom of its new members. Although both sides attempted to conscript slaves, the patriots were quite successful with regular recruitment. When a battalion of Oriental freedmen was formed in 1816, the 178 slaves who joined its ranks were freed immediately. At this time there were already 190 colored troops in the army. So important did he consider these soldiers, that Artigas himself made special reference to granting them land in his agrarian reform project.

The final defeat of Artigas's army by the Portuguese caused the same reaction among the colored troops as among the white. While a minority loyally followed their *caudillo* into exile, most of the soldiers surrendered to the enemy. Deserters in serious numbers began to trouble the patriots in 1817. Among the first to desert were several white patrician families, frightened by the increasingly radical tone of Artigas's pronouncements. The Battalion of Freedmen began to show signs of disaffection after suffering heavy losses in the Battle of India Muerta and the operations following the evacuation of Montevideo. There were desertions and finally a mutiny

[25] On the application of Artigas's *Reglamento* of 1815, Alfredo Beraza, "Nuestro más rico patrimonio," *Marcha*, Oct., 1965.

[26] Whereas the population of Montevideo remained 14,000 between 1810 and 1829, that of Buenos Aires rose from 45,000 to 60,000. Ingenieros, *Sociología argentina*, p. 469.

which was suppressed by the execution of the ringleaders. Upon hearing of these events, the Portuguese promised immediate manumission to all slaves submitting to their authority. Thereupon the colored regiments surrendered en masse on October 3, 1817.[27]

Meanwhile, several Negroes were among the 200 loyal soldiers whom Artigas led to Paraguay in 1820.[28] Two Negroes also figured in the ranks of the famous "thirty-three" whose invasion opened the final stage of the Wars of Independence in 1825. In the long campaign that followed, the colored regiments were reconstructed and many slaves won their freedom on the field of battle.

The Ideology of Abolitionism

The problem of slavery and its fundamental incompatibility with human rights was a matter of concern to the intelligentsia and the leaders of the independence movement. This may be cited as evidence of the democratic convictions of the intellectual elite, the radicalism of the movement of emancipation in the Plata area, and the development of a reaction against the colonial caste system.

Ideologically, the abolitionist movement had its roots, according to the historian Petit Muñoz, in the works of four writers of the Rio de la Plata: the Jesuit jurisconsult, Muriel; the naturalist, Azara; the colonial official, Lastarria; and Mariano Moreno, the Buenos Aires patriot leader.[29] Their thought was studied widely during the revolutionary era and had its greatest impact after 1810.

The influence of these thinkers is visible in a decree, issued by the Triumvirate of the United Provinces on April 8, 1812, which prohibited the importation of slaves, and in the resolution implementing the decree, adopted by the Cabildo of Buenos Aires.[30] Both of these

---

[27] Notice that these "slaves" had already been given the status of freedmen by the patriot government the previous year. Portuguese documentation on Negro deserters from Artigas's army, AGNM, caja 603.

[28] Paulo de Carvalho Neto, "Contribución al estudio de los negros paraguayos del Campamento Loma," *América Latina*, I–II (Rio de Janeiro, 1962), 23–40. See also H. F. Decoud, "El campamento Laurelty," *El Siglo Ilustrado* (Montevideo, 1930); Mario Petillo, *El último soldado artiguista* (Montevideo, 1936).

[29] Petit Múñoz, *La condición jurídica* . . . , p. 372.

[30] Supplement to *Gazeta Ministerial* (Buenos Aires), May 15, 1812; reprint, Buenos Aires, 1911.

[39]

acts lamented the impossibility of destroying slavery all at once and welcomed the decree's aim to extinguish it gradually.[31]

The abolitionist sympathies of some revolutionary leaders, including Bernardino Rivadavia and San Martín's aide, Dr. Bernardo Monteagudo, have been traced to their own Negro ancestry. Of course, literary figures also played a prominent role in disseminating abolitionist ideas. The poet Francisco Acuña de Figueroa wrote his ode "The African Mother" as a protest against Uruguayan participation in the human traffic on the Atlantic; later, he composed a poem in the Negro dialect of Montevideo celebrating the Law of Free Birth of 1813.[32] Lesser members of the intelligentsia expressed similar sentiments. In 1829 Juan Francisco Giró, the Minister of Government, urged the Montevideo Cabildo to prohibit the public punishment and exhibition of slaves in chains, practices he regarded as unworthy of a free nation. The same note was sounded in the following year by a Montevideo newspaper which denounced the corporal punishment of slaves as contrary to the principles of the wars of independence, fought to assure "the happiness . . . of all men of whatever class or condition." [33]

One man, the writer and lawyer Dr. Adolfo Berro (1819–1841), stands out as the greatest abolitionist of independent Uruguay. As a court-appointed adviser to the Public Defender of the Slaves, he was moved by the conditions he saw not only to defend the slaves rights in court but also to make legislative proposals (for example, the "Emancipation and Intellectual Improvement of the Colored People") and to write anti-slavery poetry.[34] His work in all fields had a profound influence on such later abolitionists as Andrés Lamas. Although he died at the age of twenty-two without seeing his dream realized, Berro's posthumously published *Poesías* was an important factor in stirring agitation for emancipation in the key year of 1842.

[31] Similar ideas were expressed in a memorandum addressed to Napoleon by Dr. Nicolás de Herrera of Montevideo and the merchant J. R. Milla de Roca. C. Parra-Pérez, *Bayona y la política de Napoleón en América* (Caracas, 1939), p. 76.

[32] Text in *El Parnaso Oriental*, I (Montevideo, 1929; new ed.), 230.

[33] Eduardo Acevedo, *Manual de historia uruguaya*, II (Montevideo, 1919), 60.

[34] Andrés Berro, *Poesías*, 2nd ed. (Montevideo, 1864).

THE PASSING OF THE AFRO-URUGUAYANS

Abolitionist Legislation in Uruguay, 1825–1853

Uruguay's national abolitionist legislation has its roots in the measures adopted by the revolutionary governments of the United Provinces between 1810 and 1813. Among these, the most important were the prohibition of the slave trade in 1812, the Law of Free Birth (1813), and the grant of freedom to all slaves arriving from foreign territory. Between 1825 and 1830, when Uruguay once more formed part of the United Provinces, several important local laws were enacted. On September 7, 1825, all persons henceforth born in Uruguay were declared free and the importation of slaves was abolished.[35] A law of May, 1829, granted freedom to any slave who had contributed personally to the cause of independence. In 1830 the state undertook to purchase the freedom of certain slaves if such action served the public interest and also proclaimed the liberty of those slaves who belonged to Uruguayan émigrés in Brazil or who had escaped from that country during the war. This last act was a reward for the military service in the Misiones campaign of many Brazilian Negroes who had been conscripted into General Rivera's army.[36]

After the final consolidation of independence in 1830, the decrees of 1825 were written into Article 131 of the national constitution. This measure was complemented by the law of 1837, which placed the freed Negroes (for three years or, if minors, until they reached the age of twenty-five) under the guardianship of publicly appointed trustees charged with clothing, educating, and giving medical and general good treatment as well as monetary compensation to their wards.[37] In 1839 the government approved a treaty with the United Kingdom (ratified in 1841), similar to other British-sponsored agreements of the time, that abolished the slave trade.[38]

By 1841 slavery existed only among those born or purchased be-

[35] Caravia, *Colección de leyes,* I (Montevideo, n.d.), 6–7.
[36] Martínez Montero, "La esclavitud en el Uruguay. Contribución a su estudio histórico social," *Revista nacional,* no. 45, p. 414.
[37] Caravia, *Colección de leyes,* I, 206.
[38] Armando Ugón, *Compilación de leyes y decretos,* V (Montevideo, n.d.), 345.

[41]

fore 1825. Its final liquidation was achieved in the 1840s, partly as a result of the "Guerra Grande" (1842–1851), a civil war complicated by the intervention of Buenos Aires. Once again, it was found that the slaves were needed as soldiers. In 1841 President Fructuoso Rivera freed his personal slaves so they could serve in the army, and soon after the government began the conscription of colored men, whatever their status.[39] The defeat of Rivera at Arroyo Grande forced the government, in its search for soldiers, to decree simultaneously the abolition of slavery and compulsory military service for the newly freed men. In face of the sketchy provisions for compensation, many slaveowners resisted the new law and several supplementary regulations had to be issued to force compliance.[40] By this time, an opposition government under Rosas's ally, General Oribe, was operating at El Cerrito. This government adopted similar measures in October, 1846, which also abolished slavery and established compulsory military service, but were more explicit about compensation to the former masters. The new freedmen were made subject to the Tutelary law of 1837.[41]

After the war, as a reward to the Negroes for their military service, the process of legal abolition was completed. Laws were passed in 1853 which ended the guardianship system for colored minors and declared the slave trade an act of piracy.[42] In effect, legal abolition in Uruguay was a twenty-five year process of expropriation of the slaves by the state, in the public interest, without adequate compensation to the owners.

The Emergence of a Class Society

The violent seventeen-year struggle for independence (1811–1828)

[39] Acevedo, *Manual de historia uruguaya*, pp. 52–53.

[40] See, for example, A. Demersay, *Histoire physique, économique et politique du Paraguay et des établissements des Jésuites*, I (Paris, 1860), 345–47; Ugón, *Compilación* . . . , II, 359.

[41] See Mateo Magarinos de Mello, *El gobierno del Cerrito* (Montevideo, n.d.), an exhaustive work.

[42] Ugón, *Compilación* . . . , III, 227. The existence of minors (under 25 years) at this time shows that the dispositions of 1825 and the constitutional declaration of the freedom of the womb in 1830 had not been fulfilled; Caravia, *Colección* . . . , I, 359.

destroyed the fabric of colonial society in Uruguay, which, more than any other part of South America, experienced social revolution during the wars. Three factors lie at the root of this phenomenon: the radical ideas of the patriot leaders, most notably Artigas; the hardships in a small territory of a long war of attrition marked by repeated foreign invasions; and the weakness of the colonial institutions themselves.[43]

In fact, the traditional colonial system had never become firmly entrenched in the Banda Oriental. Dating only from the founding of Montevideo in 1726, the colony began to develop during the reign of Charles III, which was characterized by a heavy emphasis on capitalism and rationalism, both of which had a stronger impact on the Banda Oriental than elsewhere in the Spanish Empire. Furthermore, there was no tradition of Indian servitude, of an aristocracy, nor of a wealthy and powerful Church (especially after the expulsion of the Jesuits in 1767). The population, slaves and freedmen included, was overwhelmingly urban. In fact, if the social status of the Negroes, freedmen, and Indians had not depended on racial factors (a situation of caste stratification), the society would have appeared quite similar to the estate-structured system of pre-Revolutionary France. Indeed, contradictory as it may seem, what developed in Uruguay was a capitalist society organized into castes.

With the final achievement of independence (1825–1830), there were efforts to make the country's new laws universally applicable, but a distinction was retained between slaves and free men who were also subdivided according to wealth. While the Criollo bourgeoisie, which had led the successful struggle for independence, hoped to draw the chief benefit from the collapse of the Spanish monopoly and the development of a modern state, other intermediate groups also looked forward to the fruits of peace in terms of renewed activity of the port of Montevideo and the availability of new jobs and positions from which they previously had been excluded.[44]

---

[43] Our communication at the XII International Congress of History (Vienna, 1965) on "La intervención de las clases populares en la Independencia del Río de la Plata" develops this topic further.

[44] For the impact on the lower classes see R. Bastide, *Sociologie du Brésil* (Paris, 1955), p. 29.

[43]

Perhaps the chief beneficiaries of the new situation were the freedmen, whose excellent war record was a valuable asset at the moment. Their ranks were reinforced by the absorption of many slaves who had won freedom on the field of battle so that now the freedmen were numerically important not only in Montevideo but also throughout the country. Even when performing the most menial labor, these men had a new consciousness of their importance as free wage earners.[45]

The great success of the Afro-Uruguayans in adapting to a class-based society stands out by comparison to the less successful adjustment of those other low castes of the colonial era, the Indians and the gauchos. Although both of these groups contributed as much to the wars of independence as the Negroes, they remained on the margin of society after 1828. The Indians, who had suffered heavy casualties in the fighting, were reduced to a population of 1,500 tribal nomads.[46] In 1832 these survivors were exterminated by the national army at the behest of the *estancieros*. These same landowners provided work for the gauchos, who retained a certain autonomy but also remained relatively unengaged in society because of their labor pattern. The introduction of barbed wire in the 1870s turned them into a rural proletariat, indeed a *Lumpenproletariat*.

As in Brazil, the Negro's superior adaptability to class society opened to him a means of upward social mobility unknown to the Indian.[47] Even before the abolition of slavery in 1842, the Afro-Uruguayan's position in society began to change considerably as soon as independence was achieved. Many of the older, caste-oriented men had been killed in the wars.[48] Moreover, as has been seen, among the colored population there were now more freedmen than slaves, since many slaves had won liberty, or died, on the battlefield. The resultant shortage of slaves gave rise to the contraband importation of Brazilian Negroes in unknown numbers.

A still more important factor in the changing status of the Afro-

---

[45] Cf. *Ibid.*, p. 19.

[46] A. D'Orbigny, *L'Homme américain* (Paris, 1835), I, XV; II, 84–85.

[47] Rama, *Las clases sociales* . . . , ch. 8.

[48] Cf. R. Bastide, "A propos de quelques livres récents sur les afro-américains" (Paris, n.d.) (Extrait de l'Ecole des Hautes Etudes).

Uruguayan was the wave of European immigration after 1830. In the next hundred years over 1,000,000 Europeans entered the country, making Uruguay, even more than the United States or Argentina, an immigrant land. Indeed, the old sparse population was submerged totally in this new flood of humanity. Between 1830 and 1842 the population of Montevideo increased from 14,000 to 31,000. In the same years the intensive settlement of the agricultural lands along the Uruguay River and in the South also began. Of course, these new factors produced radical changes in the national economy, which affected the colored population too.[49]

The chronic labor shortage was overcome by the influx of immigrants, whose education and skills were far superior to those of the Negroes. It was not long before slavery was eclipsed by the efficiency of the free wage system, assuring the ultimate demise of the "servile institution." The Negroes were quick to take advantage of the new economic opportunities that presented themselves. Both slaves and freedmen were put to work in the *saladeros* and on the *estancias*. These activities in time came to replace masonry and domestic service as the typically Negro occupations.

In these circumstances, the Afro-Uruguayans quickly began to develop an awareness of their civil rights, their culture, and their social status. One example of this phenomenon merits attention. In 1834 one of the important African cult organizations, the *Junta de los morenos congos de Cunga* (known in Uruguay as *naciones*), requested the Police Chief of Montevideo to lift the old colonial prohibition on the Negro groups' public fiestas and dancing. After defending the loyalty of these organizations and their lack of political aspirations, the appeal reiterated:

the regiments of free morenos have played a glorious role in all the memorable events of the patria's history as the most loyal supports of its governments. We are not so ignorant as to be unaware of the laws and liberal principles in our favor, proclaimed in the new institutions.[50]

If one considers that the author of this petition, the lawyer Jacinto

[49] For the question of their numbers, see Andrés Lamas, *Apuntes estadísticos,* 2nd ed. (Montevideo, 1928).

[50] Cf. Bastide and Fernandes, *Brancos e negros en São Paulo,* p. 62.

Ventura de Molina, was himself a moreno, the social and cultural progress of the Afro-Uruguayans becomes very clear.

Thus, by the time a capitalist class society began to emerge in 1840, slavery was no longer an obstacle to its development. Several factors may be cited to explain the evolution of western capitalism in Uruguay at this time:[51]

1) From the moment of its independence, guaranteed by Great Britain in 1828, Uruguay was drawn into the international economic structure. Its public finances throughout the period rested on loans secured from Baring Brothers and other London banks.

2) The economy was geared to supplying the British market with pastoral products. To this end, first *saladeros* and *graserías* (tallow works), and later railways, roads, and shipping lines designed to facilitate transportation through the port of Montevideo, were constructed. The economy was thus mechanized.

3) It was British, and to a lesser extent French, industry that supplied Uruguay with manufactured goods such as textiles, shoes, arms, construction machinery, and more.

4) The bourgeoisie in Montevideo and other towns grew wealthy as the middlemen in this international trade. The conflicts produced by their clashes with the landowning class were of great importance and twice expanded into international wars (the Guerra Grande and the Paraguayan War).

5) The new economic activities required an abundant supply of labor, which attracted large scale immigration from Europe. By 1842 of the 31,000 inhabitants of Montevideo only 6,000, or 19 per cent, were colored, a considerable decline since the turn of the century.

Another factor in the depletion of the Negro population was its continued interest in military service as a career because officerships were now open.[52] As a result, many Negroes perished in battle.

---

[51] A. D'Orbigny, *Voyage dans l'Amérique Méridionale*, I (Paris, 1835), 58; AGNM, doc. 31, carpeta 3, caja 336, used by I. Pereda Valdés. Notice that the term *moreno* had replaced *negro* because it did not have its pejorative connotation.

[52] The Negro Feliciano González, who entered the army in 1837 and reached the rank of colonel in 1894, exemplifies this. See the periodical *Nuestra Raza* (Montevideo), no. 18, Jan. 26, 1935, p. 6.

A further complicating factor in Negro life was the existence of a more traditional slave-based society in the region bordering on Brazil. This gave rise to a double population shift. Rather than comply with the abolition law of 1842, many owners sold their slaves in southern Brazil. At the same time many Brazilian slaves sought freedom through escape to Uruguay. This little-studied migration was important in establishing the population pattern of northern and eastern Uruguay, which even today remain the most Negroid regions of the country. The movement gained such importance, especially during the Farrapo rebellions (1835–1841) in Rio Grande do Sul, that it is mentioned in the Uruguayo-Brazilian treaty of 1851.

Had it not been for the Guerra Grande (1842–1851), the abolition law of 1842 might have remained a dead letter or, as in Brazil, the Negro's sociopolitical advancement might have lagged behind the social transformation underlying the shift from slavocracy to modern capitalism.[53] The war weakened the ability of the slaveowners to resist, and with the enactment of abolition by the El Cerrito government in 1846, the opposing factions had come down on the same side of the question. That there was no compensation to the owners may be traced to the lack of funds caused by the war. Finally, the discharge from the army of the conscripted slaves or free men in 1851 marks the definitive end of slavery in Uruguay.

The Evolution of the Afro-Uruguayan Population Since 1851

The Guerra Grande had the same importance for the slaves as the Wars of Independence (1811–1828) had had earlier for the freedmen. With the abolition of slavery and the guardianship system, the Negroes became a legally homogeneous group. By and large, they were the proletariat of Uruguayan capitalist society. There is some evidence of upward mobility among the morenos, as in the case of Jacinto Ventura de Molina, discussed earlier. Negroes at this time also seem to have entered some middle-class occupations as shopkeepers, commercial farmers, merchants, and small entrepreneurs,

[53] Cf. Bastide and Fernandes, *Brancos e negros en São Paulo*, p. 67.

although this is difficult to document in light of the absence of adequate biographies.[54]

Another factor in the advance of the Afro-Uruguayans was the national adoption of free compulsory primary education in 1878, followed by the establishment of the liceo system in 1913. It was especially helpful in drawing the Portuguese-speaking Negroes in the North into the national culture.

The relatively slow advance of the Negroes was complicated by the new wave of immigration that followed the return of peace in 1851. Between 1860 and 1870, 150,000 Europeans entered the country. By 1887 half the population of the Department of Canelones was foreign-born, the majority Italian. After 1890 immigration was supported actively by the state and reached its height between 1895 and 1914.[55] During the Great Depression the pace slackened, but has recovered somewhat since 1945. Although immigrants were to be found on all social levels, they usually remained in the lower ranks of society, at least in the first generation.

Without similar influx to sustain it, the colored population has declined relative to the white. In 1954 Angel Rosenblat, citing Ariosto Fernandes, calculated the colored population to be 58,000, of whom only 8,000 were Negroes.[56] This represents but 2.3 per cent of the national total of 2,500,000 in that year—a tremendous decline from the 26 per cent registered in 1803. The importance of miscegenation also is underscored by these figures in that only 0.32 per cent of the national and 13 per cent of the colored population was classified as Negro.

While much research remains to be done, certain important facts about the Afro-Uruguayans can be stated:

1) Until 1889 the colored population was reinforced by the arrival

[54] Much information, for example, on the first Negroes in different higher professions is given in *Nuestra Raza* (published first in San Carlos, later Montevideo, 1917–1934).

[55] According to the census of 1908, 17.4 per cent of Uruguay's population were born abroad. For Montevideo the percentage was 30.4. The Uruguayan censuses have not listed race.

[56] A. Rosenblat, *La población indígena y el mestizaje*, I (Buenos Aires, 1954), 165.

[48]

of runaway slaves from Brazil, who settled largely in the departments of Salto, Rivera, Artigas, Tacuarembó, and Cerro Largo in the North and East.

2) Throughout the century, military careers continued to attract colored men, who shed much blood in the blanco-colorado civil wars. There is a considerable popular literature about these *montoneros* who often served valiantly despite having been conscripted forcefully into the armies. To this day the Negroid element has remained an important factor in the professional army and police forces.

3) More than the white groups the Negro population was decimated by epidemics in the nineteenth century.

4) The Afro-Uruguayans have participated fully in the process of urbanization, which explains the appearance of colored *barrios* in Montevideo and other cities.

As a minority group with its origins of slavery, the colored population has tried to preserve a semblance of unity. In Montevideo this sentiment has found expression in the *naciones*, organized around the supposed tribal affiliation of the members. Aside from the *congos* mentioned earlier, there were also the *benguelas, minas, lubolos,* and more. These groups, which had permanent headquarters and organized hierarchies of offices, provided help and benefits to their members and organized traditional celebrations and fiestas, such as the *candombés*, on various holidays.[57] Whether the *naciones* had fetishist, African religious or political functions, like the *macumba* in Brazil, has been discussed widely.[58] Such purposes seem highly doubtful in light of their rejection by the membership. Today the city of Montevideo has undertaken a campaign to assure the survival of the Afro-Uruguayan traditions represented by the *naciones*. In practice, colored people, like other elements of the popula-

[57] See I. De María, *Montevideo antiguo*, 2nd ed. (Montevideo, 1938), p. 82; Lino Suárez Pena, "Apuntes y datos referentes a la raza negra" (1924; unpublished MS in the library of P. Blanco Acevedo); Marcelino Bottaro, "Rituals and candombés," *Negro* (London, 1934), p. 519 ff.

[58] The positive opinion sustained by Vicente Rossi, *Cosas de negros* (Córdoba, Argentina, 1926); the negative one by Arthur Ramos, *As culturas negras no Novo Mundo*, 2nd ed. (Rio de Janeiro, 1946), pp. 245 ff.

tion, have participated in organizations based on occupation and social status. All efforts to establish autonomous Negro churches, labor unions, schools, and political parties have failed.[59]

Racial prejudice exists in Uruguay as it does everywhere. Many examples of discrimination could be cited, from the difficulties of a Negro becoming a night watchman (*celador*) in the 1860s to the more recent examples of his problems in becoming a university professor (*docente*). However, race prejudice has been replaced generally by class prejudice, which may even be considered a sign of modernity. Thus, when confronted in 1878 by objections to integrated education which might foster social contact among the classes, José Pedro Varela, sponsor of the Primary Education Act, replied that his purpose was in fact to draw the classes together through common education.[60]

Although there is no work on Uruguay comparable to the Bastide-Fernandes study of São Paulo which confirmed the existence of prejudice in Brazil, it seems safe to assume that there is greater tolerance in the small republic thanks to the prevalence of miscegenation and the numerical insignificance of the Afro-Uruguayans of today.[61]

---

[59] The best-known effort is that of the "Partido Negro Autóctono," formed by colored intellectuals in 1937, which failed in the elections that year.

[60] The polemics of Varela with Lucas Obes. The latter did not object to *negritos* per se, but because they represented an inferior social class (see C. Rama, *José Pedro Varela sociólogo* [Montevideo, 1956].)

[61] Bastide and Fernandes, *Brancos e negros en São Paulo*, p. 370.

CHAPTER 3

Action and Ideas

in the Abolitionist

Movement in Brazil

Richard Graham

Like Professor Rama in the previous article, Professor Richard Graham of the University of Utah suggests that larger changes in the society—in this case in Brazil—demanded the abolition of slavery. The expansion of a burgeoning coffee economy and the rise of new urban groups anxious to destroy the old regime are used to explain the end of the slave institution. However, the end of the slave trade and even the "law of free birth" in 1871 were imposed upon Brazil from abroad; and the dramatic action of the slaves themselves in the last months before abolition hastened its arrival.

The basic aim of this article is to suggest the causes for the abolition of Negro slavery in Brazil. On the one hand, a specific aspect of this process which has been largely ignored will be considered: the direct action of Brazilian slaves, especially through their mass flights from the plantations. On the other, attention will be given to the general transformations of society at this time, especially the rise of new groups, which provided the basic impulse for the abolition of slavery. I do not intend to present new facts, but rather to emphasize some historical events which have not been adequately studied.

One may examine the general histories of Brazil in vain for satisfactory explanations of the passage of the law of 1888 which freed three-quarters of a million slaves, bringing ruin to many landowners and destroying the political system they had created. Although these histories mention some of the same factors with which this article is concerned, they do so only in passing and without stressing their causative importance. One is left with the general impression that the Brazilian Parliament issued the law freeing the slaves in response to humanitarian sentiments and the pressure of public opinion aroused by a propaganda campaign ably directed by a handful of abolitionists. Pandía Calógeras insisted that the step "was the inevitable consequence of irresistible national opinion." C. H. Haring, in in his summary of secondary works on Brazilian history, said that "public meetings, articles in the daily press, and abolitionist societies . . . wore down the reluctance of a Parliament dominated by slavery interests." Brazilian textbooks, not surprisingly, place their emphasis either on this same crusading effort or on the humanitarian sentiments of the emperor and princess, rather than on the pressure applied by the slaves themselves in their own behalf. The only English-language study of the question—Percy Alvin Martin's 1933 article—points to the abolitionist campaign, parliamentary activity, and voluntary action on the part of some slaveowners and refers only in passing to the failure of the army to pursue runaway slaves.[1]

Parliament did pass the law outlawing slavery by an overwhelming majority; but this Parliament represented the large landowners of the country, groups which depended for their income and way of life on the labor of slaves. Is it possible to maintain that the representatives of the slaveowners, in many cases slaveowners themselves, abandoned their clearest and most vital economic interests as

---

[1] João Pandiá Calógeras, *Formacão histórica do Brasil*, 3d ed. (São Paulo, 1938), p. 339; see the even more sterile approach of Pedro Calmon, *História do Brasil* (São Paulo, 1947), IV, 500–505, 509–15; even Caio Prado Júnior, *História econômica do Brasil*, 5th ed. (São Paulo, 1959), p. 185, places primary emphasis on public opinion. Clarence H. Haring, *Empire in Brazil: a New World Experiment with Monarchy* (Cambridge, Mass., 1958), p. 100; he adds "The Princess Regent . . . was convinced . . . that the government must keep pace with public sentiment," p. 103; Hélio Vianna, *História do Brasil*, 3d ed. (São Paulo, 1965), II, 212–15; Armando Souto Maior, *História do Brasil para o curso colegial* (São Paulo, 1965), p. 342; Percy Alvin Martin, "Slavery and Abolition in Brazil," *Hispanic American Historical Review*, XIII (1933), 172–96, esp. 193.

a result of brilliant speeches and the outcry of the press? If the answer to this question is negative, as I believe, then other reasons for the passage of the law must be found.

It is the position taken here that the ideas propagated by the abolitionists did in fact play a decisive role in bringing about the end of slavery, but not in the way generally depicted. The abolitionists appealed to the needs of the new urban groups that had emerged in Brazil after the Paraguayan War (1865–1870). Such groups, stimulated by this propaganda, encouraged and abetted the virtual revolt of the slaves.[2] The planters, faced with a *fait accompli*, preferred to legalize it in order to prevent a further decay of their position. Some of the planters were convinced of the necessity to change the system because the number of slaves was already insufficient, a situation which can be blamed on foreign pressure. The measures taken in behalf of the slaves until 1871 can also be attributed to foreign influence. This period was before the planters had felt the shortage of labor and at a time when the new urban groups were still weak.

In order to understand the interplay of forces which led to the abolition of slavery in Brazil, two major changes in Brazilian economic and social life must be mentioned. One was the rise of coffee exports and new coffee-producing regions; the other was the increasing size and importance of the cities. These two forces provided the pull and the push that led to a radical change in the nature of Brazilian life.

The major development during the latter half of the nineteenth century in Brazil was that the country was swept into the European economic vortex. The increasing momentum of the industrial revolution in Europe and the United States meant not only a rising urban population in the "developed" world and an increasing leisure with which to enjoy luxury items such as coffee, but also the application of new technology to sea and land transport significantly lessening the cost of commodities shipped to and from Brazil.[3]

[2] Webster defines revolt as "any refusal to submit to or accept authority."
[3] Sanford A. Mosk, "Latin America and the World Economy, 1850–1914," *Inter-American Economic Affairs*, II (1948), 53–82; Gerald S. Graham, "The Ascendancy of the Sailing Ship, 1850–1885," *Economic History Review*, n.s. IX (1956–1957), 74–88.

As a result, Brazilian coffee enjoyed such a marked increase in exports that the established economic and social relationships were deeply disturbed. At first the bulk of this production centered in the valley of the Paraíba River, and coffee exports from the province of Rio de Janeiro soon outstripped sugar both in quantity and value. Coffee exportation stimulated a spurt of interest in the building of railroads and, by the mid-1860s, rail connections had been established between the middle Paraíba Valley and Rio. In 1868 the ribbons of steel were stretched from the port of Santos to the rich west-central lands in the state of São Paulo, whence other railroads spread fan-like throughout a new area. By the mid-1880s the province of São Paulo produced more coffee than Rio de Janeiro. Meanwhile, Brazilian coffee exports had risen from 17,000,000 sacks (of 132 lbs.) in the 1840s to 36,000,000 sacks in the 1870s and 53,000,000 in the 1880s.[4]

With the railroads went the advancing "economic frontier," and west-central São Paulo was incorporated for the first time into the money economy. Where the railroads reached, there came the large, modern coffee plantation: straight rows of glistening bushes up and down the rolling countryside where disorderly patches of subsistence crops once had been sprinkled in the virgin forest. No longer dependent on the mule trains to carry their produce to the waiting ships in Santos, the planters could now think of moving continuously to better lands. Meanwhile, the Paraíba Valley entered a period of decline, with decaying mansions bespeaking a past grandeur.[5]

The boisterous prosperity of the São Paulo coffee area brought to the fore a new group of men, men who were not dominated by the

---

[4] William Scully, *Brazil: Its Provinces and Chief Cities. The Manners and Customs of the People; Agricultural, Commercial, and Other Statistics . . .* (London, 1866), pp. 326–30; Nelson Werneck Sodré, *História da burguesia brasileira* (Rio, 1964), p. 182; Affonso de Escragnolle Taunay, *Pequena história do café no Brasil (1727–1937)* (Rio, 1945), p. 548.

[5] On the concept of the "economic frontier" see J. F. Normano, *Brazil, a Study of Economic Types* (Chapel Hill, N.C., 1935), pp. 1–17; Pierre Monbeig, *Pionniers et planteurs de São Paulo* (Paris, 1952), pp. 83–93; Stanley J. Stein, *Vassouras, A Brazilian Coffee County, 1850–1900* (Cambridge, Mass., 1957), pp. 213–49.

traditions of a seignorial past. They were drawn from a previously unfavored group of small landowners and merchants, and with the enthusiasm of men on the way up they threw themselves at the land, driving their insufficient slaves, borrowing money, engaging in battles over land, acquiring more, pushing ever westward. They looked upon their land as capital rather than as a guarantee of position. They acquired it in order to produce wealth, and if old solutions did not work, they would try new ones. They were landed entrepreneurs and their innovating spirit was demonstrated in their adoption of a new crop, their use of novel techniques of processing it, their enthusiasm for the railroads (which they often built themselves), and their demand for a more plentiful and flexible source of labor than could be provided by slavery. When the time came, they were willing to sell off their depleted lands and invest in industry.[6]

The rise of new urban groups and general commercial growth were stimulated by the increasing export trade. No longer was it only the foreigners who became merchants. New establishments such as banks, transport companies, insurance corporations, and urban services were organized rapidly to serve the rising demands of coffee commerce. A growing number of urban dwellers administered these enterprises and performed the white-collar tasks associated with them. The expanding revenues derived from coffee also financed a proliferating bureaucracy in the capitals to deal with the increasingly complex problems of administering a prosperous country. Smaller towns such as Itú, Sorocaba, and Campinas also became more important as distributing centers for foodstuffs and supplies in a monocultural area that previously had been self-sufficient. Smaller port cities like Santos and Niterói shared in the new prosperity. The

[6] Monbeig, *Pionniers et planteurs*, pp. 121–25; 128–29; Celso Furtado, *Formação econômica do Brasil* (Rio, 1959), pp. 139–40; Florestan Fernandes, "Do escravo ao cidadão," in Roger Bastide and Florestan Fernandes, *Relações raciais entre negros e brancos em São Paulo* (São Paulo, 1955), pp. 40–41; the Paraíba planter felt that his counterpart in São Paulo, "blindly adopts the newest fad," *Novidades* (Rio de Janeiro), Feb. 28, 1888, in Stein, *Vassouras*, p. 252; Fernando Henrique Cardoso, "Condições sociais da industrialização de São Paulo," *Revista brasiliense*, no. 28 (1960), pp. 34–37.

coffee planters, bound by few ties of sentiment to the land, built town houses and occupied them for large parts of the year. One result of these changes was urban growth.

Simultaneously, new interests and attitudes arose which were not connected with the land and were skeptical of aristocratic values. The entrepreneurs were men of modern attitudes, and in the cities the complete dominance of personal relations in their dealings began to weaken. Nostalgic words were soon being uttered about the good old days in contrast to the "mercenary instinct of our time." The idea that men should be placed according to their ability began to receive wider acceptance. European standards began to be adopted and the port cities became the beachheads of European civilization. The growth of an export economy created a distinctive culture, oriented toward Europe, and the Europeanization of the cities could be seen in the fashions of clothes, the modification of eating habits, the use of novel architectural styles, and the adoption of urban improvements. European opinion came to be highly valued by these urban classes.

The three urban types which deserve special mention are the military officers, the engineers, and the industrialists. The officers had not been drawn from the landed aristocracy but from the cities, and during the Paraguayan War they had developed an antipathy toward slavery and contempt for the *bacharéis*, the graduates produced by the traditional educational institutions. They were dissatisfied with their status and looked to the future with hope of a better era. Closely linked to them were a new group of engineers, civilians who had either began their careers as military engineers or had been trained at the Escola Central created in 1858 and renamed Escola Polytechnica in 1874. One of them expressed their dissatisfaction when he cried out: "Oh, how miserable is the position of engineers in Brazil." Another new-fledged group was formed by the industrialists. The Paraguayan War had stimulated a great deal of consumer manufacturing and the upstart capitalists had turned their attention to the civilian market after the end of the war. By the mid-1870s iron foundries, textile mills, shoe factories, and hat manufacturing had all attained significant proportions. Textile manufacturing shifted away from the decadent northern areas of Bahia to invade the prospering south-central region where the industrial tradition really got its first start. To these three clusters must be added the professional men who, despite their education in the traditional law and medical colleges, were impelled by their contact with urban society to adopt the new values of the city and the new ideas imported from Europe.[7]

The urban centers, then, were filled not only with an expanding number of merchants and bureaucrats directly related to the export economy, but also with industrial entrepreneurs, engineers, military officers, and the sons of the older aristocracy who absorbed the values of these new groups. They shared an interest in change and "progress," a belief in a society characterized by social mobility and individualism, and an economy dominated by the profit motive.

They were also opposed to slavery. This seems to have been especially true of those men associated with industry, although no measurement of their opinions is now possible. Not only did they naturally oppose tying up capital in labor which could not be dismissed in bad times, but their whole way of life demanded the freedom of all men, units to be freely contracted, freely fired, freely sold to, freely moved; units to be joined and disjoined where and how economic imperatives should dictate. Brazilian entrepreneurs generally were committed to the abolition of slavery. They complained that slavery slowed down capital formation, and an industrialist in Bahia said that the best protection government could give industry was the end of slavery. André Rebouças, dock company promoter, in-

---

[7] Nícia Vilela Luz, "O papel das classes médias brasileiras no movimento republicano," *Revista da história*, no. 57 (1964), p. 21; Joaquim Nabuco, *Um estadista do imperio, Nabuco de Araujo: sua vida, suas opiniões, sua epoca,* (São Paulo and Rio, 1936), I, 188–89; Joaquim Nabuco, *Minha formação* (Rio, 1957), p. 188; Péricles Madureira do Pinho, *Luís Tarqüinio, pioneiro da justiça social no Brasil* (Bahia, 1944), pp. 71, 73; Francisco Clementino de San Tiago Dantas, *Dois momentos de Rui Barbosa: Conferências* (Rio, 1949), pp. 18–19; Percy Alvin Martin, "Causes of the Collapse of the Brazilian Empire," *Hispanic American Historical Review*, IV (1921), 4–48; André Rebouças, *Diário e notas autobiográficas* (Rio, 1938), p. 134; Nícia Vilela Luz, "O industrialismo e o desenvolvimento econômico do Brasil," *Revista de história*, no. 56 (1963), p. 276; Werneck Sodré, *História da burguesia*, p. 151; Stanley J. Stein, *The Brazilian Cotton Manufacture: Textile Enterprise in an Underdeveloped Area, 1850–1950* (Cambridge, Mass., 1957), p. 21.

sisted that "without freedom there is no industry. Freedom is the mother, the guardian angel of all industry." The nascent equivalent of a manufacturers' association joined the two major abolitionist societies as early as 1881 in advocating the end of slavery. The students and professors at the engineering school, the seedbed of the new progressive and industrial-minded elite, formed an abolitionist society. It was "in the name of Brazilian engineering" that one of them hailed the final passage of the abolition law. Industrialists believed that the substitution of a free work force for the slave one was the solution to Brazil's labor problem, and it is interesting to note how the leading São Paulo coffee-planters-turned-railroad-builders were active in the importation of European laborers to take the place of slaves.[8]

It was these two factors, the increasing demand for labor in an expanding coffee economy and the rise of urban groups dissatisfied with slavery as a system, that made the abolition of slavery a necessity. Why then, we may ask, were the first steps toward abolition taken in the late 1860s and early 1870s, before either of these forces could be considered very strong? And why was the end of the African supply of fresh slaves decreed as early as 1850? The answer to both these questions is to be found in the pressure applied by the British.

British efforts to destroy the slave trade have been much discussed and need not detain us here. A long succession of treaties, antislave-

[8] Speech of Andrade Figueira, Oct. 11, 1882, in Camara dos Deputados, *Anais*, 1882, V, 356 (Andrade Figueira's position is very ambiguous); Luís Tarqüinio, *Direitos de importação em ouro. Cartas dirigidas ao Ministro da Fazenda* . . . (Bahia, 1890), p. 32; André Rebouças, *Agricultura nacional, estudos economicos; propaganda abolicionista e democratica* (Rio, 1883), p. 10; *O abolicionista; orgão da Sociedade Brasileira Contra a Escravidão* (Rio), no. 1, Nov. 1, 1880, p. 8; and no. 8, June 1, 1881, p. 8; Rebouças, *Diário*, pp. 299, 302; Francisco Picanço, "Estradas de ferro," *Imprensa fluminense* (Rio), May 20, 1888, p. 2; Irineo Evangelista da Souza, visconde de Mauá, *Autobiografia* (*"Exposição aos credores e ao público"*) *seguida de "O meio circulante no Brasil*," 2d ed. (Rio, 1942), p. 222; Adelino R. Ricciardi, "Parnaíba, o pioneiro da imigração," *Revista do Arquivo Municipal de São Paulo*, IV, no. 44 (1938), 137–84; Nazareth Prado, ed., *Antonio Prado no imperio e na republica: seus discursos e actos* . . . (Rio, 1929), p. 30; Carolina Nabuco, *The Life of Joaquim Nabuco*, transl. (Stanford, Cal., 1950), p. 80.

trade legislation, and finally, the actual invasion of Brazilian ports by British ships are clear evidence of the United Kingdom's commitment to this goal. To what extent the British deserve the credit for the end of the slave trade has also been argued to the point of diminishing returns. It is probably correct to ascribe credit to both nations. British pressure, at a time when the Brazilian government was proud of its newly established control over the entire nation and worried about impending diplomatic and military difficulties in the Rio de la Plata, combined with a momentary surfeit of new slaves to insure the passage and rigorous application of the antislave-trade law.[9] Hard as it is at this time to see how the British could have con-

---

[9] Alan K. Manchester, *British Preëminence in Brazil; Its Rise and Decline: A Study in European Expansion* (Chapel Hill, 1933), p. 265; Nabuco, *Estadista do imperio*, I, 165; António Ferreira Cesarino Júnior, "A intervenção da Inglaterra na suppressão do tráfico de escravos africanos para o Brasil," *Revista do Instituto Histórico e Geográfico de São Paulo*, XXXIV (1938), 145–66, esp. 164. For further examination of the slave trade issue see Alfredo Gomes, "Achegas para a história do tráfico africano no Brasil—aspectos numéricos," in Instituto Histórico e Geográfico Brasileiro, *Anais do IV Congresso de História Nacional* (1949), V (1950), 29–78; William Law Mathieson, *Great Britain and the Slave Trade, 1839–1865* (London, 1929); Christopher Lloyd, *The Navy and the Slave Trade; the Suppression of African Slave Trade in the Nineteenth Century* (London, 1949); Jane Elizabeth Adams, "The Abolition of the Brazilian Slave Trade," *Journal of Negro History*, X (1925), 607–37; Lawrence F. Hill, "The Abolition of the African Slave Trade to Brazil," *Hispanic American Historical Review*, XI (1931), 169–97; Wilbur Devereux Jones, "The Origins and Passage of Lord Aberdeen's Act," *Hispanic American Historical Review*, XLII (1962), 502–20; Leslie M. Bethell, "Britain, Portugal and the Suppression of the Brazilian Slave Trade: The Origins of Lord Palmerston's Act of 1839," *English Historical Review*, LXXX (1965), 761–84; Maurício Goulart, *Escravidão africana no Brasil (das origens à extinção do tráfico)* (São Paulo, 1949), pp. 219–63; Evaristo de Moraes, *A escravidão africana no Brasil (das origens à extinção)* (São Paulo, 1933), pp. 65–99; Maurílio Gouveia, *História da escravidão* (Rio, 1955), pp. 115–35; Manoel Alvaro Sousa Sá Vianna, "O tráfico e a diplomacia brasileira," *Revista do Instituto Histórico e Geográphico Brasileiro; tomo especial . . . Congreso' de História Nacional, 1914*, V (1917), 539–64; Affonso de Escragnolle Taunay, "Subsídios para a história do tráfico africano no Brasil," *Anais do Museu Paulista*, X, 2ª parte (1941), pp. 257–72; and, on legislative aspects, João Luiz Alves, "A questão do elemento servil. A extincção do tráfico e a lei da repressão de 1850. Liberdade dos nasciturnos," *Revista do Instituto Histórico e Geográphico Brasileiro; tomo especial . . . , IV (1916), 187–258.

[59]

sidered it any of their business, the fact is that they did, and that the slave trade to Brazil was ended by their energetic actions in conjunction with propitious circumstances in Brazil itself.

Not so well known is that the end of the slave trade did not mark the end of British interest in ending Brazilian slavery, which continued until Brazil gave evidence of a firm commitment to end slavery itself. Whereas the law freeing those children of slaves born after September 28, 1871, is usually considered the first evidence of an abolitionist campaign, it was really the conclusion of the "British phase" of the story which had begun forty years earlier.

British moves to attack slavery itself revolved around three issues. One, thousands of Africans had entered the country since 1831 in violation of laws and treaties. Since they represented such a large proportion of the slave population, and since it was obviously impossible to know which ones had been smuggled in, the suggestion that those who had been imported illegally be freed was to threaten slavery itself. The British maintained a constant pressure in this regard, culminating with the demands made by the British minister William Dougal Christie, who was delighted to discover in the early 1860s that the Brazilian foreign minister "did not seek to deny the responsibility of the Brazilian government as to slaves imported since 1831."

The second issue concerned the approximately 10,000 Negroes who had been found aboard slave ships and freed by the Mixed Commission Court (which sat in Rio from 1827 to 1845) only to be deprived of their liberty nonetheless. Throughout the 1850s the British pressed for their liberation, and Christie made constant demands with the object of securing their "complete emancipation."

Finally, the larger British aim was the end of Negro slavery. As early as 1856 the British minister was suggesting to the Brazilians that they must lessen their ties to this institution. It was Christie again who thrust at the vitals of the country to which he was accredited. In 1862 he wrote Lord Russell: "I have, on various occasions, suggested to your lordship the importance of endeavoring if possible, to . . . persuade the Brazilian government to measures leading to the ultimate extinction of slavery, and in the meantime mitigating its evils."

His methods of persuasion were effective. In January, 1863, Christie was in charge of carrying out reprisals against Brazil which led to a break in diplomatic relations. It has been shown that the incidents which were the ostensible cause cannot be considered the real ones. There is much to suggest that one particular thorn in the British flesh was the re-enslaved Africans who had supposedly been freed by the Mixed Commission courts. Christie claimed that the British reprisals caused the Brazilians in 1864 to free them in truth.[10]

But, more important, these reprisals were directly responsible for the initiation of broader steps toward emancipation. In early 1864, the emperor expressed a fear that if Brazil did not move toward that end, the British might take the initiative as they had with the slave trade. Similar fears were expressed in the Senate. The emperor urged the passage of a law which would free all those born of slave mothers after a certain date. During 1865 a law along these lines was drafted and submitted to the Council of State for their consideration. It is clear that the arguments in favor were fear of eventual slave insurrections and fear of foreign intervention. "The slaves desire freedom and by the natural order of things this desire will increase steadily, and there is no way to stop it. It follows that we must prevent *external pressure* from increasing this danger, and, if we do not take measures of this sort, it will come." In May, 1867, the emperor referred to the slavery question in the Speech from the Throne; it was the first public indication that the empire might consider separating itself from the institution of slavery. The reaction in Brazil was generally one of horror and silence, but Britain prepared to repeal the arbitrary antislave-trade legislation. The eventual result was the law of 1871, which freed those born as slaves thenceforward,

[10] Sérgio Teixeira de Macedo to Paulino José Soares de Sousa, London, Oct. 8, 1852 (Arquivo Histórico do Itamaratí), 217/37, no. 18; Consulta do Conselho de Estado, March 2, 1857, in Nabuco, *Estadista do imperio*, II, 438–39; William D. Christie, *Notes on Brazilian Questions* (London and Cambridge, 1865), pp. xxxiv–xxxviii, 10, 13, 21, 22, 49, 66, 83–84; Evaristo de Moraes, *A campanha abolicionista (1879–1888)* (Rio, 1924), p. 190; Manchester, *British Preëminence*, pp. 232–33; Speech of Paranhos, June 7, 1864, Senado, *Anais*, 1864, II, 56; Richard Graham, "Os fundamentos da ruptura de relações diplomáticas entre o Brasil e a Grã-Bretanha em 1863: 'A questão Christie'," *Revista de história*, no. 49 (1962), pp. 122–23, and no. 50 (1962), p. 397; Brazilian sentiment in behalf of the *emancipados* was also inspired by the British. Aureliano Cândido Tavares Bastos, *Cartas do Solitário*, 3d ed. (São Paulo, 1938), pp. 138–45, 463–65.

but stated that they were to work for their mother's master until the age of 21 by way of compensation. Although nothing was said about eventual abolition, it was clear that slavery in Brazil was doomed.[11] It was because of British pressure that this law was passed; neither the coffee planters of São Paulo nor the new urban groups had yet emerged to exert influence in this direction.

Whether Britain's strong interest in this cause was simply the result of the British humanitarian temper or whether it was primarily a reflection of ulterior economic interests has been much debated. Some historians have suggested that British pressure for abolition sprang from a desire to increase the buying power of the Brazilian market for British goods. But the fact is that people are rarely that far-sighted. The results of abolition were uncertain and it might have plunged the country into a period of chaos and economic decline from which they could not hope to profit. The British merchants in Rio and the textile manufacturers of Manchester were loud in their protests against Christie's forceful actions, and he did not hesitate to say they were aiding Brazilian slavery. A much more defensible and sophisticated explanation is that the value system of the entire British nation was to some degree affected by the dominant position of the bourgeoisie, and slavery and the slave trade contradicted basic tenets of that system. The right to be master of one's own being was the most basic of all individual rights, and a threat to that right anywhere in the world was a threat to the validity of all

[11] Pedro II, "Apontamentos," Jan. 14, 1864 (Arquivo do Museu Imperial de Petrópolis), Maço CXXXIV, Doc. 6553, in Hélio Vianna, "Instruções de D. Pedro II aos presidentes do Conselho, Zacarias e Furtado," *Jornal do comércio*, July 3, 1964; Heitor Lyra, *História de D. Pedro II, 1825–1891* (São Paulo, 1938–1940), II, 236; Speech of Angelo Moniz Da Silva Ferraz, June 6, 1864, Senado, *Anais*, 1864, II, 49; Conselho de Estado (José Antonio Pimenta Bueno, marquês de São Vicente, *et al.*) *Trabalho sobre a extincção da escravatura no Brasil* (Rio, 1868), p. 89, italics added, also pp. 6, 62–63, 93; Joaquim Saldanha Marinho, *A Monarchia e a politica do rei* (Rio, 1885), p. 53; the Aberdeen Act was repealed in 1869. Manchester, *British Preëminence*, p. 264n; Jose Maria dos Santos, *Os republicanos paulistas e a abolição* (São Paulo, 1942), pp. 30, 49–50, 56; Nabuco, *Estadista do imperio*, I, 565–70, II, 15–54. Although there were occasional references made to the American Civil War, that sad example does not seem to have been uppermost in the minds of those who urged moves toward emancipation. They correctly perceived the differences in the respective situations of the two countries.

those rights that were considered essential by the British middle class. For the Britisher at that time it was no longer a matter of weighing the "pros" and "cons" and measuring the economic advantages or disadvantages of slavery; it was a question of asserting a principle against which no other could prevail. By the same token slavery was opposed in Brazil by those Brazilian sectors that were attacking a traditional, preindustrial, and nonindividualistic society.[12]

By the end of the 1870s the scene for the abolitionist movement had been set: the increasing demand for labor in an expanding export economy; the clearest possible signs that slavery would end sooner or later and that no new slaves would be available either from Africa or from procreation; and, finally, the presence of new urban groups who found slavery an impediment not only to their own financial success, but also to the spread of their world view. How these general forces were translated into concrete action shows the interplay of actions and ideas in human events. For the sake of clarity, it is best to jump ahead and begin with the direct causes of parliamentary action freeing the slaves, and then move backward to show the importance of these broader trends.

The most important immediate cause of abolition was the flight of the slaves from the coffee plantations of São Paulo and Rio. In the two years before the law of abolition was passed in May, 1888, the number of slaves who revolted against authority by departing from the plantations, at first secretly one by one and later in a mass and almost publicly, as enormous. It was a form of direct action against which the planters could do nothing by themselves, and the dichotomy of city and country now became evident for the first time. For in the system of escape the cities played an essential part, agents as

[12] Lídia Besouchet, *Mauá e seu tempo* (São Paulo, 1942), p. 84; Jovelino M. de Camargo Jr., "A Inglaterra e o tráfico," in Gilberto Freyre *et al., Novos estudos afro-brasileiros* (Rio, 1937), II; barão de Mauá, to marquês de Olinda, Rio, Jan. 1 and Jan. 3, 1863. AMIP, Maço CXXXIII, Doc. 6546; Carlos Americo Sampaio Vianna to Cotegipe, Rio, Jan. 21 and March 10, 1863, in José Wanderley Pinho, *Cotegipe e seu tempo: primeira phase, 1815–1867* (São Paulo, 1937), pp. 680–82; Christie, *Notes on Brazilian Questions*, pp. xxxiii, liv, livn, lxix, 133–34, 137; Eric Williams, *Capitalism and Slavery* (Chapel Hill, 1945), pp. 169–77; Roque Spencer Maciel de Barros, *A ilustração brasileira e a idéia de universidade*, Univ. de São Paulo, Cadeira de História e Filosofia da Educação, Boletim, 241, no. 2 (São Paulo, 1959), 87–88.

they were of the forces of modern change. Rio, Niterói, Petrópolis, Campos, Santos, São Paulo, and minor cities of the coffee region were all part of the network and were considered virtually free cities by the slaves. Measures were adopted there to help the escaped slaves on to the state of Ceará, where slavery had been abolished in 1884; or legal action was undertaken on their behalf to prove they were illegally held as slaves; or permanent asylum was assured until abolition became a fact.[13]

The organizer of the program of mass flights in São Paulo was Antonio Bento de Souza e Castro, who supervised the system by which slaves were lured away from the plantations, put on trains, or shepherded on foot to Santos, and installed in shantytowns. He also had the temerity to offer runaway slaves to plantation owners as hired hands during the peak harvest season, and the owners hired them. The very railways that had made the extension of coffee agriculture possible now served the slave. As one historian put it, "There was not a passenger or freight train on which a run-away slave might not find means of hiding himself, and there was not a station where someone would not discreetly receive him and help him." Almost all the railroad employees were said to be abolitionists, and not the least enthusiastic were the managers. In Santos, where all local slaves had been freed in 1886 by funds raised by public subscription, the slaves who arrived via the "underground railroad" were immediately sheltered in the outskirts of the city where 10,000 of them were sometimes gathered.[14]

In other cities the story was much the same. In the city of Rio de Janeiro, center of the abolitionist movement, the slaves had no difficulty in finding temporary asylum in the houses of interested

[13] Moraes, *Campanha abolicionista*, pp. 223–34; Haring, *Empire in Brazil*, p. 102; Fernandes, "Do escravo ao cidadão," p. 46; even Ouro Prêto played this role. José Oiliam, *A abolição em Minas* (Belo Horizonte, 1962), p. 95; Raimundo Girão, *A abolição no Ceará* (Fortaleza, 1956); on role of the cities generally, see *O Abolicionista*, no. 1, Nov. 1, 1880, p. 8; Associação Commercial do Rio de Janeiro, *Resposta da Associação Commercial do Rio de Janeiro aos quesitos da Commissão Parlamentar de Inquerito* (Rio, 1883), p. 20.

[14] Santos, *Republicanos paulistas*, pp. 170–71, 179, 181–82; Francisco Martins dos Santos, *História de Santos . . . 1532–1936* (São Paulo, 1937), II, 27, 33; Moraes, *Campanha abolicionista*, pp. 261–66; for the attitude toward slavery of railway manager J. J. Aubertin, see *Correio paulistano*, Jan. 3, 1867, p. 2.

persons, whence they were hustled to the outlying area of Leblón. Petrópolis also became a haven for escapees. In Campos, direct action took an even more overt form. Luiz Carlos de Lacerda urged slave revolts and was blamed for the burning of cane fields.[15]

Why did the government not stop the mass flights of the slaves? Although both the provincial and central governments took sporadic actions, it soon become clear that their agents—many of whom were second-generation bureaucrats with urban backgrounds—did not have their hearts in the attempt to repress slave flights. The government was located in the cities, and efforts to restrain the underground railroad there met civilian opposition at every turn. But especially significant is the fact that it was from the cities that the armed forces were recruited, especially the officers of the army. The military schools had for years been the site of abolitionist societies. There are many proofs of the reluctance of the military to act as slave hunters. Finally, in October 1887, the Clube Militar, made up of the leading elements of the army, petitioned the princess regent that they be exonerated from chasing slaves. This was an era of growing timidity on the part of the landed aristocracy in the face of the demands of the increasingly self-assertive officers, who had their way. It has even been suggested that, if the legislature had not passed the law of abolition in 1888, the cities would have risen in revolt and the military would not have defended the regime.[16]

The cooperation of urban classes can be seen in a humorous incident that took place in Santos. The government of the province

[15] Moraes, *Campanha abolicionista*, pp. 155–56, 238–50; Rebouças, *Diário*, p. 312; cf. Octavio Ianni, *As metamorphoses do escravo. Apogeu e crise da escravatura no Brasil meridional* (São Paulo, 1962), pp. 228–29; no mention of these events is made by Clovis Moura, *Rebeliões da senzala (quilombos, insurreições, guerrilhas)* (São Paulo, 1959).

[16] Rebouças, *Diário*, p. 309; Osorio Duque Estrada, *A abolição (esboço histórico—1831–1888)* (Rio, 1918), pp. 96–101; Maria Stella Novaes, *A escravidão e a abolição no Espirito Santo: história e folclore* (Vitória, 1963), p. 134; Moraes, *Campanha abolicionista*, p. 33, 167, 248, 312–14, 322–23; June Edith Hahner, "The Role of the Military in Brazil, 1889–1894" (unpubl. M.A. thesis, Cornell University, 1963), pp. 4–13; the rank and file of the army was considered untrustworthy, being generally Negroes or mulattoes, Hastings Charles Dent, *A Year in Brazil, with Notes on Abolition of Slavery . . .* (London, 1886), p. 287.

had sent a trainload of troops to capture runaway slaves there. When the train pulled into the station, the soldiers found it filled by the leading matrons of the town who jammed the doors of the cars, preventing the troops from alighting. The superintendent of the railway persuaded the half-hearted commandant of the expedition to surrender before the superior force of the buxom females and return to the provincial capital.[17] Neither the soldiers nor these representatives of the new urban groups were interested in protecting the human property "rights" of the landowners. By May it was estimated that half the slaves that had been in the Campos areas six months earlier were free; and one-third of the São Paulo plantations were being worked by recently freed slaves. Thus the law abolishing slavery was merely a formality since the process then in full swing would have ended slavery to all intents and purposes within a few months. One antiabolitionist asked "For what, an abolition law? In fact it is done already—and revolutionarily. The terrified masters seek to stem the exodus by giving immediate freedom to their slaves." [18]

This is not to say that the ideas of the abolitionists were not important in bringing about the end of slavery. It took hard work to persuade the slaves to leave the plantations.

Finally, during the first months of 1888, many planters began to free their own slaves in order to prevent them from leaving the plantations. The *Confederação Abolicionista* in Rio hired Italian peddlers to talk the slaves into leaving the plantations. They were also given leaflets to distribute throughout the interior which, presumably, were read to the illiterate slaves. Some of the peddlers were murdered by slave foremen, but the news continued to spread. The abolitionists also made it a point to convey their message to those slaves who passed through the city with their masters. On their return these slaves carried with them the idea of escape and the knowledge that they would be helped and protected.[19]

[17] Santos, *Republicanos paulistas*, p. 184.

[18] Moraes, *Campanha abolicionista*, pp. 304–309, 321–25, 339; Fernandes, "Do escravo ao cidadão," pp. 49–50; Stein, *Vassouras*, pp. 253–55; Cotegipe to barão do Penedo, Petrópolis, April 8, 1888, in Renato Mendonça, *Um diplomata na côrte de Inglaterra; o barão do Penedo e sua época* (São Paulo, 1942), p. 397.

[19] Duque Estrada, *A abolição*, p. 102; Dent, *Year in Brazil*, pp. 285–86.

One way in which this protection was realized also reflected the abolitionists' success in changing the attitudes of Brazilian magistrates. The abolitionists had hit upon the device of taking the case of slaves imported since 1831 to court, charging illegal enslavement of free persons. At first this effort had little success; at the beginning of the 1880s the abolitionists could still say, referring to the law and to the years that had elapsed since its passage, that "the judges of this country either can't read or can't count." But soon some judges, moved by the very force of the abolitionist campaign, began to hand down favorable decisions. After about 1883, few courts would deny freedom to the slave who could prove that he or his parents had been brought in after 1831, and one lawyer on a single occasion secured the freedom of 716 slaves on the basis of this law. Later, the judges placed the burden of proof upon the owner. The forceful campaign of words and ideas which preceded and accompanied the flight from the plantations had borne fruit.[20]

It was also because of the force and effectiveness of the abolitionist crusade that large segments of the urban population were persuaded to acquiesce in, or contribute to, the success of the movement. Had it not been for the abolitionists' constant effort to demonstrate the anachronism of slavery in the age of "progress," the military officers would probably have continued to cooperate to preserve the status quo. The participation of other urban groups as well was characteristic of the successful escape of the slaves.

The abolitionist campaign had begun in 1879. Since it has been examined in some detail by others, little need be said about it here.[21] Throughout the 1880s an effective group of mature journalists and publicists carried the message into the homes of the urban middle

---

[20] *O abolicionista*, no. 12, Sept. 28, 1881, p. 8; Moraes, *Campanha abolicionista*, pp. 182 ff., 203*n*.

[21] The best-known study is by Moraes, *Campanha abolicionista*, but he fails to interpret the very facts that he relates regarding slave flights. Cf. his briefer summaries in *A escravidão africana no Brasil*, pp. 147–247, and "A escravidão—da supressão do tráfico à lei áurea," *Revista do Instituto Histórico e Geográphico Brasileiro; tomo especial: Congresso Internacional de História da América, 1922* (Rio, 1927), III, 270–313. Also see Affonso Toledo Bandeira de Mello, "A escravidão—da supressão do tráfico à lei áurea," *Ibid.*, pp. 381–406; and Duque Estrada, *A abolição*.

classes. Well-financed abolitionist societies provided the direction for the many-faceted campaign. These clubs presented a series of lectures, one almost every week, and it became the fashion among those who aspired to identify with modernity to attend. On the flimsiest excuse a demonstration would be staged, with parades, banners, and speeches. Several newspapers were published, and all possible means were used to bring the cause to public attention. But it was in Parliament that the movement found its most brilliant speechmakers; and it was there that early and cautious half-measures were passed. From 1884 to 1888 this body was involved in the slavery argument almost constantly, and it was the work of the publicists in the city and the flight of the slaves in the country that were blamed for the new concern. Antônio Prado, leading coffee planter and entrepreneur, finally recognizing the approaching end, took up the leadership of the parliamentary maneuvers toward abolition and pushed it through.[22]

On May 13, 1888, the law abolishing slavery in Brazil without compensation was signed by the princess regent. Month-long celebrations ensued in almost all the urban centers of Brazil, with fireworks and speeches and parades. In the countryside, however, there was little celebration. The slaves themselves were disoriented, not knowing what to do with their freedom. Many flocked into the cities to find their fellows who had already fled the plantations. The masters, even those who had acquiesced or cooperated in the final stages of the movement, must have been dazed by the rapidity of the transformation. Depression in the countryside was the immediate result of abolition. Efforts to ameliorate this situation by government financial manipulation served only to strengthen further the urban groups of bank managers, company promoters, stock manipulators, and their employees *vis à vis* the rural powers. It is not true that abolition changed nothing. As the *coup de grâce* for the sugar zone of the Northeast and the old coffee region of the Paraíba Valley, it served to shift power definitively into the hands of the new coffee zone of São Paulo state. It increased the confidence of the new urban groups and, although their victory appeared short lived,

[22] Moraes, *Campanha abolicionista*, pp. 19, 21, 24, 25, 33, 45–171 *passim*, 321–53; Prado, ed., *Antonio Prado*, pp. 228, 243–44.

this was a significant step along the lengthy path toward modernization. It seriously weakened the monarchy, whose ties to the
landowners are well known. Even the slave-become-wage-earner,
deprived as he was of the sense of victory, was at least one degree
closer to a modern world view.

PART II

Immigration,
Stratification, and Race Relations

CHAPTER 4

Immigration and *Mestizaje*
in Nineteenth-Century Peru
Mário C. Vázquez

Immigration is one of the major aspects of Latin American social history, and in the present contribution Mario C. Vázquez—a Peruvian anthropologist connected with Cornell University—examines the numerical data regarding this phenomenon in Peru during the nineteenth century. Not only were immigrants numerically significant during this period, but also, because of governmental concessions, the British, North Americans, and Germans came to exercise important positions within the nation's economic life. The latter group, however, was precisely the one which was assimilated into the local culture with the most difficulty, while the others, not excluding many of the Asians brought in as laborers, mixed readily with the local population and intermarried to a large degree. For one thing, the constant wars and political turmoil of the nineteenth century, coupled with the shifting currents of economic development, fostered geographical mobility and encouraged new relationships between persons of different racial and national backgrounds. Since the first two factors also helped thin out the indigenous male population while the majority of immigrants were male, the process of miscegenation was further encouraged. The author also points to the original presence of many more Negroes in the highland regions than are usually thought to have been there, and contradicts the usual view of closed Indian communities into which the outsider penetrated only with the greatest difficulty.

[73]

IMMIGRATION AND RACE RELATIONS
Historical Background

Before discussing immigration[1] to Peru in the nineteenth century and the integration of the immigrants into Peruvian society, it is necessary to sketch briefly the historical background.

The most significant political events in nineteenth-century Peruvian history were the Wars of Independence, the establishment of the Republic, and the international wars. The movement of foreign and Peruvian military forces in these wars fostered both miscegenation and acculturation.

There are two important phases in the history of Peru's emancipation: the revolutionary era, and the War of Independence. The first, beginning in 1780 with the revolt of Tupac Amaru and ending in 1820 with the arrival of San Martín, was characterized by various mutinies, conspiracies, protests, and rebellions of Indians, mestizos, and *criollos*. To be sure, some of these movements, for instance, the risings in Cajamarca, did not seek national independence, but in some ways, they, too, were precursors of it.[2]

[1] References in this article to "Indian," "white," "Negro," "Asian," or "mestizo," use the social and cultural rather than the biological sense of the terms. The classifications are those adopted by Peruvian censuses. Since the nineteenth century the original classification of the population into Indians, whites, Negroes, and mestizos has been polarized into two groups (Indian and mestizo) with new sociocultural (residence and occupation) criteria. In terms of social stratification, the Indian belongs to the lower class, regionally and nationally. The mestizo, on the other hand, constitutes the provincial middle or upper class and the national middle class. There is no intrinsic relationship between biological race and the mestizo-Indian dichotomy. Genetically, many Indians would be Caucasian, as John Gillin has demonstrated in the case of the "Indians" of Cajamarca (*El mestizaje en la historia de Ibero-América* [Mexico City, 1961], p. 76). Also, as John H. Rowe ("The Distribution of Indians and Indian Languages in Peru," *Geographic Review*, XXXVII: 2 [1947], 214) states, there is no close correlation between language and race. In three provinces of Piura, from 50 to 70 per cent of the population is Indian but less than 1 per cent speaks native languages. On a national level, on the other hand, 15 per cent of those classified as whites and mestizos could speak nothing but Quechua. On miscegenation see Frank R. Ellis, L. P. Crawley, and G. W. Lasker, "Blood Groups, Hemoglobin Types, and Secretion of Group-Specific Substance at Hacienda Cayaltí, North Peru," *Human Biology*, XXXV: 1 (1963), 30.

[2] Waldemar Espinosa, "Protestas, motines y rebeliones de indios, mestizos y españoles en Cajamarca, 1756–1821," *La Causa de la Emancipación del Perú* (Lima: Instituto Riva-Agüero, 1960), p. 36.

In most instances, the participants in such rebellions and their sympathizers were punished severely by the royal authorities. Some were shot, others suffered the confiscation of property, and still others were imprisoned, persecuted, or exiled. Sometimes entire families were sent into exile. Many rebellious Indians and other insurgents were forced to live in Lima, and many *limeños* were confined to cities of the *sierra*.

The second period (1820–1825), which culminated in the defeat of the Spaniards, was characterized by the heterogeneity of those who fought the war. The ranks of the patriots were composed of Colombians, Venezuelans, Chileans, Argentines, Bolivians, and Irish, as well as of Peruvian mestizos, criollos, Negroes, and Indians. It is important to note that at first the Peruvian contingents were drawn mostly from the Lima-born, but that during the course of the war they came to include an increasing number of Indians and mestizos, enlisted by force in the various provinces, especially in the sierra.[3] This period, like the earlier era, was characterized by wholesale reprisals on the part of the victors against their defeated foes.

As we have seen, the prolonged revolutionary struggle encouraged contact among persons of different social and racial backgrounds, from various countries and various regions within Peru. Such contact occurred not only during the fighting and the occupation of the cities, but also within the plotting and periods of exile and imprisonment that were part of the war. The vicissitudes of war also induced many people to flee from their homes, especially in Lima. This phenomenon of forced internal migrations served to stimulate both national sentiment and racial mixture on a sociocultural as well as a biological level. By the end of the war there were many soldiers, Spanish and Peruvian alike, stranded in strange towns, far from their places of birth, as the baptismal and marriage certificates for the post-war years indicate.[4] Thanks to the turbulence of the first years

[3] William B. Stevenson, *Memorias de . . . sobre las campañas de San Martín y Cochrane en el Peru* (Madrid, 1919), p. 43; Joaquín de la Pezuela, *Memoria de Gobierno del Virrey . . .* , eds., V. Rodríguez Casado and G. Lohmann Villena (Seville: Escuela de Estudios Hispano-Americanos, 1947), pp. 671, 744–45.

[4] J. J. J. von Tschudi, *Travels in Peru During the Years 1838–1842* (London, 1847), p. 364.

of the Republic, this tendency toward internal population movement continued—especially for the soldiers—even after the war.

According to the historian Jorge Basadre, during the nineteenth century the Republic was characterized by

an abundance of military men because of the war, a lack of experience within the government itself, disorder that may be considered natural after centuries of subjugation, ignorance of the principles of citizenship among the masses, power-hunger in military and political circles, weakness of the state structure, a regionalism rooted in geographical remoteness, and conflict among militant nationalisms.[5]

As a result of these and other similar factors, the years between 1825 and 1900 witnessed over one hundred conspiracies, disorders, insurrections, mutinies, and revolutions. Most of these movements were headed by military or civilian *caudillos*, who, when successful, followed the precedent of inflicting such reprisals as imprisonment, exile, persecution, execution, and confiscation, upon the vanquished. During this time there were also Indian peasant uprisings in Ilave, Huancane, Huanta, Huaraz, Azangaro, Dos de Mayo, La Mar, Ayacucho, and Puno, as "protests against the abuses of the authorities and all those who felt that it was within their power to deny the Indian his dignity and rights." [6] The most important revolts occurred in Huancane in 1866, in Huaraz in 1885, and Huanta in 1896–1897. These movements, especially the one in Huanta, were repressed ferociously, with a cruelty that caused thousands of deaths and the exodus of many persecuted peasants into other regions.

Eight foreign wars were also part of Peruvian life during the nineteenth century. The country suffered three defeats, the most serious being at the hands of the Chileans in the War of the Pacific (1879–1883). According to Basadre, during this period "not a single person, young or old, man or woman, . . . was not affected in one way or another by this drama." [7] As in all wars, there were occupations, massacres, shootings, exiles, and other uses of force which created

[5] Jorge Basadre, *Perú: Problema y posibilidad* (Lima, 1931), p. 25.

[6] Santiago Távara, *Historia de los partidos* (Lima, 1951), p. 83; Jorge Basadre, *Historia de la República del Perú*, VI (Lima, 1962), 2686.

[7] Basadre, *Ibid.*, VI, 2665.

situations of contact between different peoples that in turn led to miscegenation.

Yet, not everything was anarchy, tragedy, and economic and financial depression. There were also periods of calm and of efforts to lead the country toward progress and a place of respect among nations. During these pauses, spontaneous migratory movements took place as a result of several factors. Among these were: the abolition of Negro slavery and of Indian tributes (1854); the movement to bring education to all levels of society; railroad building; the exploitation of saltpeter and guano deposits; the establishment or modernization of the textile, sugar, rubber, and wine industries; the introduction of telegraph lines, electrical services, and water and drainage systems; projects to explore and colonize the Amazon jungle; the passage of immigration laws; the regulation of commerce; the creation of banks; and the revival of mining. In most of these developmental activities, immigrants played an active role, as did many Peruvians who moved from place to place in search of better opportunities.

It should be stressed that "the people" took part directly or indirectly in the country's wars and economic development. As noted above, in wartime many persons were forced to move about, as prisoners, refugees, or fugitives; and during peacetime, movement continued as people sought work, health, or rest. Unlike the case today, the internal migrations of that period were directed not from the Andes to the coast or to Lima, but rather toward those towns which offered greater security for life and property. It is interesting that during the first half of the century the city of Lima lost population. J. J. J. von Tschudi, who visited the city in 1842, records that he found many uninhabited houses whose owners had emigrated or died during the War of Independence, the ensuing political battles, or epidemics and earthquakes.[8] Only the arrival of immigrants in the second half of the nineteenth century checked the population decline not only of Lima but of the country of Peru as a whole.

---

[8] José María Córdova y Urrutia, *Estadística histórica, geográfica, industrial y comercial de los pueblos que componen el departamento de Lima* (Lima, 1839), p. 5; Tschudi, *Travels in Peru*, p. 89.

Immigration in the Nineteenth Century

From the beginnings of the Republic, immigration was considered desirable by Peruvian officials, who sought to promote it through a series of decrees and laws which gave preference to European (that is, white) immigrants and discriminated against others. In time, however, under pressure from the *latifundistas* who needed hands to work their plantations, Negroes and Orientals were accepted. Indeed, the government itself was forced to recruit a labor force to carry out its various public works projects.

Immigrants came to Peru from five continents. It is estimated that about 200,000 arrived; in other words, about 1.0 to 1.3 per cent of the total immigration to Latin America, which has been put at 15 to 20 million for the nineteenth century. The 1876 census counted 106,962 foreigners representing 3.96 per cent of the total population.[9]

The Europeans. Despite the inducements to settlement offered them by Peruvian legislation, Europeans overwhelmingly preferred to emigrate to other countries such as Argentina and Brazil. There were several major obstacles to European immigration in Peru.

First, the *latifundistas* controlled economic and political power, which they were unwilling to surrender; and they looked upon the immigrant as a source of cheap labor on their haciendas. The Europeans, who had hoped to obtain their own land to cultivate according to European patterns, objected strongly. As Marvin Harris has written with reference to the European migrant to the New World:

The nineteenth century European migrants were animated by hope and a spirit of enterprise. They eventually came to set up their own small farms in the European mixed farming tradition, or they worked for wages in the expectation that they would soon be able to buy their own lands, or start their own business.[10]

[9] Harry L. Shapiro, "Ethnic Patterns in Latin America," *Scientific Monthly,* LXI: 5 (1945), 349; Hildebrando Fuentes, *La inmigración en el Perú* (Lima, 1892), p. 313.
[10] Marvin Harris, *Patterns of Race in the Americas* (New York, 1964), p. 98.

Second, political and economic instability had a negative influence upon the immigrants, who were looking for an improvement of the conditions under which they had lived in Europe. There is no doubt that immigration to Peru was hampered by the fact that between 1821 and 1895 Lima suffered ten military invasions.[11]

Third, Peru's foreign wars had an adverse effect on immigration, since foreigners were denied all privileges and guarantees in wartime. For example, during the war with Chile, many foreigners lost their property and even their lives; an example may be found in the execution of eleven Italian firemen by Chileans in 1881.[12]

Fourth, in international competition for immigrants, Peru had little to offer the prospective settler. With regard both to standards of living and to international reputation, it was far outdistanced by its more successful South American rivals, Argentina, Brazil, and Uruguay. And fifth, sanitary conditions were extremely poor; indeed, there were frequent epidemics of malaria, yellow fever, and typhus.

Despite these handicaps, Peru attracted about 50,000 immigrants from Spain, Italy, France, Germany, Portugal, England, Ireland, and lastly, the United States. The order of listing shows numerical importance.

The Spaniards were the largest foreign group. At the end of the Wars of Independence, some remained in Peru and others, who had left, returned. Their exact numbers are not known, since many became Peruvian citizens immediately after the Wars of Independence or the war with Spain in 1866. In 1860 three hundred Basque colonists arrived to work the hacienda Talambo (La Libertad), but six days after their arrival, they rebelled at the proposed working conditions and only one hundred eighty remained, including women and children. In 1866 Spaniards were prohibited from entering Peru and one group was forced to leave the country.[13] Nevertheless, according to the 1876 census, there were Spaniards in all of the nation's departments.

The second largest group of foreigners to enter the country during the nineteenth century were the 26,511 Italians who, according

[11] Felipe de la Barra, *Invasiones militares de Lima* (Lima, 1959), pp. 11–19.
[12] Basadre, *Historia*, VI, 2521.
[13] *Ibid.*, IV (1961), 1446; V (1961), 1299.

to official figures from Italy, emigrated to Peru largely during the ten years from 1891 to 1901, when 45.26 per cent of the total arrived.[14] According to Tschudi, the majority of Italian immigrants were Genoese sailors or adventurers who normally returned to Europe once they had made their fortunes. In 1877 the Genoese still constituted the largest percentage (42 per cent) of Italian residents of Peru and Chile.[15] According to the 1876 census, the Italians lived in all the departments of Peru. In Lima they were the second largest foreign group, accounting for 3 per cent of the city's total population and 19.18 per cent of the resident foreigners. It is estimated that in 1900 there were over 10,000 Italians in Peru.[16]

The French, who came to Peru both before and after Independence, occupied third place among the European immigrants in Peru, accounting in 1876 for 9.21 per cent of Lima's foreign population. Several Frenchmen or their Peruvian sons participated in the revolutionary stage of the Wars of Independence.[17]

Germans came to Peru both in groups organized for settlement and individually as immigrants. Various bands of settlers arrived at several different times:

Year	Germans Arriving in Peru
1851	1,000
1857	294
1868	314
1871–1926	1,115

The first group was to have settled Lower Huallaga, but only a small number ever traveled even as far as Tarapoto and Moyobamba. The majority stayed in Lima as domestic servants or artisans. According to Del Rio, many German immigrants walked the streets of Lima asking for charity.[18] The second group, composed of one

[14] *Annuario statistico italiano 1904* (Rome, 1904), p. 119.

[15] Tschudi, *Travels in Peru*, p. 121; *Statistica della emigrazione italiana ca nell' anno 188*7 (Rome: Direzione Generale della Statisti, 1888), p. 9.

[16] Marie Robinson Wright, *The Old and the New Peru* (Philadelphia, 1908), p. 433.

[17] Walter F. Willcox, *International Migrations,* I (New York, 1929), 110.

[18] Willcox, *Ibid.*, I, 121; Mario E. del Hío, *La inmigración y su desarrollo en el Perú* (Lima, 1929), p. 53.

hundred Catholic families from the Tyrol and fifty from the Rhine, was sent to colonize the Pozuzo area of the Amazon jungle, where, in 1858–1859, a total of 247 persons arrived. Although they were abandoned by the Peruvian government, which did not comply with the contract it had signed to aid them, some remained in the settlements. Despite great difficulties and vicissitudes, many found success in cocoa-tree plantations, the exploitation of cocaine, and the distillation of cane *aguardiente*. A third group, also from the Tyrol and Rhine area, was sent to the Pozuzo colony, but half of them returned to Lima and other coastal cities to take up commerce. At the end of the century, some descendants of the first two groups moved to Oxapampa and took part in the settlement of that area. The fourth "group" probably was made up of individual immigrants, since there is no official record of their arrival as a group. Between 1885 and 1887 only ninety-two German immigrants traveled to Peru.[19]

The English and Irish apparently constituted a large foreign colony until the middle of the nineteenth century, since it was the only group to obtain permission from the Peruvian government to maintain a private cemetery, in Bellavista, Callao. These foreigners worked for English import-export, shipping, manufacturing, and mining companies. One of these immigrants was the founder and owner of the Casa Grace y Cia. It is well known that many Irish mercenaries fought on the side of the patriots during the Wars of Independence and that after the wars many remained in Peru. In 1851 three hundred twenty additional Irish farm laborers arrived in Peru to work on the Gallagher hacienda near Callao.[20]

Lesser numbers of Portuguese, Belgians, Danes, Swedes, Dutch,

---

[19] Willcox, *International Migrations*, II (1931), 355; Juan F. Pazos Varela, *Tesis sobre la inmigración en el Perú* (1891), p. 30; Basadre, *Historia*, II, (1961), 953; Hío, *La inmigración*, p. 53. The Pozuzo colony was visited by Antonio Raimondi in 1880; see his *Apuntes sobre la Provincia Litoral de Loreto* (Iquitos, 1942), p. 127; René Gonnard, *L'émigration européenne au XIXᵉ siècle* (Paris, 1906), p. 175; Wolfram U. Drewes, *The Economic Development of the Western Montaña of Central Peru as Related to Transportation* (Lima: Peruvian Times, 1958), p. 13.

[20] Basadre, *Historia*, II, 453, 563; Brian Fawcett, "How China Came to Peru," *The Geographical Magazine*, XXXVII: 6 (1964), p. 427.

Swiss, Greeks, and others also emigrated to Peru, settling mostly in the urban centers.

There were North Americans in Peru from the onset of the Wars of Independence. With the advent of the Republic they, like the English (with whom they identified), organized commercial enterprises and mining companies.

The Asians. Although controversial, immigration from Asia was more successful than European settlement for the following reasons: first, sale of semi-slaves in Peru was a lucrative business, without responsibilities, for Asian slave traders because the Peruvian government paid a premium of thirty pesos per head for the arrivals; second, slave traffic was supported by the *latifundistas* and businessmen who held economic and political power; third, these immigrants, "accustomed to humble work, were happy with the little they got" and resigned themselves to working as semi-slaves and serfs, agricultural laborers, or in urban services;[21] and fourth, the governments of China and Japan which supplied most of the Asiatic immigrants displayed little interest in the welfare of their subjects.

Immigration from Asia began when the *latifundistas*, who were unable obtain further concessions for the importation of Negro slaves from British colonies, obtained the passage of laws permitting them to "import" Chinese from Hong Kong and Macao between 1849 and 1874. During these twenty-five years, 90,000 to 150,000 Chinese arrived in Peru.[22] It is believed that they belonged to the Huach'iao group; linguistically, they were Cantonese and Hakka.[23] All were males under forty years of age, who "contracted" to work for eight years as "braceros" on coastal plantations, guano islands, in mines, in railroad construction, or as servants. It is estimated that

[21] Luis Pesce, *Indígena e inmigrantes en el Perú* (Lima, 1906), pp. 128–29.

[22] Emilio Choy, "Reseña: Chinese Bondage in Peru," *Folklore Americano*, II:2 (1954), 162. According to Watt Stewart, *Chinese Bondage in Peru* (Durham, N.C., 1951), p. 74, they were 90,000; according to Eugenio Chang-Rodríguez, "Chinese Labor Migration into Latin America in the Nineteenth Century," *Revista de Historia de América*, No. 46 (Mexico City, 1958), 391, they were more than 100,000; according to Choy, "Reseña," p. 165, they were 150,000.

[23] Alice Jo Kwong, "The Chinese in Peru," in Morton Fried (ed.), *Colloquium on Overseas Chinese* (New York: Institute of Pacific Relations, 1958; mimeogr.) p. 41.

90 per cent of these coolies worked on plantations, on the haciendas on the coast and of the sierra, such as Cajatambo, Huarochirí, Tarma, Arequipa, and Moquegua. Although the Chinese died by the thousands, they remained the largest single foreign group in Lima, accounting for 36.57 per cent of that city's total foreign population in the census of 1876.[24]

Japanese immigration began after 1873. The 1876 national census counted only fifteen Japanese, but by the end of 1899, according to Titiev, there were 1,200 of them living in Peru.[25] After 1899 their numbers increased sharply as more and more contracted plantation workers arrived. The first such group, consisting of 790 men who were divided among twelve plantations, disembarked in April, 1899. By December, only 449 remained working on nine haciendas. Of the rest, forty-two were employed as house servants and seventeen as free laborers in Lima, four were in Callao, five had deserted and emigrated to Bolivia, and the rest had died.[26]

The Negroes. The Negroes arrived in Peru together with the Spaniards during the Conquest and throughout the colonial period. The 1791 census, ordered by Viceroy Gil de Taboada, reported 41,398 mulattoes and free Negroes and 40,337 Negro slaves. According to Viceroy Avilés, as quoted by Palma, 65,747 Negroes were brought to Peru between 1790 and 1802. Another group arrived in 1814 during the administration of Viceroy Abascal. Palma also notes that in 1821 the number of Negro slaves in all of Peru was 41,228, of which 33,000 were involved in agricultural work.[27] In 1847 Negro slaves from New Granada (Colombia) were brought to Peru, but the venture was discontinued because it proved unprofitable and because the Congress of New Granada prohibited the ex-

---

[24] Chang-Rodríguez, "Chinese Labor Migration," p. 389; Stewart, *Chinese Bondage in Peru*, p. 89.

[25] Mischa Titiev, "The Japanese Colony in Peru," *The Far Eastern Quarterly*, X, No. 3 (1951), 228.

[26] Toraji Irie, "History of Japanese Migration to Peru," HAHR, XXXI (1951), 444–45, 651.

[27] Rubén Vargas Ugarte, *Manuscritos peruanos*, II (Lima, 1938), 370; Ricardo Palma, *Tradiciones peruanas completas* (Madrid, 1953), pp. 138–39

odus of its slaves.[28] Palma estimates that at the moment of Abolition in 1854 there were about 17,000 slaves in Peru, although by falsifying documents the slaveowners "raised" the number to 25,505 in order to draw more compensation from the government.[29] The 1876 census placed the Negro population at 44,224, 92 per cent of which lived on the coast, and the rest in the jungle and the sierra.[30]

The South Americans. Immigration to Peru from other South American countries existed throughout the nineteenth century, but it had begun in the middle of the previous century with the arrival of certain Argentines and Chileans. Besides taking part in the revolutionary movements of emancipation, these settlers also controlled Peru's commerce. Proctor, who visited Lima in 1823–1824, wrote that "there should not be more than two or three Peruvian mercantile establishments in Lima and Callao: commerce may be said to be engrossed by foreigners, amongst whom are many natives of Chile and Buenos Aires." [31]

In 1842 Tschudi noted that "settlers from the other American republics have of late considerably increased in Lima. After the Chilean expedition of 1838 many Chileans established themselves in Peru, and numbers of Argentines, escaping from the terrorism of Rosas in Buenos Aires, have taken refuge in Lima." [32] Between 1850 and 1879, thousands of Chileans and Bolivians came to Peru to work as *braceros* on the guano islands and in the building of railroads. Stewart believes that 25,000 Chileans and 10,000 Bolivians worked in the construction of the Mollendo-Arequipa, Lima-La Oroya, and Arequipa-Puno railways between 1868 and 1872. He notes that when in 1879 their expulsion was decreed by the Peruvian government,

[28] Basadre, *Historia*, II, 833.

[29] Palma, *Tradiciones peruanas*, p. 141.

[30] Fernando Romero, "The Slave Trade and the Negro In South America," *The Hispanic American Historical Review*, XXIV (1944), 381.

[31] Robert Proctor, *Narrative of a Journey Across the Cordillera of the Andes, and of a Residence in Lima and Other Parts of Peru in the Years 1823 and 1824* (London, 1825), p. 235.

[32] Tschudi, *Travels in Peru*, pp. 121–22.

there were 20,000 Chileans in the country.[33] Of course, the expulsion was only partial.

Many Colombian and Venezuelan soldiers in Bolívar's army also remained in Peru. Only 8,000 of the original 13,000 troops returned to their country. The rest were replaced by Peruvian soldiers, repatriated in part in 1852 and 1857.[34] The 1876 census listed the Chileans and Ecuadorians in, respectively, the fourth and fifth positions among foreigners resident in Lima.

The Polynesians. Immigration to Peru from Polynesia was small but not insignificant and involved only one group, the 1,680 Polynesians or "canacas" who arrived in Peru in 1862 to work as semi-slaves on the plantations and farms along the coast. Most succumbed to disease, and the survivors were expatriated by the Peruvian government because of French pressure.[35]

Mestizaje and the Integration of the Immigrants

Mixture of immigrant ethnic groups with the native-born population and integration into the social and cultural life of Peru were fostered by the high proportion of male immigrants and by the existence of a large, mostly Indian, lower class. According to the 1876 census, 84.86 per cent of all foreigners in Peru were males. Among the native born, on the other hand, as a result of the wars women were in a clear majority. Marriage between foreign men and Peruvian women helped redress the balance. Thus, although there were 2,786 more women than men in the city of Lima in 1854, twenty-two years later, males (23.64 per cent of whom were foreigners) outnumbered the females by 4,322. In Callao, the male majority was 5,838 according to the same census of 1876. The situation changed after the war with Chile; in 1891, there were 4,256 more women than men in Lima.[36] The decline of the foreign-born population of

[33] Watt Stewart, "El trabajador chileno y los ferrocarriles del Perú," *Revista Chilena de Historia y Geografía,* LXXXV, No. 93 (1938), 135–36, 163.

[34] Basadre, *Historia,* I, 161–62.

[35] *Ibid.,* III, 1450.

[36] Tschudi, *Travels in Peru,* p. 91; Juan Bromley and J. Barbagelata, *Evolución urbana de la ciudad de Lima* (Lima, 1945), p. 92.

[85]

Lima from 15.35 per cent in 1876 to 11.85 per cent in 1891 also contributed to this imbalance. At the same time, there was an increase in the number of widows (from 6.15 per cent in 1876 to 8.59 per cent in 1891) largely as a result of the War of the Pacific.

The presence in the cities of a large lower class, composed mainly of Indians (who accounted for over 50 per cent of the country's total population) and poor mestizos, facilitated ethnic mixing. Copelo estimates that in 1894, servants, two-thirds of which were women, accounted for 30 per cent of the population of Lima.[37] Especially in the cities and on the plantations, lower-class women engaged in sexual relations with the immigrants either as legitimate wives or as concubines. When they visited Peru in the nineteenth century, Tschudi and Gibbs observed quite correctly that in the choice of husbands, Peruvian women preferred immigrants to the native-born.[38] This selective criterion still exists.

From the colonial epoch to the present day, the very generalized practice of extra-marital relations between men and their Indian or Negro female servants has been an important element in *mestizaje*. Although theoretically it follows that the mestizo population should have increased as a result of unions between foreigners and Peruvians, the percentage of mestizos in the total population actually declined between 1791 and 1876, as can be seen from the following table:

Ethnic Groups	1791	1876	1940
Indians	56.58	57.60	45.86
Whites	12.67	13.75	
Mestizos	26.56	24.80	52.89
Negroes	3.75	1.95	0.47
Asians	—	1.90	0.68
Unknown	0.34	—	0.10

The mestizo group accounted for 26.56 per cent of Peru's population in 1791, 24.80 per cent in 1876, and 52.89 per cent (including whites as well as mestizos) in 1940. That is to say, the percentage of mestizos fell by 1.78 between 1791 and 1876. Undoubtedly the de-

[37] J. Copelo, *Sociología de Lima* (Lima, 1895), p. 84.
[38] Tschudi, *Travels in Peru*, p. 122; Stewart, *Chinese Bondage*, p. 122.

cline can be explained by the participation of mestizos in the various wars of the period. The effects were most noticeable in Lima, where the percentage of mestizos decreased from 52.92 per cent in 1820 to 48.79 per cent in 1842, or 4.13 per cent in twenty-two years.[39] These figures remained static until 1876, when the percentage of mestizos declined even further, to 47.96 per cent, or a loss of 0.63 per cent from the 1842 figure.

The decline can be explained partially by the absorption of immigrants and their descendants into the Indian communities that surrounded them. In light of the absence of "Europeanizing" acculturative agents such as schools and modern communications media, the new generation tended to become "Indian," though biologically it was mestizo. If we compare the mestizos with the Indian, white, Negro, and Asian groups, we notice that the first two increased equally (by 1.12 per cent) between 1791 and 1876. According to Kubler, the increase of Indians occurred throughout Peru, while the increase of whites can be explained by the great influx of European immigrants during that period.[40]

Let us now turn to a brief analysis of the process of *mestizaje* and the social integration of the different immigrant groups which arrived in Peru during the nineteenth century.

The Europeans. Among European immigrants, the Spaniards and Portuguese mixed most readily with the Peruvian population. Concentrated in the cities and mining areas, they left a large number of descendants by native women. Such unions gave rise to an Indo-mestizo population which was culturally Indian although it possessed some Caucasoid features, such as lighter complexion, blond hair, light eyes, and substantial pilosity. These types still persist in the mining region of Conchucos (Ancash) and among some ethnic groups in the Department of Puno.[41]

[39] Córdova y Urrutia, *Estadística histórica*, p. 57; Tschudi, *Travels in Peru*, p. 91.
[40] Direccion Nacional de Estadística, *Censo Nacional de Población y Ocupación* (Lima, 1944), p. XXXIII; George Kubler, *The Indian Caste of Peru, 1795–1940* (Washington, D.C., 1952), p. 59.
[41] Emilio Romero, *Monografía del Departamento de Puno* (Lima, 1928), p. 177.

The Germans, English, and North Americans made the fewest marriages with Peruvian women, probably because of religious barriers and racial prejudice.

Thanks to the exemptions and privileges they enjoyed immediately after Independence, the British and North Americans came to dominate mercantile activities, especially international commerce. By the end of the nineteenth century, foreigners owned most of the important industrial establishments and commercial firms, and the railroads and guano industry were almost entirely in the hands of the English.[42] Since they were involved in commerce, most Europeans lived in the principal cities. For example, of fifty merchants in the city of Huaraz in 1841, 25 per cent were foreigners: three English, three French, three Spanish, one Argentine, one Bolivian, and one Ecuadorian. In Cerro de Pasco, commerce was in the hands of Europeans and white *criollos*. According to Basadre, for a long time "to say foreigner was to say merchant." [43]

Aside from the Spaniards, the Italians most readily became a part of Peruvian society. They were involved in various activities throughout the country as bankers, industrialists, merchants, *hacendados*, farmers, urban laborers, owners of grocery stores and restaurants, and settlers of the jungle in the valley of Chanchamayo and La Merced. Larrabure mentions that in 1898 a group of Italian immigrants arrived in the valley of Cañete to work as *peones*, only to return to Callao within a week of their arrival.[44] According to Hammel, the Italians rather than the Chinese triggered the most important economic and social changes in the Ica Valley after 1850, managing to gain great power and economic influence and even to displace some Spaniards. At the beginning of the twentieth century, Italian capital invested in commerce and industry amounted to some

[42] Wright, *The Old and the New Peru*, p. 431.

[43] Archivo Histórico del Ministerio de Hacienda, Lima: "Matrícula de contribuciones de la Povincia de Huaraz"; Tschudi, *Travels in Peru*, p. 336; Basadre, *Peru: Problema*, p. 116.

[44] Río, *La inmigración*, pp. 51, 59; Drewes, *Economic Development*, p. 18; Basadre, *Historia*, V, 2073; Fuentes, *La inmigración*, p. 52; Wright, *The Old and the New Peru*, p. 432; Carlos Larrabure y Correa, *Colonización de la Costa Peruana* (Lima, 1900), p. 28.

thirty million dollars.[45] In the area of health and charity, the Italian community made a significant contribution, establishing a hospital where famous Italian doctors practiced, and also the *Sociedad Italiana de Beneficiencia*, which played an important role in aiding immigrating compatriots.[46]

The French settled mainly in the cities, where they became jewelers, pharmacists, small tradesmen, tailors, photographers, dressmakers, and teachers.

The English and North Americans, involved in foreign trade and mining, became integrated into the community economically but not socially or culturally.

German interests in Peru at the end of the nineteenth century were almost entirely commercial, although there had been some settlement in the Chanchamayo and some valleys of the interior. Many German professionals, technicians, and educators came to Peru under government contract. Thus in 1876 eleven German teachers arrived to teach in the national schools of Cuzco, Piura, Puno, and Chiclayo.[47]

The Asians. Once the Chinese had fulfilled their forced labor contracts, a few stayed on as small farmers and merchants near the plantations they had worked originally, and others emigrated to the sierra. The majority, however, moved to the large urban centers, especially Lima, where after 1850 they established the Colonia China. In Lima, many took jobs as cooks, washers, and servants, slowly coming to own small grocery stores, rooming houses, *fondas* (small restaurants), and *chinganas* (small liquor stores). Some even became *curanderos* (curers and herbalists). The more industrious became successful merchants, often amassing great fortunes. Examples are the developers of the Pow Lung and Weng Company, established in 1866,[48] and the Chong Company, which exploited the

---

[45] Eugene A. Hammel, *Wealth, Authority, and Prestige in the Ica Valley, Peru* (Albuquerque, N.M., 1962), pp. 51–52; Wright, *The Old and the New Peru*, p. 433.

[46] Basadre, *Historia*, VI, 2956.

[47] Wright, *The Old and the New Peru*, p. 432; Basadre, *Historia*, V, 2092.

[48] Kwong, "The Chinese in Peru," p. 43; *Lima, la Ciudad de los Reyes en el IV Centenario de su fundación* (Lima, 1935).

cotton plantations in the Chancal and Huaral Valleys at the beginning of the twentieth century. These plantations were administered exclusively by Chinese who possibly had worked on them once as *braceros.*

Since the assimilation of the Chinese into urban life already has been described by Alice Jo Kwong, we shall limit our brief discussion to their integration in the provinces. They first emigrated to the sierra not only as servants of the rich or as *braceros,* but also through marriage to Andean *cholas* who returned from the coast to their original communities. Over the years, genetic and social fusion with the local groups occurred. Apparently, the Chinese lived throughout the sierra, especially in the center and north. According to the census of 1876, the 238 Chinese of Ancash were distributed over twenty-eight of the province's sixty districts. Between 1880 and 1900, the Chinese expanded into districts they had not inhabited previously. This was the case in Huaylas, where eight Chinese, married to local women, emigrated,[49] and in Aquia (Provincia de Bolognesi),[50] Pariahuanca (Provincia de Carhuaz), and other places where the mestizo descendants of these Chinese became totally assimilated, as did their own descendants. In Apurimac, it is known that thirty coolies were living in five of the department's thirty districts, but after 1876 there are no more figures.[51]

Upon marriage, the Chinese and Japanese espoused Catholicism, adopted Peruvian names, or kept those which had been assigned to them by immigration officers. The majority took the names of their baptismal godfathers, but some of the children preferred the mother's name. The sons of Chinese men and Peruvian women, known as *injertos,* born in small towns, found no obstacles to social advancement if they were well off or had a formal education. In some instances, they even became the highest social class, as in the Huaylas district of Ancash.[52]

Mestizaje and social integration among the Japanese were less

[49] Paul L. Doughty, "Peruvian Highland in a Changing World: Social Integration and Culture Change in an Andean District" (Ph.D. diss. in Anthropology, Cornell University, 1963), pp. 149–50.

[50] The author of the present article is a native of this community.

[51] Census of 1876.

[52] Doughty, "Peruvian Highland," p. 150.

complete. The Japanese established associations of people from the same "home town." This practice limited the number of marriages between Japanese men and Peruvian women and tended to keep each group in unassimilated isolation. According to Del Río, the Japanese immigrant was not able to adapt to agricultural work nor was he interested in establishing close ties with the native population.[53] As a result, once their contracts had expired, some returned to Japan and the rest drifted into cities where they obtained easy jobs as domestic servants, in cafeterias, barbershops, and candy and ice cream businesses. This view of the Japanese coincides with Irie's impression of a group of farmers and poor laborers, who immigrated in 1899:

Their only interest was to earn higher wages than in Japan and to accumulate some savings so as to improve their condition upon return home. They were brought together by this incentive.[54]

The South Americans. Since they had the same background as the Peruvian mestizos and *criollos,* South American immigrants experienced no difficulties in social integration. They were accepted as equals in all economic, political, social, and cultural activities, including the armed forces. In 1845 there were ninety-seven foreign officers in the Peruvian army who ranked from lieutenant to marshal.[55]

As noted above, the Chileans constituted the largest South American group in Peru. Next came the Bolivians and Argentines. Many of the Chilean *braceros* who went to Peru to work in railroad construction married Peruvian women and lived on in Andean towns. For example, in the district of Aquia (Department of Ancash) there lived three Chileans whose Peruvian wives had given birth to many children.

The Negroes. Despite legal restrictions to the contrary, throughout Peruvian history, Negroes and Indians have engaged in sexual

[53] Titiev, "The Japanese Colony," pp. 230–32; Río, *La inmigración,* p. 62.
[54] Irie, "History of Japanese Migration to Peru," p. 443.
[55] Basadre, *Historia,* II, 550.

relations, as the case of the Campa and Amuesha tribes of the Amazon clearly shows.[56] The incidence of mestizaje was greater in the case of free Negroes and became more frequent in the middle of the eighteenth century. Harth-terré analyzes a number of cases of Negroes who were freed by their Indian masters, and even mentions marriages between Indians and freed Negresses. This explains why in 1791 there were more free Negroes and mulattoes (41,398) than Negro slaves (40,337).[57]

With Independence, unions between Negro men and "cholas" became more numerous, especially after 1854, when Negro slavery was abolished. According to Hammel, after Abolition many Negro families stayed in the Ica Valley where the men worked for wages, cultivated their own plots, or became *aparceros* (share croppers). They enjoyed an active social life with the Indians who also formed part of the lower class.[58]

Another example of miscegenation and integration is provided by the "Indian community" of Aucallama in the northern part of Lima, most of whose inhabitants are descendants of Negro peons from the neighboring haciendas and Indian women from the community. Almost all students of the Negro population in Peru believe this pattern exists exclusively on the *Costa* and in some valleys or towns where the Negro predominated.[59] It seems to us, however, that the mixing of Negroes and Indian women in the Andes was greater than usually is believed, since some Negro slaves were taken to the sierra by their Spanish or Indian masters during the colonial period.[60] Moreover, Romero's analysis of the 1876 census takes into account only political departmental divisions and fails to consider that some

[56] Antonine S. Tibesar, "San Antonio de Eneno: A Mission in the Peruvian Montaña," *Primitive Man*, XXV (1952), 32.

[57] Emilio Harth-terré, "El esclavo negro en la sociedad indoperuana," *Journal of Inter-American Studies*, III (1961), 333–40; Vargas Ugarte, *Manuscritos peruanos*, p. 370.

[58] Hammel, *Wealth, Authority, and Prestige in the Ica Valley*, p. 52.

[59] Virgilio Landazuri, "¿Quienes son comuneros en el Perú?," *Mensajero agrícola*, No. 155 (1963), 13; Romero, "Slave Trade . . . ," p. 380; Roberto Mac Lean y Estenós, *Negros en el Nuevo Mundo* (Lima, 1948), p. 124.

[60] Emilio Harth-terré, *Informe sobre el descubrimiento de documentos que revelan la trata y comercio de esclavos negros por los indios de común durante el gobierno virreinal en el Perú* (Lima, 1961), p. 12.

departments have provinces and towns in the sierra. For example, Romero classifies the Department of Ancash as "coastal" (*costeño*) when actually it includes 60 Andean districts inhabited by 701 Negroes. In most of these towns, the Negroes have been disappearing as an ethnic group through fusion with the local population. For example, in the city of Carhuaz, not a single Negro is to be found, although a large slave colony existed there in the eighteenth century, and as late as 1876 there were still seventy-one Negroes. A similar phenomenon must have occurred in the Quechua community of Paucarcolla (Puno), where a team of serologists has estimated that 14.6 per cent of the population is the product of Indian-Negro mestizaje, and only 1.1 per cent of white-Indian mixture.[61] Undoubtedly, Negroes became better assimilated into Peruvian society than Europeans or Asians because they did not preserve any nationalist feelings toward their homeland.

In summary, it may be said that miscegenation and the integration of immigrants into Peruvian sociocultural life was not a uniform process. The Chinese, South Americans, and Negroes became the most assimilated. The Europeans were less successful in this respect, especially the English and the Germans, who integrated themselves into Peruvian society economically but not culturally. An example is the German colony in the eastern jungle, which after a century in Peru still maintains itself as an endogamous group. Nevertheless, the contribution of the European immigrants to the development of the country has been very important, thanks to the support and exemptions granted them by the Peruvian government. Not only did they stimulate commerce, industry, and education, but they also lent a new dignity to manual labor and made possible the rise of an upper middle class based on wealth. Many immigrants, beginning with small grocery and hardware businesses, accumulated fortunes which they invested in great estates that afforded their descendants the upward mobility needed to attain high status in the national society.

[61] William R. Best, M. Layrisse, and R. Bermejo, "Blood Group Antigens in Aymara and Quechua Speaking Tribes From Near Puno, Peru," *Physical Anthropology*, XX (1962), 328.

Conclusion

It is most difficult to assess the effects of immigration on the ethnic and cultural structure of Peru in quantitative terms. There can be no thought of racial or cultural "purity" in a land that since colonial days has been subject to a permanent process of mestizaje and the assimilation of immigrants.

Mestizaje reached its greatest importance in the nineteenth century, especially after 1850. The historical events of the period, together with immigration, gave rise to mixtures, not only between members of different ethnic groups but also between various types of mestizos, mestizos and Indians, and between Indians from different places and sociocultural backgrounds. Therefore, the classification of Indians and mestizos should be based on sociocultural factors rather than biological considerations.

It should be stressed that the mixing of ethnic groups and sociocultural change took place throughout the country, and not merely in the capital. The census data of the nineteenth century do not reflect this fact adequately. They give the impression that the greatest concentration of immigrants was in Lima and Callao, although mestizaje was intense on the coastal plantations which contained many of the foreign immigrants and native migrants. Similarly, mestizaje occurred even in places not considered conducive to it, such as the Andean communities which were often seen as closed, isolated, and inaccessible societies. The use of genealogical methods and techniques, employed successfully in Peru by the Department of Anthropology of Cornell University, bears out these assertions. In Vicos (Ancash), a Quechua Indian community, we have found that 72.46 per cent of the family genealogies include immigrants from other communities, some from other regions.[62] This figure is confirmed by the findings in another Andean community, Aquia (Ancash), where the ancestors of 72 per cent of the families were immigrants—including foreigners such as Spaniards, Chileans, and Chinese—who settled there during the eight-

[62] Mario C. Vázquez and Allan R. Holmberg, "The Castas in Vicos, Peru," *Ethnology*, V (1966), 284–303.

eenth and nineteenth centuries. Eighty per cent of the surnames in the coastal town of Virú (La Libertad) come from the sierra, other towns of the *Costa*, and from Italy, China, Japan, France, and Germany as well.[63]

It should be stressed that many of the old great families historically associated with these three towns have disappeared, largely through lack of male heirs. In most cases, they have been replaced by the descendants of migrants, among whom the proportion of males has been higher.

Finally, it should be noted that the mestizos continue to consolidate their position as a dominant social group, and that racial prejudice against them has practically disappeared. Paradoxically, prejudice and discrimination against the Indian, Negro, and Asian have persisted among the mestizos and "pseudo-whites" who form the provincial elites or hold important positions in public administration, institutions such as the Peruvian Navy, or in professional spheres. Usually, those who practice discrimination do so out of ignorance or in order to hide their own mestizo origins. There are, to be sure, families with racist ideas, but fortunately they are few in number.

In short, it is evident that the population of Peru today is genetically and culturally mestizo as a result of the historical mixing of various ethnic groups. At the same time, the Indian retains his numerical preponderance in Peru, because society has not found any adequate means of integrating him into modern life.

[63] Mario C. Vázquez, *Virú: Land and Society* (Cornell University, Dept. of Anthropology, Ithaca, N.Y., 1965), p. 33.

CHAPTER 5

The Dominican Republic in the Nineteenth Century: Some Notes on Stratification, Immigration, and Race

Harry Hoetink

An understanding of class and race in the Dominican Republic during the nineteenth century presupposes knowledge of that country's "internal" history: the interaction of economic, social, and political factors which form the basis for the periodicity of its past. Harry Hoetink, a sociologist who until recently directed the Center for Latin American Research and Documentation at the University of Amsterdam, here presents a broad historical framework according to which the past experience of the independent republic after 1844 is rather sharply divided around 1875. During the last quarter of the nineteenth century the spread of a modern sugar economy transformed both the political relationships and the relative social position of its inhabitants. The rise of an economically powerful social elite, the immigration of workers from other Caribbean areas, the arrival of other immigrants from the old world anxious to establish their economic position, and the increasing emphasis on racial criteria designed to maintain social control were all characteristic of this latter era. Dr. Hoetink believes that the master-slave relationship does not suffice to explain the character of race relations both outside and after slavery. In his words, these relations were "consistently milder in the Caribbean areas colonized by Iberians than in those governed by West Europeans."

Introduction: Political Background

In the second half of the eighteenth century, the commercial policy of the Spanish Bourbons gave rise to a relative upsurge in the economic situation of the colony of Santo Domingo. It may be assumed that this increasing prosperity caused a reshaping of the quasi-feudal structure which had been weakening in the previous periods of stagnating poverty and underpopulation. That the social and political convulsions which began around 1790 in the French part of the island of Hispaniola did not, however, leave the Spanish colony untouched is demonstrated by the emigration of people and capital to Cuba, Puerto Rico, Louisiana, and the northern parts of South America.[1] In 1795, by the Treaty of Basel, Spain ceded its colony on Hispaniola to France, which in turn proved initially unable to occupy the country. Instead, the nineteenth century started under Haitian occupation, which only accelerated the emigration of well-to-do whites when Toussaint L'Ouverture crossed the border from the east in 1800.

Some years before, undoubtedly under the influence of events in Saint-Domingue, there had been a number of slave revolts (beginning with a rising on the Boca Nigua plantation of the Marquess of Iranda),[2] all of which had been suppressed rapidly. On January 28, 1801, one day after his entrance into the capital, Toussaint proclaimed the abolition of Dominican slavery. In the following year, when pressure from French troops under the command of Generals Ferrand and Kerverseaux, who had been drawn from General Leclerc's expeditionary army, forced the Haitians to withdraw, they succeeded during their retreat in provoking some local rebellions—all without lasting consequence—among the Dominican Negro population.[3]

Though French troops elsewhere on the island were withdrawn, General Ferrand chose to disobey orders and remain in Santo Domingo, where he proclaimed himself governor on January 1, 1804. He acted to strengthen the decadent agrarian economy by authorizing the resumption of the slave trade for a period of twelve years in the case of the local Spanish inhabitants, six for foreigners. A provi-

---

[1] Sumner Welles, La Viña de Naboth, transl., I (Santiago, Dom. Rep., 1939), 32. See also Juan Bosch's Trujillo: Causas de una tiranía sin ejemplo (Caracas, 1959), p. 61. This little book, in spite of its title, may be considered the first attempt toward a sociological interpretation of Dominican history. Unfortunately, like many other serious Dominican works, it lacks references and bibliography.

[2] Welles, La Viña de Naboth, I, 34.

[3] Ibid., 40.

sion in the same decree for the enslavement of Haitian prisoners of war[4] was cited later by Dessalines as justification for a new effort by Haiti to conquer its eastern neighbor in 1805. The attack failed, but the attendant cruelties committed by the Haitian troops were recorded in vivid detail by Dominican historians. Ferrand's active economic policy, which had enabled a number of emigrants to return, came to an end when one of these, Juan Sánchez Ramírez, in conjunction with some members of the military and clergy, and aided by Pétion and Henri Christophe in Haiti, overthrew the French regime. The Spanish Crown then was offered sovereignty over the colony, which the *Junta Central* of Seville accepted in 1810. Forthwith, all French inhabitants were expelled from the colony.

The period of renewed Spanish domination ("*La España Boba*"), thus begun, developed into a serious economic depression under Governor Urrutia. Poverty, it was said, was so general and so severe that "hardly any classes" were to be distinguished, since the buying power of the *hacendado* and the free mulatto were equally small.[5] In 1821 José Núñez de Cáceres proclaimed the independence of "Spanish Haiti," and meeting no opposition from the Spanish colonial administration, sought—unsuccessfully—integration into Gran Colombia. In January of the following year, however, President Boyer of Haiti sent an army against the country, which hardly defended itself. By February, Núñez de Cáceres voluntarily had offered Boyer the keys of the capital. Thus began the "Haitian occupation," which was to last twenty-two years; only in 1844 would the Dominican Republic start life as an independent country for the second time.

The Proclamation of Dominican Independence on February 27, 1844—associated with the names of the "Founding Fathers," Duarte, Sánchez, and Mella—was followed in the course of a dozen years by several Haitian invasions, which were all repelled by improvised armies under the command of the *caudillo*-President Santana, a cattle rancher from the eastern region. Yet, this continuing threat from Haiti, which remained militarily and economically the stronger of the two countries through most of the nineteenth century, was an

[4] *Ibid.*, 43.
[5] *Ibid.*, 58.

important factor in the ever-greater efforts of Dominican politicians to place their land under the protection of a European power (Britain, France, or Spain) or of the United States. Finally, Santana succeeded in reannexing the Republic to Spain, which then exercised sovereignty from 1861 to 1865. In that year, as the result of a rebellion begun in 1863 (the "War of Restoration"), a third period of independence was begun, which lasted until the United States intervention in 1916. Even after 1865, however, Dominican leaders formulated several plans to place the country under foreign control. The efforts of the *caudillo* Baez, who occupied the presidency several times, to annex the Republic to the United States (1868–1870), after previously having failed to interest France in a similar agreement, are well known, since the proposal reached the United States Senate.

The first dozen years of the post-1865 era, as the years between 1844 and 1861, were characterized by internal political instability; revolutions were many, and governments short-lived. The situation became more stable only at the end of the 'seventies, when the political leader Gregorio Luperón, whose fame had grown out of military accomplishments in the War of Restoration, established the supremacy of his political "party," the *Azules,* over other factions. After that, thanks to a "party dictatorship" which, in fact, depended completely on the authority of Luperón as *caudillo,* a number of governments led by men of Don Gregorio's choice—such as Father Meriño, President from 1880 to 1882, and Ulíses Heureaux, 1882 to 1884—peacefully succeeded each other in office. In later years, however, Heureaux rejected Luperón's leadership. Between 1887, when he regained the presidency, and 1899, when he was assassinated, Heureaux developed into an absolute dictator who no longer restricted himself to old political friends from the *Partido Azul* in the selection of close collaborators.

The Period 1822–1844

Traditional Dominican historiography considers the Haitian domination "a death-like dream." [6] It accepts the arguments enumer-

<hr>

[6] *Ibid.,* 61.

ated by the Founding Fathers in the Proclamation of Independence from Haiti. Although these patriots admitted that Boyer had been welcomed at first, they held that he

soon forced the principal and wealthiest families to emigrate, and with them went talent, riches, commerce and agriculture; he alienated from his council and from the most important posts the men who could have represented the rights of their fellow citizens; he brought many families to poverty, taking their properties from them in order to enlarge the domain of the Republic or to donate these properties to individuals from the western part, or to sell them at very low prices . . . ; he robbed the churches of their wealth. . . . Later he proclaimed a law according to which the goods of those absent would become . . . the property of the state.[7]

In the last century, only the sociologist Hostos saw the effects of the Haitian period more objectively. Though he agrees that the "African wave" over the country caused barbarism to predominate so that "the family system, property, the progress of ideas and the course of civilization suffered deeply," he is nevertheless of the opinion that this era brought

the invaluable advantage of democratizing political society and equalizing it to the point where the notions of privileged authority and difference of caste were deleted from mind and custom. Thus . . . when the hour for the expulsion of the Haitians struck, a government of equals could be constituted for whites, Negroes and mestizos without the whites disputing the mestizos or the Negroes their political and social elevation, and without the mestizos and Negroes becoming dissatisfied about obeying leaders who were white.[8]

Juan Bosch goes yet further, stating that economically too the country became more stable under Haitian rule. According to him, the population increased and at least one new town (San Cristóbal) was founded. Indeed, "the country had recuperated from its former misery." Bosch considers that Boyer's policy favored the *latifundis-*

[7] Gregorio Luperón, *Notas autobiográficas y apuntes históricos* (2d ed.; Santiago, Dom. Rep., 1939), I, 37 ff.

[8] E. M. de Hostos, "Quisqueya, su sociedad y algunos de sus hijos," in E. Rodríguez Demorizi (ed.), *Hostos en Santo Domingo*, I (Ciudad Trujillo, 1939), 266.

tas, who then must have become more powerful by it. The success-ful Haitian revolt against Boyer in 1843 which brought a liberal government to power in Port-au-Prince was anti-*latifundista*, and precisely for this reason it must have reinforced separatist tendencies among the big Dominican landowners and the higher clergy.[9] Here, there is much room for doubt and, consequently, for further inves-tigation. It may be that the *Código Rural*, introduced by the Haitian government in an effort to develop a system of non-free labor, had some favorable effects on agricultural production, but it would have taken considerable time for the damage caused by the emigration of capital and know-how to be repaired.

The only immigrants during the Haitian period were several thousand North American free Negroes who began to arrive in 1824.[10] According to the nineteenth-century Dominican historian, García, the motive behind Boyer's immigration scheme was not so much to provide the country with able laborers and artisans as to change the "social physiognomy" of the Spanish area of the island and to awaken "racial preoccupations" in the minds of immi-grants which would tend to foster their identification with the Haitians.[11]

The Period 1844–1875

Let us compare some of the scarce population estimates for the period between the end of the eighteenth and the end of the nine-teenth century: 1789, 125,000;[12] 1819, 63,000;[13] 1871, 150,000;[14]

[9] Bosch, *Trujillo*, pp. 75–76.

[10] They settled in different parts of the country and were fused with the Dominican population in the course of a few generations, except for the few hundred settled on the Samaná Peninsula who have conserved their Methodist religion and English language to this day; H. Hoetink, "Americans in Samaná," *Caribbean Studies*, II (1962), no. 1, pp. 3–23.

[11] José G. García, *Compendio de la Historia de Santo Domingo* (3d ed.; Santo Domingo, 1893), II, 121–22.

[12] M. L. E. Moreau de Saint-Méry, *Description de la Partie Espagnole de l'Isle Saint-Domingue* (Philadelphia, 1799).

[13] Junta Central Organizadora del Concurso de la Exposición de Bruselas, *La República Dominicana en la Exposición Internacional de Bruselas* (Santo Domingo, 1897), p. 98.

[14] E. Rodríguez Demorizi (ed.), *Informe de la Comisión de Investigación de los E. U. A. en Santo Domingo en 1871* (Ciudad Trujillo, 1960), p. 75. A trans-

1887, 382,312;[15] 1897, 486,000;[16] 1898, 458,000.[17] It would seem that a pronounced population increase occurred after the 1870s when, as has been shown, political stability also increased. A similar trend emerges from analyzing the distribution of the founding of new towns (and the elevation of existing settlements to the status of *común*) during the course of the century. Under the Haitians only two new towns were founded, one of which (San Cristóbal) increased in population only because of the decay of nearby sugar plantations. Between 1844 and 1861, three new towns were established; one of these, San José de Ocoa, was populated by refugees from the border area. For the Spanish period (1861–1865) one town can be listed and for the turbulent decade after that, two. In the 1875–1899 era, however, no fewer than thirty new towns—of a total of thirty-eight for the entire century—were founded or elevated.[18]

These data suggest the convenience of dividing the 1844–1899 period in two, with the year 1875 as an approximate borderline. In what follows, I hope to show more clearly the usefulness of such a periodization, from the viewpoints both of economic structure and social stratification.

Defective infrastructure, political instability, and underpopulation in the three decades after 1844 led to the predominance of labor-extensive cattle farms, "*hatos*," in the eastern and western regions of the country. Individual property was not the general rule. Several factors are mentioned frequently to explain the institution known as "common lands" (*terrenos comuneros*): the sparse population and the consequently low value of land; the absence of competent public officials to measure plots; finally, the difficulty of dividing a *hato* among several heirs so that each of them would come into possession of sufficient meadows, woods, brooks, palm trees, and

---

lation of: *Report of the Commission of Inquiry to Santo Domingo* (Washington, D.C., 1871). Hereafter: *Informe.*

[15] Junta Central Organizadora, *La Republica Dominicana.*

[16] *Ibid.*

[17] Fernando Arturo de Meriño, *Elementos de Geografía Física, Política e Histórica de la República Dominicana* (3d ed.; Santo Domingo, 1898).

[18] Conclusion based on data in Meriño, *Ibid.*

conucos to make ranching possible.[19] Instead of inheriting ownership of a specific part of the *hato*, every heir received shares called
acciones or *pesos* or *acciones de pesos* in accordance with the portion of the inheritance to which he was entitled. As the word "*peso*"
indicates, the worth of these shares was measured in monetary units.
The nineteenth-century historian Del Monte y Tejada has shown
that *terrenos comuneros* existed as early as the seventeenth century;
by the middle of the eighteenth century, fifty *hatos* in the eastern
sector of the country, once individually owned, had become *terrenos comuneros*.[20] Although these lands had been made part of the
state domain by the Haitians, after 1844 the system began to flourish
once again. The chaotic nature of the institution becomes clear
when we realize that the possession of *acciones* was not limited to
the descendents of the original landowner since shares were traded
to others as well. Until approximately 1875, only the low value of
land made the legal confusion tolerable. The *ejidos*, the lands belonging to an *ayuntamiento*, were also often considered *de facto*
common property, unless they were rented for a nominal sum or
simply given away.[21]

In 1871 the number of big landowners, those who possessed between 1,000 and 10,000 acres, was estimated to be very small indeed. They were to be found in the eastern cattle area and in the
region around the southern town of Azua, where there were several
plantations which still used the traditional *trapiche* for sugar production. In this period, the Church, whose original landholdings had
been confiscated by the Haitian government, an act confirmed by

---

[19] A. Albuquerque, *Títulos de los terrenos comuneros de la República Domi-
nicana* (Ciudad Trujillo, 1961). See also J. R. Abad, *La República Dominicana:
Reseña general geográfico-estadística* (Santo Domingo, 1888); M. R. Ruíz
Tejada, *Estudio sobre la propiedad inmobiliaria en la República Dominicana*
(Ciudad Trujillo, 1952); H. Hoetink, "Materiales para el estudio de la República
Dominicana en la segunda mitad del siglo XIX, I: Cambios en la estructura
agraria," *Caribbean Studies* (October, 1965).

[20] *Historia de Santo Domingo* (4 vols; Santo Domingo, 1890–1892), III, 19,
quoted in Albuquerque, *Títulos de los terrenos*, p. 19.

[21] *Informe*, p. 548; see also S. Hazard, *Santo Domingo, Past and Present, with
a Glance at Hayti* (London, 1873), p. 484.

the successive independent regimes, re-established itself as an important landowner. However, its lands, like those of the State, which in 1871 owned between one-quarter and one-third of the national territory, lay fallow for the most part. Even in the fertile Cibao Valley, in the same year, it was estimated that nine-tenths of the land was fallow, and "shifting agriculture" was the common technique.

In comparing the 1844–1875 period with the most flourishing years of the Spanish colonial era (and perhaps also with the Haitian domination) when a stable quasi-feudal structure was, if not completed, at least in the process of development, we may surmise that a regression to more diffuse and confused forms of land tenure as well as to comparatively more primitive agrarian techniques occurred. Consequently, lesser significance was given to agrarian property as a criterion for social stratification. The "democratization" which Hostos considered an effect of the Haitian period encountered no obstacles in the agrarian sector which might have hindered its continuation in the years 1844–1875.

Although sugar and its secondary products, as well as wax, honey, and fine woods, were exported at this time, tobacco was undoubtedly the main commercial crop. Linked exclusively to Hamburg, the tobacco trade was controlled by German buyers who lived in the northern harbor town of Puerto Plata and used local merchants in Santiago and the surrounding Cibao Valley (where the tobacco and also some coffee were grown) as their intermediaries in purchasing. The existence of this German monopoly, together with an agrarian situation characterized by an abundance of fertile land (as described above), make it credible to estimate that the economic power of the merchants was much greater than that of the planters. An observer in 1871 noted that, "After Puerto Plata, Santiago de los Caballeros is the most important city of Santo Domingo. It is a city of merchants who govern the smaller merchants in the interior and who, in their turn, are governed by the foreign merchants of Puerto Plata and Saint Thomas." [22]

Besides their close contacts with mostly Jewish financiers and traders in Saint Thomas, Dominican politicians and merchants also

[22] *Informe*, p. 283.

maintained relations with the rich Sephardic merchants of the Dutch island of Curaçao. Curaçaoan Sephardim were living in Santo Domingo even during the Haitian domination, but their number became significant only after 1844. Sometimes sent to the country on a temporary basis as representatives of family merchant houses, growing numbers of them decided to stay in the Republic. They or their children married Catholic Dominicans, and the third generation conserved no more of the Jewish portion of their heritage than the proud memory of it. Initial resistance to the Sephardim's commercial activities, illustrated in a petition to President Santana from a group of residents of the Cibao in 1846, met with a negative reaction from the government. The good reputation of these people with the politicians rested not only on the financial help they gave to different factions, but also on the personal ties created through Masonry. Several Dominicans of Curaçaoan origin attained high governmental posts in the nineteenth century and later.[23]

Political activity sometimes was desirable for the merchants and nearly always unavoidable, but it involved economic risks, especially in the politically unstable period under discussion. Thus, the *afrancesados*, who had backed Baez's plans for annexation to France, lost the money invested in his campaign when he fell. For German and other foreign merchants, with the exception of the Spaniards, the 1861–1865 period was disastrous because of the economic policy of Spain. It would be worth while to investigate the role played by foreign capital in the War of Restoration. Of course, the Dominicans had their own complaints against Spanish domination. Madrid, as had Port-au-Prince earlier, reserved the highest government posts for its own representatives. In remarkable contrast to the criticism leveled against the Haitians, however, the Spaniards aroused resistance by their severity in implementing the laws of marriage and the ban against Masonry—in which so much of the Dominican clergy always had been active![24] Once independence was restored in 1865, the *españolizantes*, of course, had to suffer "lamentable transgressions," against which the government tried to pro-

[23] E. Ucko, *La Fusión de los Sefardíes con los Dominicanos* (Ciudad Trujillo, 1944).
[24] Luperón, *Notas autobiográficas*, I, 82 ff.

tect them "because they had money and credit, and could give movement, progress and life to the Province [of Santiago]." [25] In this way protection was offered not only to the Hispanophile Dominicans but also to the considerable number of Catalans and other Spaniards who had arrived in the country as soldiers or merchants during the annexation and after 1865 decided to stay.[26] Next to the German and Sephardic traders, these *peninsulares* "little by little . . . came to exert dominant commercial and political influence in the Cibao. This was to be the cause of grave consequences for many of them who were ruined by having involved themselves in politics which could offer them no favorable results." [27]

Enough examples exist to suggest that, because of its political instability, the 1844–1875 period did not foster the formation of a solid commercial elite, just as the continuing troubles and civil wars made the growth of a prosperous landowning class virtually impossible. Certainly every region knew some "respectable" families who acted as social leaders, and certainly nuclei of well-to-do merchants existed, but both groups contained relatively large numbers of foreigners with double national loyalty, at best. Furthermore, the defective infrastructure made contact between the regions extremely difficult, and it also appears that intimate social contacts between *hacendados* and urban traders were infrequent in this period. Insofar as one can speak of an economic elite with a degree of social cohesion, it is the merchant groups of Puerto Plata and Santiago that best approximate this concept, perhaps. These Cibao cities were also the political center of the country at this time. Most of the revolutions began here, and several governments had their seats here, although Santo Domingo was the official capital. In the Cibao, too, one found the largest number of people who had been educated in Spain, England, and Germany and thus expressed most articulately their longing for liberal and democratic forms of government. The failure of one of them, Ulíses Francisco Espaillat, an apothecary, as President of the Republic can be ascribed to his alienation from the sociopolitical milieu in which the essence of

---

[25] *Ibid.*, p. 159.
[26] *Informe*, p. 286.
[27] Luperón, *Notas autobiográficas*, I, 358.

political power lay in the hands of those persons, drawn mostly from the lower social strata, who had made a career of the politico-military struggles by leading small armies of loyal *clientes* in the civil wars and revolutions. Some of these leaders attained the presidency themselves: Santana was a cattle ranger from the East; Luperón came from a poor, fatherless family in Puerto Plata; Guillermo was an illiterate Negro; Heureaux, also very dark-skinned, came from a similar background of poverty in Puerto Plata. According to Luperón, at the close of the war against Spain in 1865, the country had forty-five "generals," and in the following decade, filled with civil strife, more than a thousand appointments to this rank were made.[28] In 1881 twenty-three generals were to be found in the little town of San Cristóbal alone.[29] These and other high military commissions were given on an *ad hoc* basis for politico-military merits mostly to economically weak landowners who occupied themselves with agriculture during the short periods of peace but who were always ready to exploit the material advantages of their "military" function. Such activity involved a risk similar to that which confronted the merchants *in politicis:* if the political choice proved "correct," profits could be great indeed; if not, it would cost much *suspicacia, malicia,* and *oportunismo* to keep one's life and goods.

In the period under discussion, the political, economic, and military structures of Dominican society would seem to be understood better if they are analyzed sociologically in terms of "markets" rather than of "organizations." The substantial vertical mobility within these structures was not limited to those immediately involved; rather, due to the extended family, patronage, and ritual kinship systems, it influenced *clientes, compadres, ahijados,* and *primos segundos* in different regions and social strata. Small wonder that Hostos's attention was drawn to "the sudden social and political ascents favored by the vicissitudes of revolution." [30]

[28] Luperón, *Ibid.,* III, 35. It should be kept in mind that in the absence of a national military organization, the political and military aspects of Dominican history during this period can hardly be separated.

[29] E. Rodríguez Demorizi, *San Cristóbal de Antaño* (Ciudad Trujillo, 1946), p. 102.

[30] Hostos, "Quisqueya," 275.

The Period 1875–1899

Toward the end of the seventies, modern sugar plantations and sugar processing appear in the Dominican Republic, especially in the southern and eastern provinces which then gain economic and political weight proportionately in relation to the Cibao. These agricultural innovations clearly were stimulated by the immigration of sugar planters from Cuba, who had fled the war in their country. Between 1875 and 1882, thirty modern sugar plantations were founded. In addition to the Cubans, several Puerto Rican and North American entrepreneurs were attracted by the sugar boom. Soon, besides sugar, North American companies were planting bananas and other fruits, too. In these years, the cultivation of coffee and cocoa also becomes much more important and modern. The rapid increase in land value caused falsification and fraud in the system of *acciones* and the trend toward a fixed pattern of land tenure was intensified. Many *ejidos* were sold, divided, and developed for construction by private persons. Archaic techniques of sugar production vanished; labor-extensive cattle farms decreased in number; traditional small-scale cultivation of fruits and vegetables diminished as many small farmers were attracted by the relatively high wages on the big plantations. Thus, geographic mobility also increased among the lower economic groups. A general improvement of the infrastructure made communication throughout the country easier as ports and railroads were built or improved, railroads and telegraph lines constructed.

Now that economic opportunities had improved, the relative scarcity of labor forced the government to adopt an active immigration policy. Sugar workers from the British West Indies and Haiti, and artisans from the Dutch Antilles arrived, and contracts were made with and land distributed to farmers from the Canary Islands. In 1882 Luperón tried in vain to organize a group immigration of East European Jews.[31] However, new bands of *peninsulares*

---

[31] Luperón, *Notas autobiográficas*, III, 137; see also M. Wisnitzer, *Historical Background of the Settlement of Jewish Refugees in Santo Domingo* (unpublished MS.).

did arrive, as did Italians, Chinese, and Arabs; in 1895 a company
of 295 Cubans disembarked. The country's first ministers in France,
Holland, and Germany were instructed to foment emigration to
Santo Domingo,[32] and in several Dominican towns, interested employers founded *Juntas Directivas de Inmigración.* When an economic crisis made itself felt at the end of the nineties, a number of
foreigners, mostly Cubans and some Curaçao Sephardim, left the
country;[33] however, the greater part of the newcomers chose to
stay. Spaniards, Italians, and other Europeans dedicating themselves
to commerce, agriculture, or the professions did not provoke resistance, and soon they mingled with the older nuclei of "respectable" families. More protest was heard initially against the immigration of Negro laborers from the adjacent area,[34] but in that case too,
assimilation, this time with dark-skinned Dominicans, took place
without further friction.

While the Chinese group has preserved its identity until today,
the "Arabs" (*sirios, turcos*) not only have succeeded in winning a
respectable position within the commercial elite during this century, but in recent decades a rather strong intermingling with other
prosperous groups has been taking place. In the period with which
we are dealing, however, this was not yet the case. A campaign
against the commercial practices of these "áraves," even more
violent than the one against the Sephardic traders fifty years earlier,
was launched by the settled (mostly Spanish) merchants in the
nineties. The Arabs' practice of ambulant selling was considered
unjust competition, and appeals for protection were made to the
government,[35] which as it had fifty years before, defended the immigrants. In the official documents one finds the importance of
prosperous and/or energetic immigrants for the progress of the
country emphasized repeatedly. Further proof of the government's
sympathy for the newcomers was the declaration in the 1890s that
foreigners were eligible for political office in the *municipios.* Perhaps some immigrants showed pride in their material success with

[32] Luperón, *Ibid.,* III, 56.
[33] *Listín Diario,* enero 1899 (*Archivo General de la Nación*).
[34] *Ibid.,* 2 de enero 1899.
[35] Hoetink, "Materiales."

insufficient tact, as when the Spaniard Enrique Vélez declared that without the foreigners the Republic would be a primitive country, a statement which caused lively discussion in the *Listín Diario* of 1896. Certainly, the economic benefits of the import of capital, know-how, and energy cannot be denied. Another question is whether these immigrant groups have been able to preserve their original powers of economic initiative and innovation. The answer must be that those which mingled most easily with the local elite, that is, those immigrants who *grosso modo* had the greatest somatic and cultural affinity with the elite, assimilated the economic mentality of the Latin American "aristocracy" most rapidly. Soon they began to invest newly-acquired capital in land and houses and to educate their sons in the favorite academic subjects: law, medicine, philosophy, and literature. On the other hand, others, such as the Arabs, who were subjected for a prolonged period to a minority position within the higher economic strata, could better maintain their original economic ethos in their relative isolation.

Reviewing the 1875–1899 period, we may conclude that in these years of relative political stability, during which several groups of immigrants came to fill the vacuums existing in the socioeconomic structure, conditions were created for the formation of a national, economically powerful social elite, consisting of the nuclei of the "autochthonous" prosperous, or "respectable" families, combined with those economically successful immigrants who were somatically and culturally acceptable to those nuclei and vice versa. The improved infrastructure which lessened the isolation of the old regionally closed social systems; the growth of the general population and of the economically privileged groups; the sharp increase in the value of land—all served to interrelate the originally rather separated groups of merchants, landowners, and intellectuals.[36] At the other end of the social scale, the proliferation of modern capitalist agricultural enterprises stimulated the formation of an agrarian proletariat which also consisted of intermingled groups of Dominicans and immigrants.

Thanks to its long duration, the "unifying autocracy"—to use

---

[36] Cf. Bosch, *Trujillo*, p. 31.

Germani's term[37]—of President Heureaux's regime lessened not only the insecurity of the merchants but also that of the politico-military leaders who had backed Heureaux's ambitions. These men from the lower social strata now had the opportunity to improve their own economic position and also to increase their social respectability by educating their children abroad (often with presidential scholarships) and then carefully choosing their offspring's marriage partners. Thus, toward the end of the Heureaux era, a number of these leaders had stabilized their social positions sufficiently to become absorbed in the national bourgeoisie in *statu nascendi.*

While I would characterize the 1844–1875 period as one in which the political, military, and economic sectors of society, sociologically speaking, were *markets* with a strong speculative element and corresponding risks, in the period we are discussing now the dictator succeeded in dominating and organizing the political and military sectors. A monopoly mechanism, similar to the one N. Elias observed in medieval Europe, changed the horizontal competitive relations into a vertically organized hierarchy of power and rank.[38] Simultaneously, as we have described above, a process of clear hierarchization in the socioeconomic sector was started.

It must be emphasized, of course, that the fall of Heureaux's regime implied the corrosion of the political and military organizations he had built. However, the national bourgeoisie which had emerged during his period of government could for the most part maintain itself. To a certain extent it was even responsible for the dictator's fall, for in dethroning Heureaux, the new bourgeoisie hoped itself to monopolize political power in the name of democracy.

By the use of the term "organization" instead of "market," I do not want to imply that in the 1875–1899 period a greater efficiency in the governmental system or in the mechanism of the selection of government employees per se, as compared to the earlier periods, can be discerned. The political system did preserve its patrimonial traits; the patronage system, the significance of ritual and blood

[37] G. Germani, *Política y Sociedad en una Epoca de Transición* (Buenos Aires, 1962), p. 148.
[38] N. Elias, *Ueber den Prozess der Zivilisation* (2 vols.; Basel, 1939).

kinship in the allocation of positions did not change. It is simply that in the last decades of the nineteenth century the political structure was more stable, and therefore tenure in official positions was more permanent than previously. Coincidentally, this may have produced a greater capability in the civil servants because of their longer experience. I may repeat further that the clearer hierarchization in the economic, political, and military sectors, described above, was evolving *during* the last two decades of the century; it was a process taking place. Mobility (for example, of the immigrants) towards the socioeconomic groups-in-formation and the adoption of adequate patterns of behavior can be observed throughout the period.

These patterns of behavior were, of course, connected with the "aristocratic" pattern of thought, of Iberian origin, which had become part of Dominican culture. Here I speak in Karl Mannheim's terms of an "aristocratic culture" in which the concept of *distance*, horizontal and vertical as well as temporal and, in certain cases, mythical, is emphasized heavily in all layers of society. In regard to social stratification, such a society imposes upon its members an *image* of social hierarchy in which the social categories are precisely defined and allocated. Such an image need not correspond at all closely to social reality, nor need it prevent social mobility.[39] In the Dominican Republic the image of social stratification was based on a dichotomy: *la gente bien, la gente culta, la clase pensante* vs. *el pueblo, el vulgo, la plebe.*

Yet, we have seen that during the greater part of the nineteenth century it was hardly possible to speak of a higher "estate" in the sociological sense unless one considers as such the small number of families of Spanish colonial origin whose prestige was based more on ancestry (*abolengo*) than on economic position or political influence. Only when these *dones* began to intermingle with the newly risen *señores* (mostly immigrants) did an influential "estate-conscious" group emerge.

Between this latter group and *el vulgo* were those elements which distinguished themselves from the lowest strata by their style of liv-

[39] K. Mannheim, "The Democratization of Culture," *Essays on the Sociology of Culture* (London, 1956), pp. 171–246.

ing, their economic situation, and their somatic traits—but which, for similar reasons, were not acceptable to the highest strata. These "middle groups" were very heterogeneous. They comprised artisans, small merchants and shopkeepers, teachers, and even lawyers of Dominican or Caribbean origin whose overly dark appearance made further social rise difficult. Also included were those white immigrants who had not achieved sufficient economic success to become acceptable to the higher classes. Where such groups were sizeable enough, as in the case of the Canary Islanders in the capital, they lived apart in their own *barrios*. Although undoubtedly a heterogeneous middle group of *"familias de segunda"* also had existed in the first three quarters of the nineteenth century, its numbers and stability increased considerably in the last three decades of that century.[40] To speak of class consciousness in a society with an aristocratic culture would be a contradiction in terms. As recently as 1953, it was remarked of the "middle groups": "As a group, they cannot rise in the social scale. They seek individual ways which isolate them from their equals . . . in order to elevate them from the social level on which they live . . . while they demonstrate deep gratitude to him who belonging to a superior group, treats them on a level of equality." [41] In the period under consideration one cannot speak of socially relevant resentment *vis à vis* the higher social strata, although a man like President Heureaux privately directed many cynical remarks to the "honorables." The vertically structured patronage system, which linked all social layers, remained the principal mechanism for individual social betterment. Thus, the aristocratic concept of the protector and his clients formed an obstacle against social action based on "horizontal" solidarity. Given the fact that, on the one hand, aristocratic culture emphasized distance in *all* social layers, while, on the other, some mobility did occur, one can state safely that there were few cultural or structural factors to lead to collective frustration. Such frustration could be

[40] Cf. Bosch, *Trujillo*, pp. 28 ff., who, in my opinion, lays too much stress on the social importance of the "familias de segunda" during the earlier periods of Dominican history.

[41] M. A. Mejía Ricart, *Las Clases Sociales en Santo Domingo* (Ciudad Trujillo, 1953), pp. 45, 47.

experienced subjectively only in a much later period of Dominican history, which falls outside the scope of this article.

Let me conclude this section by quoting an observer of late nineteenth-century social stratification in the capital:

There were *Dones* and *Seños*. Those persons of *el pueblo* who distinguished themselves by their respectability and decency were called *Seño* or *Seña*. There were three social classes: those of the first category (*los de primera*), those of the second category (*de segunda*), and those of the anonymous mass (*el montón anónimo*). The most distinguished families lived in the center of town. Between the corners of El Conde and José Reyes Streets and the western walls of the city there was a *barrio* called El Navarijo which was inhabited by good people of the second category, dedicated to [small] commerce, something which no proud family would be. From the corners of Emiliano Tejera Street to Santa Bárbara, the *barrio* took the name of La Estancia, also second class, whose inhabitants were in the majority Curaçaoans, honest laborers, carpenters, cabinet makers, . . . proprietors of cheap eating places and second hand shops . . . The poorest people lived in the uptown *barrios* consisting of rustic *bohíos* covered with palm leaves.[42]

Within the "anonymous mass" there was, of course, social differentiation according to occupation, somatic traits, influence in the patronage system, and so forth. This differentiation escaped the observation of those manipulating the image of social stratification which their aristocratic culture imposed.

The Influence of "Race" on Social Stratification

Around the year 1845, the French consul in Haiti, Raybaud, tried to explain the difference in the development of race relations in Haiti and the Dominican Republic. Looking back at the Spanish part of Hispaniola at the time of the Haitian turbulence, he wrote:

The double layer of free blood which the conquering race and the last nucleus of the Indian race mixed with the blood of Africa could hardly be distinguished after the second generation. Indeed, the bronzed skin of the Spaniard, the copper-colored complexion of the Indian and

---

[42] L. E. Gómez Alfau, *Ayer, o el Santo Domingo de hace 50 años* (Ciudad Trujillo, 1944), pp. 123 ff.

the tan coloring of the mulatto tended to merge under the influence of a common hygiene and climate. If there had been interested observers at the time, they often would have found it difficult to discover in a face the secret of a genealogy lost in the savanna and the forests. This process of fusion, hindered neither by European immigration from a moral viewpoint, nor by African immigration from a sociological point of view, is summed up in the following figures for population at the moment of the revolution: 25,000 pure Spanish whites; 15,000 Africans who had not succumbed to revolutionary propaganda thanks to their dispersion and who felt too proud of the social superiority over their counterparts in the French zone, which they derived from daily contact with their masters, to follow the example of the Haitians; finally, 73,000 mulattoes who began by calling themselves white and, in the absence of any injurious objections, ended by considering themselves such. Thus, the separatist element in the French colony was converted into the conservative element of the Spanish colony. Vanity, which had dug an abyss of hate between the three classes in Haiti, had operated for cohesion here.[43]

The character of race relations always must be distinguished carefully from that of master-slave relations; the latter do not exclusively explain the former. In the institution of slavery, an economic and juridical subordination usually coincides with a racial one, but the character of master-slave relations as well as the frequency of manumissions are determined to a high degree by economic factors. During successive economic phases in one and the same society there may exist benign and harsh relations within the slavery system, as the histories of "West European" and "Iberian" societies in the Caribbean both show. Yet, racial relations among whites, coloreds, and Negroes outside (and also after) slavery, have been consistently milder in the Caribbean areas colonized by Iberians than in those governed by West Europeans. This difference can be explained partly by cultural factors, but, with Raybaud, I consider the different positions of the colored (mulatto) part of the population to be of the greatest importance. As I have tried to show elsewhere, the white "somatic norm image," that is, the definition of whiteness, is

[43] G. d'Alaux (pseudonym for M. Raybaud), *L'Empereur Soulouque et son Empire* (Paris, 1856); Spanish trans. in E. Rodríguez Demorizi (ed.), *Documentos para la Historia de la República Dominicana*, III (Ciudad Trujillo, 1959).

somewhat darker in the Iberian Caribbean variant than in the West European. This means that the "somatic distance" between white and colored is smaller in the former, since a part of those who "biologically" are colored fall within the margin of the prevailing white somatic norm image. Thus, a continuous absorption *by marriage* of coloreds into the "white" group occurs, provided the former are somatically, and also economically, acceptable to the latter. As a consequence, in the Iberian variant, of which the Dominican Republic forms a part, the colored group functions as an important mediator and as a channel of mobility—both social and cultural—between whites and Negroes. The mulatto's possibility for greater identification with the white group, in comparison to his position in the West European areas, leads to less frustration and therefore to less aggression.[44] Although, thus, on general grounds a comparative mildness in the relations among Negro, colored, and white in the Dominican Republic during the period under consideration may be postulated, I do not want to suggest that the racial factor was not of social relevance. In Dominican society, as in all multi-racial societies of the Caribbean, the white somatic norm image is dominant in regard to social prestige. Discussing the situation, Mejía Ricart writes:

The Dominicans have an ethnic complex . . . Since racial purity is very rare and a mixture of the different variations prevails: white, near white, mulatto and Negro, the consequence is that one is constantly observing the differences in skin color, hair texture and more or less white origins. Such an importance ascribed to this aspect of the individual naturally produces the aspiration to become white on the part of those who are not and the aspiration to improve their color on the part of those who are nearly white, while those small groups who have all white ancestors aspire to preserve this gift (*ese don*) which they consider a real family patrimony.

Mejía Ricart is of the opinion that the racial factor, more than any other, determines whether one may be accepted as a member of the highest social group.[45] In this context, it may be observed that the

[44] Cf. H. Hoetink, *The Two Variants in Caribbean Race Relations* (London, 1967).
[45] Mejía Ricart, *Las Clases Sociales*, pp. 27, 28.

"improvement" and growth of the Caucasoid element in the population always has been cited publicly as one of the motives of Dominican immigration policy.

As yet, but few Dominicans have not judged the period of Haitian domination a black page in the history of a people that would have liked to be white. The opinion of Luperón, that in the struggle against Haiti the Dominican people defended "its language, the honor of its families, the freedom of its commerce, the morality of marriage, the hatred of polygamy [and] a better destiny for its race," still prevails. Yet, one must question whether this cultivation of appraising the Haitian domination as a traumatic collective experience did not also serve the purpose of alleviating the pains of the internal situation of the Republic. Since this period, it has been possible to attribute Negroid traits in members of respectable families to the barbarian cruelty of the Haitian conquerors. At the same time, as Hostos noted earlier, the Haitian occupation had a cohesive effect on the relations of the different racial groups within the country; even the darkest were Dominicans and took part in the struggle for independence. Cultural identity then proved stronger than racial identity, although the Negro was still required to demonstrate his cultural competence more than were others, as the saying "He who is black must speak clearly" shows. The Haitian was and is the racial scapegoat and escape valve upon whom feelings of racial uneasiness can be projected. Dominicans often depict their "own" Negroes (who are concentrated mostly in the southern and eastern parts of the country in contrast to the Cibao, which has a proportionately greater number of whites and colored) as being racially less "pure" and therefore esthetically more attractive than those from Cuba, Haiti, or the Virgin Islands.

Given the important social position and the numerical superiority of the Dominican colored group, including the "near-white," and the paucity of either "pure" whites or "pure" Negroes, it is easy to understand that the coloreds tended to view themselves as more "Dominican" than the others and sought rationalizations of this conviction. Thus, Luperón, who sprang from this element, claimed that "The mulatto group, by the law of climates, [tends] to become identical (*volver a*) to the aboriginal race of the island."[46] In 1887, when Luperón became a candidate for the presidency, one of the leading intellectuals of the Cibao applauded him as follows:

The government that rules us . . . should begin to think seriously about the destiny reserved by Providence for the Negroes and mulattoes of America. From now on, this destiny is manifest, given the present numbers of this race; and I believe the island of Santo Domingo is called to be the nucleus, the model of its glorification and individuality in this hemisphere. And who better than you could begin to lay the groundwork, the foundation of this greatness? Who better than you could know how necessary the white race is for the achievement of this goal, but at the same time recognize the superiority of the combinations of this great race? And who better than you could melt, amalgamate and shape a homogeneous whole from the wisdom and ignorance of one and another family so that from today, we as a model of tolerance and restraint, may attract the benevolent gaze of the universe and place ourselves, robust and free, in a highly enviable position?[47]

It must be kept in mind that the author of this passage was supporting the candidancy of the mulatto Luperón against that of the Negro Heureaux, who, besides being unfortunate enough to be of Haitian descent on his father's side, was too Negroid to be considered a colored. His political enemies, including some very liberal thinkers, reminded him of his racial status in unequivocal terms such as "*mono*" and "*antropoide.*"[48] In the many anecdotes about Heureaux, which even today form a part of Domican political folklore, the racial factor plays a substantial role. These stories clearly reflect the ambivalence of the Negro: Heureaux sometimes accepts the prevailing prejudices, while other times he takes revenge and punishes his often "respectable" offenders.

The future of the non-white population always became a factor, clearly inserted to stimulate popular political action, in the discussions that arose over the many projects to yield the national sover-

[46] Luperón, *Notas autobiográficas*, I, 27.
[47] *Ibid.*, III, 250.
[48] *Ibid.*, III, 343, 345.

eignty to one or another foreign power.[49] In the nineties, when it was rumored that Heureaux secretly was negotiating for annexation to the United States, Luperón tried to mobilize public opinion by declaring that the North Americans

> plan to seize the island without regard to any rights and by means of crimes and outrage, because what interests them is not the people but the island—to which they would like to send their 4,000,000 African freedmen; the Yankees will exterminate our race because it is not theirs. It is to this North American people, enemy of the Indian race, of the yellow race, of the mestizo race, of the African race, and, above all, of the Latin race that the traitor General Heureaux tries to sell and surrender the Dominican Republic.[50]

In the last two decades of the nineteenth century when Dominican social stratification became more stable and the racial factor acted as one of the main determinants of social status, the chances of maximum mobility for decidedly Negroid persons must have grown smaller. A social rise like that of the American freedman Eliah Gross, who arrived in the country in 1824, immediately was appointed Postmaster General by the Haitian government, and later served as a judge under all successive regimes until 1871, must have become quite exceptional in a time when the growth of a stable bourgeois group had made the lack of higher public servants with a minimum education less acute. Similarly, the attainment of the presidency by an illiterate Negro like Guillermo, or even by somebody like Heureaux himself, became difficult to repeat, precisely because of the social changes that took place during the latter's government. A later self-made dictator, Trujillo, would have his origins in the provincial *familias de segunda* milieu.

Although through today the army has remained one of the main channels of vertical mobility, the change from a "market" into an "organizational" structure it experienced during the Heureaux regime probably increased the weight given to the racial factor. Since the bureaucratization of the military apparatus required staff person-

[49] Welles, *La Viña de Naboth,* I, 205, 305, 373.
[50] Luperón, *Notas autobiográficas,* III, 328 ff.

nel with better education, it was the mulattoes who profited. Besides, once organized, the military sector must have tended to apply the same determinants for social promotion—of which physical appearance was one—as did society as a whole. On the other hand, for a long time to come a military career would not enjoy the same social prestige as the traditional bourgeois professions; therefore, the number of whites in the army remained proportionately low. When in 1895 José Martí inspected one of the well-trained battalions of Heureaux's army, he observed that there were mestizos and Negroes amongst the officers, only Negroes amongst the soldiers.[51]

Further, it is probable that the sheer numerical growth and the increasing social consciousness of the national bourgeoisie increased the social relevance of the racial factor, if only because through it, the mechanism of social control could be manipulated more effectively. In the last decade of the nineteenth century, we find frequent use of such pejorative terms as *culebrón* for a social climber.[52] Finally, urban growth in the eighties and nineties may have caused more pronounced segregation, specifically between the Negroes and the other population groups. There are too many exceptions to allow for dogmatism on this point, however. For example, at the end of the century, the San Carlos *barrio* of the Canary Islanders was the home of one Negro family "which they called black Islanders because its members were honest, industrious, and good." [53] Just as the new bourgeoisie founded its exclusive social clubs in these years, so, too, the dark-skinned groups started their "social centers," and "in their statutes restrictive rules abounded. One of the most prestigious of these clubs was . . . the 'Black Pearl.' " [54]

It might be fair here to warn that the trends we have observed or surmised in the development of social structure and race relations in the nineteenth-century Dominican Republic cannot simply be extrapolated into present-day Dominican society, because in the pres-

---

[51] Jóse Martí, *Apuntes de un viaje* (La Habana, 1938), p. 40.
[52] Gómez Alfau, *Ayer*, p. 123.
[53] M. A. González Rodríguez, "Apuntes y Recuerdos de San Carlos," *Clio*, CVI (Ciudad Trujillo, 1956), 93–95.
[54] Gómez Alfau, *Ayer*, p. 124.

ent as in the previous century, periods both of relative political stability and relative chaos do occur. Given the patrimonial character of the political structure, this means that today, too, frequent changes in government cause increased vertical mobility, both upward and downward, in many social institutions.

CHAPTER 6

Immigration and Race
Relations in São Paulo

Florestan Fernandes

European immigrants and Afro-American slaves have long been considered alternative rather than mutually consistent solutions to the manpower problems of the New World. Generally, immigrants have gone to areas where slavery has not been pronounced. Yet in Brazil, and most especially in São Paulo, large numbers of immigrants flooded an area previously dependent largely on slave labor. Florestan Fernandes has long been concerned with the question of race relations in that area and, as a sociologist at the University of São Paulo, has steadily encouraged research on this subject by word and example. In his view, the demands of capitalistic society for free labor after the abolition of slavery did not offer any opportunities for the ex-slaves, but only for the newly arrived immigrants. Only after 1930 did a "second Industrial Revolution" in Brazil absorb the Negro and mulatto, as witnessed by the new "immigration" from the country to the city. He thus followed the steps of the immigrant first by forming protective associations and then by searching for integration. Immigration thus served to worsen the climate of race relations in Brazil, although it certainly cannot be maintained that the immigrant introduced prejudice there.

Scholars are familiar with a double paradox: slavery is usually pointed out as an obstacle to immigration, which in turn is generally mentioned as contributing to the spread of free labor and capitalism. Thus, the relation of immigration to the crisis it precipitated in the slave-based production system has been much emphasized.

[122]

In the present paper we do not intend to discuss these problems. Rather, taking the city of São Paulo as the source of our empirical investigation, we wish to answer a few questions concerning the recent past and the present. What has been the role of immigration— in a sociological sense—as a structural and dynamic factor in the perpetuation or change of adjustments? Has immigration contributed to modifying the patterns of racial relations themselves?

Our plan is simple and direct. We are concerned with three basic questions: (1) how immigration affected the pre-existing forms of adjustment of the Negro and the mulatto to the economic structure of the community; (2) how the Negro and the mulatto reacted to the presence and noticeable influence of the immigrants and their first generation descendants; (3) how immigration influenced the system of racial relations either for persistence or alteration. For none of these points was it possible to deepen, develop, or corroborate the conclusions empirically. Our conclusions, however, do show something that seems of relative theoretical and practical interest. Immigration adapted itself to the inconsistencies of the Brazilian racial relations system. Therefore, it did not even contribute to eliminating or changing the archaic or archaizing elements that prevented that system of race relations from playing a role in the cultural and socioeconomic modernization process of the community. If immigration has had any major significance, in this respect, it is because of its powerful contribution to bringing about a world in which free competition and democracy tend to became social values.

The Displacement of the Negro Populations

The increase in immigration constituted, in the beginning, a function of the disintegration of the servile system. Thus, when it became clear that free labor should replace slave labor, the flow of immigration gained sudden momentum. The total of immigrants entering São Paulo during the last five years of the nineteenth century amounted to more than four and one-half times the number of immigrants who entered between 1827 and 1884. Later, this acceleration reached its peak in the history of immigration in São Paulo as a

[123]

result of the manpower requirements of the reorganization of the labor system. Because of the demands for agricultural manpower, the effects of such reorganization were acutely felt from 1889 to 1899, the years following Abolition. However, the whole period from the last quinquennium of the nineteenth century until approximately 1930 was one characterized by rapid substitution of the organization patterns of economic activity and by the introduction, consolidation, and expansion of a free-labor-based economy. The following data indicate the trends of this immigration movement:[1]

Years	Arrivals	Departures
1827–1884	37,481	
1885–1889	168,127	
1890–1899	735,076	
1900–1909	388,708	65,262 (1908–1909)
1910–1919	480,509	247,927
1920–1929	712,436	234,342
Total:	2,522,337	547,531

The demographic studies made by Samuel Lowrie show that, strictly speaking, there was no substitution of the native population by immigrants. Nevertheless, especially with regard to the city of São Paulo (and not the State of São Paulo as a whole), urbanization also meant Europeanization, both extensively and in depth. It seems beyond doubt that a population substitution occurred with the Negro and mulatto segments of the urban population. The appearances of the phenomenon were concealed by the heavy mobility of the colored population and by the increases that resulted from the excess of arrivals over departures which characterized the internal migrations of Negroes and mulattoes during this period.[2] In order to deal with the sociohistorical process which have structural significance, it is necessary to distinguish three large global tendencies which in turn reveal that the impact of immigration on the Negro

[1] "Movimento Migratório no Estado de São Paulo," *Boletim de Directoria de Terras, Colonização e Immigração* (São Paulo, 1937), 29–75.

[2] On these phenomena see Roger Bastide and Florestan Fernandes, *Brancos e Negros em São Paulo*, (2nd ed., São Paulo, 1959), Chap. 1; Florestan Fernandes, *A Integração do Negro à Sociedade de Classes* (São Paulo, 1964), Chap. 1.

and mulatto segments of the São Paulo population varies according to the historical period which one considers.

First, there is the long period from approximately 1827 to 1885, during which immigration was curtailed by the socioeconomic contingencies of the servile regime. During that time, the immigrant did not threaten the racial adjustment patterns resulting from slavery. As Couty rightly suggests,[3] slave labor economically eliminated free labor. As long as he had a slave, the master had the greatest interest in exploiting him as intensively and extensively as he could. Nevertheless, the immigrant's presence was not entirely neutral. All over Brazil the economic development of agriculture under the servile system brought about and conditioned the formation of urban centers within which it determined a certain differentiation in the occupational system. Although it constitutes no exception to this trend, São Paulo went through it under peculiar social and historical circumstances. While cities such as Recife (Pernambuco), Salvador (Bahia), and even Rio de Janeiro offered opportunities for the reabsorption of freed slaves as free workers, even before Abolition—in the public services, or as craftsmen or small merchants—in São Paulo an early tendency developed to grant such opportunities to the immigrants.

Thus, even though the population of the city had a sizeable number of freed slaves,[4] they were not able to take advantage of the free labor opportunities offered by a "slavocratic" and manorial society. On the contrary, as the yearbooks and statistics reveal, the immigrants who were concentrated in the city absorbed the more advantageous job opportunities. As a result, the number of freed slaves who were able to find a good position in the socioeconomic structure of the city was relatively small,[5] in contrast with what occurred in other Brazilian cities in which the mestiços came to be considered as the most important demographic and economic ele-

---

[3] Cf. Louis Couty, *Le Brésil en 1884* (Rio de Janeiro, 1884) and, especially, *L'esclavage au Brésil* (Paris, 1881).

[4] Cf. Bastide and Fernandes, *Brancos e Negros em São Paulo.*

[5] On this point, see Ernani da Silva Bruno, *História e Tradições da Cidade de São Paulo* (3 vols.; Rio de Janeiro, 1954), and Richard Morse, *De Comunidade a Metrópole*, Trans. (São Paulo, 1954).

[125]

ments for the future of Brazil. Thus, before the collapse of the servile regime, the Negro and the mulatto suffered very definitely the negative effects of competition with the immigrants. They lost the only available avenues to stability and security in the complex of free occupations connected with the structure and function of the slave-holding economy. This fact had a specific dynamic meaning, since it led to the devastating effects that the immigration influx would have on the different strata of the colored population.

In the second place, we must consider the years from 1885 to 1930 as a period of consolidation and rapid expansion of the competitive social order. During this period, although not a direct, exclusive, or dominant factor, immigration acquired the proportions and meaning of a social calamity for the Negro and the mulatto. Slavery had only prepared its workers for the socioeconomic roles of slaves and freedmen in the midst of a slavocrat social order. When the system went into crisis and broke down, the only economic and sociocultural conditions that protected and guaranteed the social and economic adjustments of the Negro to the work system disappeared with it. Suddenly free but unprepared to fill the roles of the *free man*, the Negro found himself in a city that was rapidly becoming the main stronghold of the bourgeois revolution in Brazil. As a result, his lack of ability for free labor, for inter-racial competition, and for an urban style of living, was aggravated by the presence of a mass of foreigners who were avid to seize existing or emerging economic opportunities and who were absolutely preferred in the labor market. Moreover, the Negro himself had to learn the social behavior of the free worker and how to deal with an urban economy without having enough time to do so. Things had moved too fast. The Negro's maladjustment, which could have been only a passing phenomenon, became a structural maladjustment. Instead of being reabsorbed by the urban labor organization and the competitive social system, the Negro was pushed to the outer fringes of the urban society where were concentrated the lowest and most unsteady occupations, economically as well as socially.

Within this context, then, the expression "displacement of the Negro populations" does not mean that the immigrant may have picked up jobs or economic situations previously belonging to the

"Negro element." Such a statement would not be historically precise, since the labor relations patterns and the organizational arrangements of the productive system had already changed during the transition period. In this case, "displacement" simply means that in the course of the changes that occurred, the "Negro element" lost its status as a privileged (or inevitable) manpower source for several types of manual labor and craftsmanship or other economic activities which were usually associated with urban services and small businesses. This status, as a natural result of Abolition, was transferred to the "white man," which meant particularly the "white foreigner." A few data are sufficient to indicate the nature and the direction of this process. In 1893, for example, immigrants constituted 79 per cent of those employed in manufacturing; 85.5 per cent of those employed as craftsmen; 81 per cent of those in transportation and related activities; and 71.6 per cent of those in commercial activities. Their participation in the higher levels of the occupational structure was still small (only 31 per cent of the property owners and 19.4 per cent of the capitalists were foreigners). However, they were included in these activities, in contrast with the Negro and the mulatto, who were not. Even in the area of less attractive jobs they were well represented; 58.3 per cent of those in domestic occupations and 32 per cent of those in agricultural jobs were foreigners. As a whole, 71.2 per cent of the working population of the city were foreigners.[6] Although the competition from the immigrant affected the whole native population, only the Negroes and mulattoes suffered its impact as a kind of social cataclysm. Excluded from the labor market or forced to its fringes, the colored men found themselves condemned to chronic unemployment, seasonal work, depressed wages, and adjustment to a type of life in which, inevitably, misery went hand in hand with social disorganization.[7]

In the third place, we should consider the period of consolidation after 1935, when internal migrations became more important as a

---

[6] *Relatório apresentado ao Cidadão Dr. Cezario Motta Junior, Secretário dos Negócios do Interior do Estado de São Paulo pelo Director da Repartição da Estatística e Arquivo Dr. Antonio de Toledo Piza, em 31 de julho de 1894*, pp. 68, 71–72.

[7] Cf. Fernandes, *A Integração*, Chap. 2.

manpower source. During this period the acceleration of economic growth gave rise to new job opportunities for native elements. It became much less of a problem for the Negro and the mulatto to secure a permanent job, and, correlatively, a steady source of income. A new trend then set in to absorb the "colored population" in the occupational system resulting from the universalization of free labor. The opportunities were still, however, largely concentrated in the lower job classifications of an urban economy. Even so, after a delay of more than fifty years, the Negro and the mulatto entered the new era, and began to draw their due share of the economic guarantees assured by the competitive social order. The results of a survey made in 1951 indicate through the sample taken how this trend manifested itself: craftsmen, 29.39 per cent; domestic work, 20.76 per cent; government employees, 9.18 per cent; industry (skilled or semi-skilled workers), 8.13 per cent; office workers, 7.08 per cent; retail business (salesman, etc.), 4.46 per cent; seasonal workers, 3.93 per cent; horticulturists and gardeners, 2.33 per cent; other occupations, 14.69 per cent.[8] These figures show that even "proletarianization" of the colored population is a recent phenomenon. The 1940 census data indicate something analogous (although indirectly): compared to 15,261 white employers (97.04 per cent) there were only 123 Negro or brown employers (0.78 per cent). To be comparable to the demographic proportions indicated by the same census data, the latter figure should be 13.5 times larger. Nevertheless, incipient proletarianization and the appearance of middle-class Negro families reveal a new reality: the disappearance of the inhibiting effects of immigration on the processes of absorption of the Negro and the mulatto into new job categories and social classification.

This rapid survey suggests two considerations. First, it is unquestionable that immigration constituted a highly constructive revolutionary force. If it produced some negative or even destructive effects for the Negro populations, this was due to the peculiar conditions that surrounded the emancipation process and the creation of a competitive social system. Second, the circumstances of the

[8] *Ibid.*, p. 426.

creation, consolidation, and growth of the competitive social system did not help to minimize the negative or destructive impact of immigration on the socioeconomic adjustments of the Negro populations. On the contrary, they created a sociocultural, economic, and political context that prolonged and intensified the negative influences. These conclusions show once again that the sociodynamic influences of immigration depend, structurally and functionally, on the organization of the social milieu. It is not immigration per se that produces this or that effect. Rather, the manner in which it is converted into a sociohistorical factor determines the quality, variety, and degree of persistence of its direct or also of its indirect effects.

The Reaction of the Negro and the Mulatto

The reaction of the Negro and the mulatto to the presence of the immigrant varied as time went by. Moved by a disposition to social integration and frequently cast aside in his competitive relations (more or less confined to the white man's world), the Negro and the mulatto tended to give vent to their resentment on the basis of their frustrations in those two areas. Thus, the character of the reactions varied historically, according to the social configuration of the possibilities for integration and inter-racial competition. In general, it is possible to distinguish four reactive polarizations that are characteristic.

During the period of slavery, the presence of the immigrant introduced an upsetting element in the cultural horizon of the slave and, in general, in the self-evaluation of the Negro. For the master, as well as for the slave or the freedman, the immigrant presented himself as a human equivalent of the servile laborer. The immigrant rejected this classification, impelled by two concomitant pressures: 1) the growing crisis of the labor market; 2) the drive for the implantation and generalization of free labor. On the other hand, the immigrant's cultural traditions and social aspirations protected him from the authoritarianism and harshness of the masters. The latter were forced to review their attitudes and behavior, since the immigrants kept their contractual obligations and demanded their fulfillment, calling on their consulates. Consequently, before the total breakdown of the slavocrat and manorial society, the immigrant already played economic, social, and legal roles typical of a competitive structure. This meant wages commensurate with the kind of work freely contracted for, minimal human respect, and social guarantees for the personal freedom of the worker and his family. Both the slave, being almost completely deprived of these advantages or enjoying them only in a limited way, and the freedman, because he was hurt by the social and economic degradation of "work for Negroes," reacted to the situation in a rather crude and violent manner. The following words put in the mouth of a slave by a commentator give us an idea of their inconformity: "The master is good—he won't mistreat us—but the master who gets rich and happy gives land to the foreigner, pays him for his services, and leaves us as we were before." [9] It was in inconformity, though, that did not pit the slave against the immigrant. The slave began to repudiate the condition that made him a victim of the slavocrat exploitation and intended to demand treatment analogous to that dispensed to the foreigner. Two commentaries of the time pointed out the trend as follows:

By force of the circumstances, the slave compares himself with the free worker and he feels the long distance that separates them; he understands, then, the lowliness of his position, without much hope for better days and from this discouraging situation are born all the follies of which a crude kind of organization is capable, and all the reactions which a man who feels despised by a pitiless fate will resort to. This clearly means that side by side with the free, remunerated worker and the immigrant, there is no place for non-compensated work, slave work, done exclusively for the benefit of the proprietors; that immigration, as a social institution, irresistibly repels the servile institution; that this great factor of our progress makes the slave impossible.[10]

(The slaves) escape and abandon the farms because their minds, accompanying our evolution, no longer can understand work without remuneration; because they know that the rural settler who no longer has enough strength to work in the fields, has savings, has his joys and,

[9] *A Província de São Paulo*, Nov. 9, 1887.
[10] *O Correio Paulistano*, Nov. 13, 1887.

lives much better. . . . The Negro race is capable of the same noble feelings as the civilized races.[11]

During the period that goes from Abolition (1888) to the end of the First Republic (Revolution of 1930), the "Negro" in São Paulo faced the worst imaginable vicissitudes.[12] During that time two things should be stressed. On the one hand, the tendency of the Negro was to handle his freedom in an extremely irrational manner. Feeling that he was now "master of his fate," the Negro put into practice certain adjustments that ran counter to the very nature of free work, contractual relations, and the competitive bases of the new social structure. Thence resulted a deep structural maladjustment which severely contributed to eliminating the Negro from the labor market, even in those areas regarded as "Negro jobs." On the other hand, there was a growing tendency toward the racial concentration of income, social prestige, and power. Abolitionism is typically part of a social revolution made by whites for whites. Thus, the competitive social system did not realize, at once, any of the hopes of correcting the racial inequities of the *ancien régime*. Initially, it aggravated them in an extreme and sometimes shocking way. In opposition to the Negro, the immigrant was part of the process through which the bourgeois revolution took place in São Paulo.[13] As a result, he rapidly attained a class status and was able to use it as an adaptive mechanism of competition and social mobility. The Negro found himself between these two contradictory pressures. One of them eliminated him at least from the center of the work and the status system of the competitive social structure; the other stressed this effect very clearly, making it look even more apparent and blatant, thanks to the seemingly shining success of being an "equal"—the imperfect external resemblances of the point of departure encouraged that image in the Negro community.

Since he did not have the mechanisms to absorb the resulting psychological and sociological frustrations, the Negro expressed his

[11] *O Correio Paulistano*, Nov. 16, 1887. On this subject, also see José Maria dos Santos, *Os Republicanos Paulistas e a Abolição* (São Paulo, 1942), pp. 315–16.

[12] Cf. Fernandes, *A Integração*, pp. 118–98.

[13] *Ibid.*, esp. pp. 30 ff.

resentment in a bitter and destructive manner. It was then that certain ambivalent representations appeared and spread among the Negro community. These ideas have been cultivated to this day among some Negroes. The immigrant was seen as a companion, as one who had suffered with the Negro and who, along with him, had "eaten the bread of affliction." But, at the same time, the immigrant was a "stuck-up type" who forgot his Negro friends and left them to their own devices when he "made the grade." In particular, the immigrants were held responsible for the policy of rejecting the local people and favoring only "other foreigners like them." Related to these general evaluations was a strong tendency to impute race prejudice to the foreigner who would have been responsible for introducing it to the country.[14] Such ideas, however, never became factors of systematic hostility. Because of the lawless conditions of social life and its limited competitive character, the Negro and the mulatto never found themselves in a position to compete effectively with the immigrants and their descendents. Thus, these reactions were part of the Negro folklore. On a psychosocial level, however, they were no more than devices to preserve the integrity and equilibrium of the ego. In any case, they furnished plausible and impersonal explanations for the "successes" of some and the "failures" of others. There do not appear to be any relations to open conflicts or tensions. This is an important point, because it reveals something basic. Even where the reaction to the immigrant reached its strongest negative intensity, it did not lead to his being defined, sociologically speaking, as an enemy and did not imply the need to treat him as such.

During the period that began with the structural crisis of the First Republic, the Negro and the mulatto also presented themselves, in a rather timid and irregular way, in the trends for social reconstruction that were stirring Brazilian society. They even attempted to take a stand, in racial terms, in the face of such trends, by organizing some major social movements, approximately from 1927 to 1948. They were thus led to equate, historically, the aims and social

[14] Another equally strong alternative tendency inverts the explanation. "Color prejudice" would be acquired in Brazil, thanks to the influence of the traditional families over the immigrants.

aspirations of the colored people with the organized and conscious struggle against the causes and effects of the racially based concentration of income, social prestige, and power. The *Manifesto to the Brazilian Colored People* stated that:

The Brazilian Negro Problem is that of the absolute and complete integration of the Negro in all aspects of Brazilian life (political, social, religious, economic, labor, military, diplomatic, etc.); the Brazilian Negro must have the fullest training and the fullest acceptance everywhere and for everything, given the proper conditions (which should be encouraged)—physical, technical, intellectual, and moral—required for "Equality Under the Law." Brazil must absolutely stop being ashamed of its Race here at home, and abroad, in international life. . . . Therefore, we repeat, we must fight for a Negro Association, but—let us stress—one that is radically Brazilian and affirms Tradition, and extends wherever there exists any problem.[15]

Within the emotional and logical context of such a vision of reality, the Negro directly attacked the factors of racial inequality and the effects that tended to perpetuate it indefinitely. The Negro's inconformity assumes, therefore, a socially constructive aspect, leading him to ask himself why "equality under the law" did not produce practical results, and to uncover, with acuteness and objectivity, the myth of the nonexistence of color prejudice in Brazil. In these circumstances, the Negro and the mulatto did not turn against the immigrant. The latter was diluted in the framework of the system that produced the racial concentration of income, social prestige, and power. Although it was still believed that the immigrant tended to pass over the natives, favoring his countrymen and preserving prejudice and discrimination, the new social movements introduced an unexpected and revolutionary appraisal of the immigrants' success. The leaders of these movements had had, for one reason or another, more or less intensive experiences with foreign families, particularly Italian.[16] Consequently, they were better able to evaluate the reasons for the immigrants' success and, at the same time, to

---

[15] Arlindo Veiga dos Santos, "Manifesto à Gente Negra Brasileira," Dec. 2, 1931, transcribed from the original.

[16] José Correia Leite, one of the principal leaders of these movements, could be taken as an example.

exert some influence toward encouraging the Negro to develop constructive forms of imitation. It was in this context that concern first appeared for the value of an integrated family, domestic cooperation, systematic savings, owning a home, and putting an end to man's sexual irresponsibility and the cult of the "Negro mother." Taking the immigrant as a point of reference, the Negro discovered that he lacked the social techniques which could allow his integration in society and assure bases for inter-racial competition. Thus it was that the foreigner appeared here in two aspects: 1) as a white—pure and simple—who should be seen and represented as any other white (including those of native origin); and 2) as a source of emulation. Just as the immigrant had faced difficulties analogous to those of the Negro, the latter could repeat his feats. The explicit attacks appeared to be polarized around the social interests of the Negro himself. Frequently, they had to do with accusations made against the traditional families who allegedly would have "sacrificed the Negro" to an "immigration policy" designed to bring economic advantages. But there were also concrete cases of color prejudice expressed by the immigrants. These cases were dealt with directly and particularly, according to the events that brought about the conflicts or misunderstandings.

Finally, during the period that could be described as the "second industrial revolution" in São Paulo, especially from the 1940s on, the rate of economic growth was reflected in the job opportunities and the tendencies to classify the Negro in the social and economic structure of the community.[17] The Negro seemed to repeat the immigrant's past, albeit in harsher and less promising competitive conditions. He rose in the segments of the population which were in the mainstream of events and were actors of the historic drama. This process was, however, uneven and not very intense. Only a few were able to cross the racial barriers of concentration of wealth, social status, and power, and reach a social position comparable to that of the whites who had risen in the competitive social system. Nevertheless, the number is constantly growing. This means that it is a clear and constant trend which—if certain sociohistorical and

[17] Cf. Fernandes, *A Integração*, pp. 415-52.

economic conditions are maintained—can be assumed decisively to favor the progressive integration of the Negro and the mulatto in typical class situations. The significant element in this whole broad process is the emergence of a new type of Negro with a new mentality, a new behavior, and new social aspirations. The new Negro has benefited from the constructive influences of the old social movements; thanks to these movements, he has learned not to fear the white and to have sounder judgment about the extrapersonal factors of racial inequality. Because of his identification, however, with the aims of vertical social mobility that he can exploit effectively, he turns his back on and even fights the humanitarian goals of the social movements, preferring to use accumulated experience to achieve personal, direct, and selfish objectives. The new Negro no longer values the white, socially, as a *white;* he sees the white only in terms of his class situation and may reject him if he finds that he is in a lower position. On the other hand, as the Negro has learned about the working of institutions and the selective criteria in a competitive society, he is less inclined to overestimate the power of certain groups of people. Hence, he tends not only to restrain his enthusiasm in face of the foreigner simply because of color, but also to curtail unfounded retaliations because of any alleged "protection of fellow countrymen." Furthermore, as he understands better the structure of competitive relations, he ends up by upsetting the balance of racial adjustments. In the confrontation with the foreigner or his descendants, this assumes particular relevance. Both the immigrant and his descendants, as well as the Negro, are led to reinforce the traditional representations, perhaps as a superficial defense mechanism and a way of neutralizing potential conflicts. In spite of this, the cases that could be systematically analyzed suggest that the Negro tends to adopt quite rational attitudes and behavior patterns, considering the nature of the social interests of the isolated individual. Instead of aggravating the tensions, causing direct accusations and irreparable breaks, he prefers to get around the situation. If he feels injured by some foreigners, he turns to other whites for support and thus tries to rise above the causes of personal tension. The relevance of these attitudes is clear. They indicate that the factors related to the national or ethnic origin of the immigrants are secondary in the motivation and organization of competitive relations between "Negroes" and "Whites."

The total results of the discussion of this topic show the existence of a general and constant trend. In the several historical and social conditions in which he confronted the "immigrant," the Negro did not go against the "foreigner." Even when the latter's influence was felt and represented as specifically unfavorable, it never came to be systematically formulated in aggressive or opposing forms. The reason for this seems simple. What concerned the Negro in any of these phases was not the position of the immigrant and his descendants in the community structure, but the fact that the Negro himself was not—or was only partially—a part of that structure. His inconformity took him, then, invariably in the same direction: the extension of the benefits of an open society to all segments of the Negro people. The reactions of the Negro against the immigrant were softened by this tendency, which diluted and socially restructured the motives for frustration and aggression, turning them into active dispositions of racial accommodation and desire for integration on equalitarian bases.

Immigration and the Race Relations System

Immigration did not contribute to changing either immediately, or on a long-term basis, the structure of the pre-existing race relations system. It did help, though, from 1880 onwards, to bring about the collapse of the servile regime. But immigration itself began and grew during the nineteenth century as the historical result of the manpower and labor relations crisis of the slavery system.

The explanation for this phenomenon is relatively simple. The rapid and intense changes that affected the development structure of São Paulo did not have any repercussion on the position of the Negro in the social system or on race relations patterns. Basically, the status change implied in the transition from the condition of slave or freedman to that of citizen[18] did not find the economic,

[18] Besides the works cited in Note 2, also see Octavio Ianni, *As Metamorfoses do Escravo* (São Paulo, 1962), Chaps. V and VII, and Fernando Henrique Cardoso, *Capitalismo e Escravidão no Brasil Meridional* (São Paulo, 1962), Chaps. V and VI.

social, and political support that would make it a historical reality. It was a semantic operation or—as one liberal leader put it—"an atrocious irony." In the areas of intense economic growth, it consolidated the last plundering suffered by the slave and the freedman, and practically purged them from the labor system without any economic compensation or social guarantees.[19] Hence, the Negro was to prolong the human drama of the slave, and more than half a century was needed before the situation would begin to change. The traditional race relation patterns[20] remained almost untouched during that half century, maintaining an atmosphere of inter-racial relations that differed very little from that prevailing in the previous historical situation.

This background helped to keep up the racial attitudes and evaluations transplanted by the immigrants along with their cultural heritage. Most of the immigrants, regardless of their provenance, had had no experience in dealing with the Negro and looked at him ethnocentrically, as if he were biologically, psychologically, and culturally inferior to the white. It was easy to dissimulate such attitudes behind the race relations pattern imposed by the surrounding atmosphere. These attitudes and evaluations did not, however, create racial prejudice and discrimination in the forms in which they presented themselves in Brazilian society. They both appeared long before, as part of and in answer to the need to give moral foundation and social legitimacy to slavery and its consequences in a society with Christian mores.[21] These attitudes were maintained during the creation and development of the competitive social system, first, because of the persistence, and later, the aggravation of the racial concentration of income, social prestige, and power (in other words, the intensification of racial inequality itself). The immigrant, in other areas, did not have to resort to prejudice or discrimination to protect his chances for social climbing, defend a certain income level, or maintain a certain style of living. At no time did the Negro

---

[19] Cf. Fernandes, *A Integração*, pp. 30 ff.; Roberto Simonsen, "As Consequencias Economicas da Escravidão," *Revista do Arquivo Municipal*, Year IV, Vol. XLVII (São Paulo, 1938), 257–68.

[20] On this pattern in São Paulo see Fernandes, *A Integração*, Chap. 3.

[21] Cf. Bastide and Fernandes, *Brancos e negros em São Paulo*, Chap. II, *passim*.

ever constitute a threat to the white, his social values, or human destiny.

Nevertheless, immigration worsened the climate of racial relations for four different reasons. The first has to do with the way of redefining the customs of the country. Anxious not to be different from Brazilians, the immigrants tried to adjust themselves to the situations in which they had to live with the Negro, keeping to the formula that "even though inferior. Negroes are still people." This formula could be successfully applied only when and where the two parties observed the bases of the traditionalist race relation that gave the Negro a heteronomous position. For lack of experience, and also because social distance sometimes made the game somewhat difficult, the immigrant would fail in the application of the formula and find himself caught in his own trap. The Negro would start "taking liberties," "getting too familiar," or "too fresh," "not keeping his distance," "taking advantage of people's good faith," "getting too nosey," and so on. Within a short while, the immigrant would learn his lesson and would go to the other extreme. With rather discrepant and ostensible behavior and attitudes, although shunning anything that might appear as "insulting" or "degrading," he started to avoid the Negro. Even so, his action represented a deviation from the conventional racial treatment.

The second reason is linked to certain modes of "exploitation of the Negro" that, consciously or unconsciously, were practiced by many immigrants during the hardest time of their struggle to make good in the New World. During the first steps of capital accumulation, the immigrant depended on certain forms of cooperation that resulted in getting people to work for subsistence wages. This stratagem could only be successfully applied in the family or household milieu. Thanks to the many abandoned Negro children and the inclination of many mothers to "give their children a trade," the Negro and the mulatto fell prey to this artifice (which, incidentally, was also quite common among traditional white families, even during the first quarter of this century). In terms of socialization, this represented an asset for the youngsters. Many learned the three R's, got a job, and found out what life was like in an organized home. On the whole, this experience was to be very useful for some of the leaders of social movements that developed in the Negro milieu. In some areas, however, it produced disturbing consequences. From his youth, the adopted "brother" discovered that his real condition did not give him the right to have the same aspirations as the others. Friendly relations would turn sour. In their stead were bitterness, frustration and, sometimes, implacable hatred. On the white's side, the self-defensive reactions produced conventional retaliations (such as, "you can't lend a hand to a Negro," "ungrateful people," or "people who bite the hand that feeds them"). The Negro or the mulatto would go further because they felt that their security and aspirations had no meaning, and this often led them to place their hopes in collective protest movements.

The third reason is indirect and involves immigration only partially. The growth in population and the consequent Europeanization of the city did not have the character of a population substitution with regard to the white natives.[22] With regard to the Negro, however, the population substitution took on a specific and drastic character.[23] For this reason, the phenomena of social anomie which took place in the Negro milieu found one of their root causes in this process that conditions and worsens the displacement of the Negro populations. This topic should be mentioned here because of two particularly important implications. On one hand, chronic maladjustments were connected with these phenomena of anomie and produced a greater visibility of the Negro and the mulatto as "rowdies," "vagrants," "bums," "thieves," and so on. It was precisely this visibility that nurtured the perpetuation of the old racial stereotypes and channelled the social redefinition of the Negro in an extremely unfavorable direction. Although the immigrant was neither personally nor morally responsible for what happened, his presence was related to the process in an easily perceptible way. On the other hand, when the Negro and the mulatto questioned immigration, they tended to see it from an emotional and moral angle, in the light of this impact. Immigration was not the only (or the main) cause of the phenomenon; and, in many respects, it was nothing more than an effect

[22] Cf. esp. Samuel H. Lowrie, *Imigração e Crescimento da População no Estado de São Paulo* (São Paulo, 1938).
[23] Cf. Fernandes, *A Integração*, pp. 81–118.

of the same series of factors that led to disintegration of the servile society and to bourgeois revolution. But the Negro who lived in the city during that period (and sometimes his descendants, also) could free himself from the compulsion to relate his shame to the immigrant's deeds. In this case, the latter did not become a scapegoat. He did appear, however, as the missing piece that would explain the beginnings and the dimensions of the drama that befell the colored people.

The fourth reason operates all along the situation of racial contact and seems to be, from a dynamic point of view, the most important of all. We refer to the direct or indirect effects of social rise on race evaluations and relations. In many respects, the immigrant's situation was always very similar to that of the Negro and the mulatto. The immigrant had a quite modest point of departure, although he was white; he often had to struggle hard to attain social status and, later, to enjoy the benefits of social mobility. However, because he had some (or complete) knowledge of the social techniques that govern human relations in a competitive society, the immigrant attained his two objectives quite rapidly. The point worth stressing now is that a clear distinction was established between the "poor" immigrant and the "rich" immigrant. As he climbed the social ladder, the immigrant went through a period of crisis, during which he broke his moral and physical ties with his old social world. In contrast with the traditional Brazilian families, especially those that did not lose status throughout all the changes taking place in the city, the immigrant did not have enough social prestige to face the demands of his newly acquired social level, while at the same time maintaining seemingly spurious connections with the past. Such connections aroused in him the fear of social degradation, as if the visibility of the Negro affected and spread to those who were seen with him. Furthermore, the tendency to avoid the Negro during the crisis period became a sort of convention. The immigrant and his descendants wound up building a world in which there is no place for the Negro. Neither of the effects mentioned were the product of his cultural tradition. They derived, rather, from the complex tensions created by social climbing in a class society. Other groups, however, did not see things from this angle. The white native, from the higher class, simply disapproved of what he believed to be an intolerable manifestation of racial prejudice. The middle-class Negro, for his part, ran into the spiteful character which avoidance assumed in the immigrants' behavior. Therefore, on two social levels, the immigrant was seen as if he were introducing "race prejudices" into Brazil. Immigration became accused, although, from what we know, it was only indirectly related to the foci of tension.

The results of this analysis clearly suggest that immigration did not contribute in fact to including race relations in the sphere of social change and modernization. On the contrary, where immigration did not adapt itself—by its direct or indirect effects—to the pre-existing race relations system, it aggravated it, stimulating the persistence of inter-racial adjustments tinged with prejudice and discrimination. Nothing justifies the tendency to attribute to the immigrants the "introduction" of race prejudice and discrimination into the city, however. At least in the known manifestations of both phenomena, the immigrants simply absorbed attitudes and behavior patterns previously incorporated in the Brazilian race relations system. It seems that immigration became a neutral factor with respect to the democratization of race relations because what could be called "the Negro problem" did not affect the development of the competitive social system. Ceasing to be a privileged manpower source and—for some reason—a factor or impediment of economic growth, the Negro lost his historical importance to the white. Nothing, then, could involve the immigrant in the mesh of interests and social values that would become linked to the implantation of racial democracy. Immigration would also have been neutral with regard to the structure itself of race relations, had it not been for the historical circumstances that spontaneously and inevitably turned it into a factor of concentration of income, social prestige, and power. It was for this reason that it contributed clearly to worsen the appearances and the reality of racial inequality. However, we must here distinguish conditions, causes, and effects in the intricate historical and social context under consideration. The immigrant did not introduce himself—nor did he find himself introduced—into a structure of racial competition with the Negro and the mulatto. If immigration had a dramatic effect on the manifestations of racial inequality, this happened because it was one of the accelerating factors in the economic growth and social development of the community. The groups that had more or less advantageous positions in the power structure and the competitive system obviously had also the best opportunities to participate in these two processes. In fact, since the structure of the race relations system excluded the "Negro" from such opportunities, the whites practically monopolized the advantages which derived from them. Immigration as a historical factor simply aggravated the different forms taken by racial inequality in the social life of the Negro and the mulatto.[24]

[24] Other works to which reference should be made include: J. R. Araujo Filho, "A População Paulistana," *A Cidade de São Paulo* (Associação dos Geógrafos Brasileiros: (São Paulo, 1958); Salvio de Almeida Azevedo, "Imigração e Colonização no Estado de São Paulo," *Revista do Arquivo Municipal*, Year IV, Vol. LXXV (São Paulo, 1941), 105-57; José Francisco Camargo, *Crescimento do População do Estado de São Paulo e seus Aspectos Econômicos* (São Paulo, 1952); Samuel H. Lowrie, "O Elemento Negro na População de São Paulo," *Revista do Arquivo Municipal*, Year IV, Vol. XLVIII (São Paulo, 1938), 5-56; Odilon Nogueira de Matos, "São Paulo no Seculo XIX," *A Cidade de São Paulo* (Associação dos Geógrafos Brasileiros, São Paulo, 1958).

PART III

Change in Indo-America During the Nineteenth and Twentieth Centuries

CHAPTER 7

Mestizaje in Mexico

During the National Period

Moisés González Navarro

In Mexico "race" mixture has proceeded even more rapidly since independence than it did in colonial days. The statistical evidence for this assertion is, however, scanty. Moisés González Navarro, a historian who teaches at the Colegio de México, here notes, however, that although legal distinctions as to race were terminated in 1822, in many cases racial terminology continued to be applied in official documents. Admittedly, statistical data based on "race" do not suffice to determine the spread of *mestizaje*, but the author believes that data based on language and illiteracy may be used for the same purpose. In his view, the process of mestizaje was facilitated by the violent struggles that characterized Mexico during most of the nineteenth century.

The Spanish conquest united the scattered groups of Indians who were then inhabiting the territory of present-day Mexico. In principle, the Crown strove to keep the conquerors and conquered segregated except when the Indians were forced to labor for the colonists. To these two major groups soon were added Negroes and, little by little, there appeared mestizos or *castas*, mixed bloods, the result of the inevitable mixing of the races. Since most of these unions were illegitimate, the term "mestizo" became synonymous with bastard, a stigma that was to disappear only after the Revolution of 1910 rehabilitated Indian culture.

In the nineteenth century (1810–1910), the hierarchical estate

[145]

system was abolished legally, but in reality only a start toward ending it was made. Legislation by both the Spanish liberals in 1811, 1812, and 1820 and the *criollo* conservatives (*Plan de Iguala*, 1821) established the equality of all inhabitants of New Spain. On September 27, 1822, the Sovereign Constituent Congress, implementing the *Plan de Iguala*, ordered that classification of persons by race not be permitted in official documents.[1] Nevertheless, it was necessary to consider race in attempting to destroy peculiar Indian institutions, especially the agrarian ones. Actually, the definition of the concept of "Indian" in regard to the questions of disamortization and redistribution of their landholdings lay at the heart of the problem of referring to the Indians in racial terms. For example, in 1826 the Senate of Jalisco adopted the premise that since very few "pure-blooded Indians" remained, those whom "public opinion" considered Indians would be regarded as such whether or not there had been any racial mixture (except with Negroes). Nevertheless, this same state returned to a strictly racial classification in 1862, when the lands belonging to the brotherhoods (*cofradías*) were being distributed. It was decided then to divide ownership among those who could be certified as Indian according to the Registration Book of *Indígenas*.

On the other hand, with the exception of Puebla and San Luis Potosí, in their first constitutions all the states restricted the civil rights of domestic servants and illiterates. In the case of illiterates, however, implementation of these restrictions was delayed for periods of from ten to twenty-five years. The 1836 *"centralista"* constitution imposed similar handicaps. Although no such restrictions appeared in the *"federalista"* constitution of 1857, in practice little progress was made because despite a decrease in illiteracy the rapid development of peonage impeded the greater part of the indigenous population from actively participating in national life. Several states, especially in the North and South, contradicting the express text of the Constitution of 1857, made criminal the violation of a contract of tenancy and labor when prior payment had been

[1] Moisés González Navarro, "Instituciones indígenas en México Independiente," *Métodos y Resultados de la Política Indigenista en México* (Mexico City, 1954), pp. 115–30, 143–65.

made. The Supreme Court of Justice did, however, grant protection to the Indians in some instances.

It would seem that the interests of the *criollo latifundistas* constituted a factor which influenced the success of the new policy. Immediately after Independence, the landowners demanded, in the name of equality, that indebted Indians be obliged to remain on the haciendas. In their view, justice required that, as free and equal citizens, the Indians had the right to make contracts and the obligations to fulfill them. José María Luís Mora stated clearly that the new legislation replaced the old distinction between Indian and non-Indian with a new division between rich and poor, "thereby extending to everyone the benefits of society." Similarly, many years later Francisco Pimentel fought on behalf of the landowners against the establishment of the Society for the Protection of the Poor, favored by the Emperor Maximilian, since equality required that an analogous organization be founded to defend the "rights of the rich."

Nonetheless, governmental authorities sometimes were forced to recognize the independent existence of indigenous groups, principally of the nomadic tribes of the North. Until 1850, the governments of Coahuila and Chihuahua made treaties with the Comanches and Apaches despite the advice of Lorenzo de Zavala, who urged them to "force the barbarians to organize themselves into regular societies or leave the national territory, as the North Americans are doing with their Indians."

During most of the nineteenth century, the sedentary Indian tribes, which included the majority of the country's population, were in revolt throughout Mexico. Although both local and federal congresses had granted to the Yaquis the right to have their own government and laws, in 1825 this tribe began a campaign to exterminate the white man. In response to the "War of the Castes" (*Guerra de las castas*) begun in Yucatán in 1847, Justo Sierra O'Reilly sought the expulsion of the Indians from the peninsula because they had refused to "mix" with the rest of the population. The Mayas responded to this argument by defending their right to the land being threatened by the "King" and the "Spaniards," that is, by the government and the non-Indian Mexicans. This dated concept of the country's political structure laid bare how completely the absolute separation of the races had been maintained. Whatever the consequences might be, in 1848 Justo Sierra O'Reilly requested aid from the United States and José María Luís Mora help from Great Britain so that the white man could defeat the Indian rebels of the Yucatán. At mid-century the revolt of the Indians of the *Sierra Gorda* affected a wide area of the central region. The clearly agrarian character of the revolt elicited the description "communist" from General Anastasio Bustamente, who was charged with quelling it. As a matter of fact, according to Francisco Pimentel's description of the situation years later, the Indians faced the dilemma of "kill or be killed" because, as Guillermo Prieto explained, independence turned the Mexicans into the"*Gachupines* of the Indians." [2] At the root of these revolts Lucas Alamán saw the criollo mentality which, in seeking to differentiate itself from the Spanish, held that independence meant a return to the pre-Conquest era.

Together with the violent racial and social struggle of this period, the process of mestizaje gained momentum. Several confused if picturesque expressions of this phenomenon appeared at the time. An example is the plan for an indigenous monarchy proclaimed in 1834 by the priests Carlos Tepisteco and Epigenio de la Piedra, who proposed that a constituent congress consisting of the twelve youths most closely descended from Moctezuma should name an emperor. If he were an Indian, he should marry a white woman; if white, a pure-blooded Indian. A council composed of Indians and non-Indians would advise him, and he would distribute governmental positions equally between the races. Twenty years later, the Rodeo plan for regenerating the country proclaimed Augustín de Iturbide the Elder (son of Augustín I) Emperor, and in the case of his refusal nominated Antonio de Haro y Tamariz or whomever the Cortes should appoint to succeed to the throne. If the Emperor were single, he would marry a Mexican Indian. These initiatives reveal the country's growing awareness of its mestizo character, a positive aspect of the egalitarian policy since it favored contact, mixture, and,

[2] The phrase is "gachupines de los indios." Gachupín is a derogatory term for peninsular Spaniards (ed.).

ultimately, fusion of the races—"In preparation for the emergence of one single race." [3]

Although fragmentary and arbitrary, statistical estimates of the racial composition of Mexico during the Porfiriato confirm that whereas the mestizo element of the population increased in size, the Indian sector declined. Various calculations of that era characterize 44 per cent of the population as mestizo. According to Antonio García Cubas, the Indian population was in absolute numbers the same in 1877 as in 1810, but this fact in itself implied a relative decline. Everyone seems to have agreed that the Indian population was decreasing because of unfavorable sanitary conditions, poverty, ignorance, isolation, and so on. In 1893 Adolfo Duclós Salinas predicted that within a century the Indian population would be assimilated into the mestizo group which, in the opinion of Justo Sierra, constituted the true family of Mexico. Similarly, Andrés Molina Enríquez described the mestizo as the strongest, largest, and most patriotic element in the country since it possessed a common origin as well as unity of religion, physical characteristics, language, values, and aspirations. Toward the end of the Porfiriato, Molina Enríquez devised an elaborate theory of Mexican social stratification with an ethnic basis. Foreigners (North Americans and Europeans), the criollos, parts of the mestizo group, and the lower clergy (even if Indian) composed the higher classes. The middle classes consisted of small landowners and shopkeepers. In the lower classes were to be found most of the Indians, be they soldiers, day workers, or communal landholders. [4]

After 1810, under the stimulus of the abolition of slavery and the declaration of formal racial equality, a new national society of classes began to emerge from the colonial estate system. The movement was quickened, at least theoretically, by the fragmented process of disamortization culminating in the Lerdo law of 1856. Although

[3] González Navarro, "Instituciones indígenas. . . ."

[4] Moisés González Navarro, "El Porfiriato. La Vida Social," in D. Cosío Villegas (ed.), *Historia Moderna de México*, IV (Mexico City, 1957), 33–35, 383–84. See also Juan Comas, "Razas, mestizaje y clases sociales en la obra de A. Molina Enríquez: 1909," *Cuadernos Americanos*, 150:2 (Mexico City, 1966), 153–60.

in principle this process was intended to transform the Indian communal farmers into the proletariat of a national class society, in point of fact the identification between race and social class continued. During the Porfiriato, officials often resorted to euphemisms to resolve these questions. For example, at the end of the nineteenth century when a law to distribute free land to poor Indians was under consideration, Juan A. Mateos suggested the omission of the word Indian so that the law would not make distinctions between them, the mestizos, and the Negroes. The solution was found by Joaquín Casasus, who substituted the term "poor farmer." In this way, there would be no question of "helping a specific social class because of its race, but rather because of its poverty."

The Mexican Revolution marked the definitive period of transition from a caste system to an open class society. Thus, the law of January 6, 1915, which established the *ejido*, specified that the measure was designed as alleviation of the Indian's inability to adapt to the concept of private property rather than as a reconstruction of the old Indian community for its own sake.

However that may be, the first three national censuses (1895, 1900, 1910) contained no questions about race. It remained for the fourth, in 1921, deficient on so many other accounts, to add this further item of confusion and uncertainty. According to this compilation, almost six-tenths of the population was mestizo, less than a third Indian, and a tenth, white. The census of 1930 no longer contained questions regarding race, in keeping with a new criterion of social classification that reflected the incorporation of many indigenous groups into the mainstream of national life. In this process, they tended to lose their distinctive ethnic characteristics, including language. Thus, Mexican social stratification, especially since the Revolution, has come to have an economic rather than an ethnic basis, so that data on race, besides being unscientific, were seen as false.[5]

Nevertheless, from 1930 to 1940 marriages still continued to be registered according to the race of the parties. Figures from these years indicate that approximately three-fourths of the white males

[5] *Quinto Censo de Población. 15 de mayo de 1930. Resumen General* (Mexico City, 1934), p. xv.

married white girls; the rest, mestizos. According to these same questionable sources, in 1930, 94.6 per cent of the pure-blooded Indians married women of their own race, and in 1940, this percentage increased to 98.4. The 1930 data indicate that 0.28 per cent of the pure Indian males married white women; in 1940, it was 0.42 per cent. In 1930 and 1940 alike, 99 per cent of the mestizos married into their own group. Among oriental "yellow" men, 75 per cent married mestizo women according to both the 1935 and 1940 censuses, whereas in 1930 only 25 per cent married women of their own race. This figure decreased to 10 per cent in 1940 due to an increase in the number of marriages with white women. Whereas 91.3 per cent of the Negroes married within their own race according to the 1930 data, this figure fell to only 50 per cent in 1940 because of a sharp increase in the number of Negro marriages with mestizo women.[6]

In keeping with a more modern approach, the 1940 census made no mention of race but increased the number of questions about certain cultural characteristics of the population such as eating habits, clothing and footwear, sleeping facilities, and so on.[7] Nonetheless, an occasional official source continues to classify population by racial origin.[8]

Given the fact that since the nineteenth century it has been valueless to classify the population by race, one must seek other criteria to determine the state of mestizaje in Mexico. In general, a language criterion has come to replace the racial standard. At the beginning of the nineteenth century, only very weak attempts were made to extend the use of Spanish as the national language in the schools. For example, the Constituent Congress of Chihuahua decreed in 1826 that Indians be admitted to the primary schools. Two years later, the state of Occidente passed a law establishing primary

[6] *Anuario Estadístico de los Estados Unidos Mexicanos 1939* (Mexico City, 1941), pp. 122–23. *Anuario Estadístico. . . .* (Mexico City, 1943), p. 156.

[7] *Memoria de la Secretaría de la Economía Nacional presentada al H. Congreso de la Unión por el C. Secretario del ramo Efraín Buenrostro, sept. de 1939–agosto de 1940* (Mexico City, 1940), p. 86.

[8] *Informe rendido ante la H. Legislatura constitucional del Estado, de la gestión realizada por el Poder Ejecutivo, 16 de sept. de 1944 al 15 de sept. de 1945* (Chihuahua, 1944–1945).

schools in the Indian towns and requiring each tribe to send a literate Indian to Guadalajara or Mexico City to be trained in the Lancastrian system so as to be able to teach on returning home.

In Mexico City until the *Reforma*, the Colegio de San Gregorio was dedicated exclusively to instruction of the Indians. There, and at the Seminary of Puebla as well, the Mexican language was taught. After the Reforma, the indigenous languages received some attention but only in isolated instances. For example, during the Porfiriato the *Secretaría de Fomento* made the study of local Indian tongues obligatory in its hacienda schools. Similarly, Nahuatl was taught in the *Escuela Nacional Preparatoria* from 1884 and in the *Museo Nacional* after 1908. During this period, the general policy was to teach reading and writing directly in Spanish, as was the case in Chiapas, Guerrero, Chihuahua, the state of Mexico, and Jalisco. On the other hand, in areas that previously had suffered Indian rebellions, such as Tancahuitz in San Luis Potosí, it was decided to teach the alphabet in the local native languages. Toward the end of the Porfiriato, when the Federal Government was extending instruction in Spanish to the highlands of Xochimilco, only 364 children learned the language because of failure to solve their parents' work problems. Apparently, the Church adopted a more realistic approach than the government since it insisted that the clergy learn the language of its flocks and provided translations of the catechisms and other holy books in the more important Indian languages. The barracks, too, were an effective center of acculturation where conscripted soldiers were transformed forcefully from nomads into sedentary, Spanish-speaking citizens.[9]

According to an 1877 estimate, 38 per cent of the population spoke indigenous languages. In 1910 it was only 13 per cent (13.1 per cent female, 12.7 per cent male). Indians older than five years who spoke only a native language decreased from 14.7 per cent in 1921 to 3.8 per cent in 1960, or from 1,820,844 to 1,104,955 in absolute numbers. The percentage of bilingual persons (speaking Spanish and an Indian tongue) declined from 7.6 in 1930 to 6.6 in 1960, although in absolute terms, their numbers increased from

[9] González Navarro, "Instituciones . . . ," pp. 132–38.

1,065,760 to 1,925,299. On the other hand, between 1921 and 1960, the percentage of Spanish speakers increased both relatively (84.19 to 89.11 per cent) and absolutely (10,498,626 to 25,968,301).[10] According to a rather more refined criterion, the Indian population, defined as monolingual speakers of indigenous tongues, diminished from 7.6 to 3.2 per cent of the population between 1940 and 1960. At the same time, the percentage of "mesti-indios," that is, Indian-Spanish bilingual persons, declined from 7.4 to 5.4 per cent and likewise, mestizos, who speak Spanish but conserve Indian food, clothing, and shelter habits, fell from 37 to 30.6 per cent of the population. On the other hand, the "mesti-blancos," who speak Spanish and are predominantly Western by culture, increased from 47 to 60.2 per cent.[11]

Illiteracy is another good measure of mestizaje in Mexico. Since the last years of the Porfiriato, the percentage of illiterates has declined considerably; by 1910 they constituted only half of the population older than ten years, and by 1960 this figure had fallen to 38 per cent of those over six years of age.[12]

Without doubt, many social and geographical factors have done much to effect rapid and profound changes in the Indian population. The opening of new highways, both local and long-distance, and industrialization have stimulated new migration patterns: from the center to the North; from the mountains to the tropical lowlands; and, above all, from the countryside to the cities. Radio, television, and motion pictures also have been instruments of change which tend to break down the identification of rural Mexico with the Indian and of the city with the mestizo. Probably these changes have given greater stimulus to acculturation than have two governmental agencies, the *Departamento de Asuntos Indígenas* and the *Instituto Nacional Indigenista*, both of which were resisted initially by some who contended that for the same reason agencies for

---

[10] *Resumen del censo general de habitantes de 30 de Nov. de 1921* (Mexico City, 1928), p. 69; *Quinto Censo . . .* , p. 122; *Octavo Censo General de Población. 18 de junio de 1960* (Mexico City, 1962), pp. 649–50.

[11] Jorge L. Tamayo, *Geografía general de México*, III (Mexico City, 1962), 452.

[12] Moisés González Navarro, *Estadísticas Sociales del Porfiriato 1877–1910* (Mexico City, 1956), p. 125; *Octavo Censo General . . .* , p. 290.

[153]

Negroes, whites, and mestizos should be organized. Those who resisted apparently had forgotten that the purpose of these institutions, as stated by Lázaro Cárdenas at the Interamerican Congress of Pátzcuaro in 1940, is "to Mexicanize the Indian." [13]

In the nineteenth century, the country was ruled by the criollos, liberal or conservative, who sought—especially during the Porfiriato —to "whiten" the population by encouraging European immigration and prohibiting the entrance of Asians and Negroes. Today racial and color statuses no longer have legal force; in this sense Mexican society can be called "open," as the expression "Money whitens Indians and mixed-bloods" indicates. So, too, does the growing identification between the words *"indio"* and *"campesino"* seen in the use of the term *"indios gueros"* (blond or fair) to describe peasants who do not have the physical features of pure-blooded Indians. The Revolution rehabilitated the image of the Indian, to a degree sometimes approaching demagogy, as when the Indian was considered always right, whatever the facts. Of course, this policy was the exact opposite of Dr. Mora's mid-nineteenth-century plan for the population of the country by white foreigners who should be given preference over the "colored" races in everything that did not constitute a "clear violation of justice." [14]

Years later, attempts were being made to tie the foreign colonies within Mexico to the life of the country and to encourage race mixture by establishing Mexicans within these groups.[15] The outcome of these efforts to foment mestizaje was highly unsatisfactory, especially among the Mormons and Mennonites. Nevertheless, the Revolutionary government has found the strength to oblige most foreigners to become naturalized Mexican citizens, although this does not necessarily mean that they have mixed with the rest of the population.[16]

At any rate, it should be kept in mind that the preponderance of

[13] *Seis Años de Gobierno al Servicio de México* (Mexico City, 1940), p. ix.

[14] González Navarro, "Instituciones . . . ," pp. 153, 166.

[15] Moisés González Navarro, *La colonización en México* (Mexico City, 1960), p. 3.

[16] *Quinto Censo* . . . , pp. 108, 117–18; *Octavo Censo General* . . . , pp. 251–63, 461–93.

males in the foreign population may have facilitated miscegenation. For example, in 1895 70 per cent of the 116,437 foreign-born residents of Mexico were men, whereas in 1910 the figure had fallen to 54 per cent of the 223,468 foreigners. An analysis of population figures for foreigners who retained their original nationality shows that in 1895, 66 per cent of 46,163 were men and in 1960 84 per cent of the 52,276.[17]

In short, the classification of race has followed these criteria: 1) Legally, the use of racial terminology in official documents was ended on September 27, 1822. However, it continued until 1832 in certain remote or heavily Indian areas. In some states, the practice went on irregularly throughout the nineteenth century; indeed, with regard to marriage statistics, it extended to 1940; 2) the payment of a special Indian tribute persisted until 1824 in Chiapas; 3) in some churches, different fees were charged to Indians and non-Indians. For example, according to a regulation of March 22, 1899, in Chilapa, non-Indians paid eighteen pesos to get married whereas Indians paid only eight; 4) although in theory the disamortization proclaimed in the Lerdo law of 1856 ended economic differentiation by race, in 1940, 1,895 Indian communities owning 6,096,359 hectares remained; in 1960 these had grown to 1,915 communities in control of 8,735,449 hectares; 5) cultural distinctions (that is, language, food habits, dress, housing) are currently the best criteria for analyzing Mexican society. It is, however, also possible that some people might belong to one race by some standards and to a different one by others.

---

[17] In 1921 of the 108,433 persons born outside of Mexico, 84.6 per cent maintained allegiance to a foreign government. By 1960 of the 223,468 persons born outside of Mexico only 23.4 per cent were not Mexican citizens.

APPENDIX to Chapter 7

Table I gives chronological listing of the dates on which various parishes ended racial classification in their records. In some states, Jalisco for example, the practice had ceased even before the order issued by the Constituent Congress and the Plan of Iguala.

TABLE I

Arandas (marriages)	November 8, 1820
Plan of Iguala	February 24, 1821
Arandas (baptisms)	May 25, 1821
Guadalajara, cathedral (baptisms)	May 18, 1822
Ameca (marriages)	May 19, 1822
Constituent Congress	September 17, 1822
Mexico City, cathedral (baptism of orphans)	September 19, 1822
Monterrey, cathedral (baptisms)	September 22, 1822
Mexico City, cathedral (baptisms)	September 25, 1822
Monterrey, cathedral (marriages)	September 25, 1822
Mexico City, cathedral (marriages)	September 27, 1822
Tomatlán (marriages)	October 6, 1822
Guadalajara, cathedral (marriages)	November 6, 1822
Tuito (marriages)	October 14, 1822
Tomatlán (baptisms)	December 1, 1822
Xochimilco (baptisms)	November 2, 1830
Xochimilco (marriages)	January 2, 1831
Tecpan (marriages)	April 15, 1831
Tecpan (baptisms)	March 5, 1832
Pitic (baptisms)	May 25, 1832
Hermosillo (marriages)	October 8, 1832
Ameca (baptisms)	July 7, 1822

Table II shows the race of baptized children as recorded in various baptismal registers, 1821–1832.

[157]

TABLE II, SECTION A

Race as Recorded in Various Baptismal Registers, 1821–1832

Parish and Race	1821	1822	1823	1824	1825	1826	1827	1828	1829	1830	1831	1832
Amcca												
Coyotes	12	10	—	—	—	—	—	—	—	—	—	—
"Citizens"	9	11	—	—	—	—	—	—	—	—	—	—
Unknown, orphans	51	18	—	—	—	—	—	—	—	—	—	—
Spaniards	180	96	—	—	—	—	—	—	—	—	—	—
Indians	111	58	—	—	—	—	—	—	—	—	—	—
Mestizos	80	38	—	—	—	—	—	—	—	—	—	—
Mulattoes	96	46	—	—	—	—	—	—	—	—	—	—
No data	—	1	—	—	—	—	—	—	—	—	—	—
Total	539	278	—	—	—	—	—	—	—	—	—	—
Arandas												
Spaniards	21	—	—	—	—	—	—	—	—	—	—	—
Indians	1	—	—	—	—	—	—	—	—	—	—	—
Mestizos	1	—	—	—	—	—	—	—	—	—	—	—
No data	615	—	—	—	—	—	—	—	—	—	—	—
Total	638	—	—	—	—	—	—	—	—	—	—	—
Guadalajara (Sagrario)												
Coyotes	1	1	—	—	—	—	—	—	—	—	—	—
"Citizens"	1	5	—	—	—	—	—	—	—	—	—	—
Unknown, orphans	119	48	—	—	—	—	—	—	—	—	—	—

	1	2	3	4	5	6	7	8	9	10	11	12
Spaniards	270	118	—	—	—	—	—	—	—	—	—	—
Indians	102	56	—	—	—	—	—	—	—	—	—	—
Mestizos	24	11	—	—	—	—	—	—	—	—	—	—
No data	12	6	—	—	—	—	—	—	—	—	—	—
Total	529	245	—	—	—	—	—	—	—	—	—	—
Hermosillo												
Apaches	—	1	—	—	—	—	—	1	—	—	—	—
Neophytes	—	—	—	—	—	—	—	—	—	1	2	—
"Citizens"	—	8	265	338	348	226	422	—	—	—	—	—
Unknown	—	—	1	1	—	—	—	—	4	1	—	—
Spaniards	—	148	3	1	—	—	—	—	—	—	—	—
Spaniards (surnames)	—	—	—	—	—	4	4	263	225	168	356	—
Pagan Indians	—	—	22	9	7	—	—	4	2	2	—	—
Indians (surnames)	—	—	—	—	—	—	—	13	1	52	69	—
English	—	—	—	—	—	—	—	—	—	1	—	—
Mestizos (surnames)	—	—	—	—	—	—	—	7	2	1	4	—
No data	45	84	1	—	—	—	—	—	—	—	—	—
North Americans	—	—	—	—	1	—	1	—	—	—	—	—
Papagos	—	—	—	—	—	—	—	1	—	—	—	—
Pimas	—	—	—	—	—	—	—	1	1	—	—	—
Seris	—	—	—	—	—	—	—	1	—	—	—	—
Vagabonds	—	—	—	—	—	—	—	—	—	—	—	—
Yaquis	3	—	—	—	—	—	9	140	75	4	—	—
Yumas	—	—	—	—	—	—	3	—	—	—	3	—
Total	48	241	292	349	356	230	439	434	310	230	434	—

TABLE II, SECTION A (*Continued*)

Race as Recorded in Various Baptismal Registers, 1821–1832

Parish and Race	1821	1822	1823	1824	1825	1826	1827	1828	1829	1830	1831	1832
Mexico (Sagrario: legitimates)												
Castizos	9	7	—	—	—	—	—	—	—	—	—	—
Spaniards	935	826	—	—	—	—	—	—	—	—	—	—
Indians	126	111	—	—	—	—	—	—	—	—	—	—
Mestizos	58	31	—	—	—	—	—	—	—	—	—	—
Mulattoes	—	1	—	—	—	—	—	—	—	—	—	—
No data	—	3	—	—	—	—	—	—	—	—	—	—
Germans	—	1	—	—	—	—	—	—	—	—	—	—
Total	1128	980	—	—	—	—	—	—	—	—	—	—
Mexico (Sagrario: orphans, and children whose parents are not known)												
Castizos	3	—	—	—	—	—	—	—	—	—	—	—
Spaniards	171	156	—	—	—	—	—	—	—	—	—	—
Indians	76	39	—	—	—	—	—	—	—	—	—	—
Mestizos	22	12	—	—	—	—	—	—	—	—	—	—
Mulattoes	—	1	—	—	—	—	—	—	—	—	—	—
No data	—	5	—	—	—	—	—	—	—	—	—	—
Total	272	213	—	—	—	—	—	—	—	—	—	—
Tecpan												
"Citizens"	3	—	—	—	—	—	—	—	—	—	—	—
Unknown	5	2	—	—	—	—	—	—	—	—	4	3
Spaniards	37	1	—	—	—	—	—	—	—	—	18	3
Indians	58	1	—	—	—	—	—	—	—	—	94	15

Mestizos	3	1	—	—	—	—	—	22	2
Mulattoes	41	—	—	—	—	—	—	—	17
No data	86	95	—	—	—	—	—	1	22
Total	233	100	—	—	—	—	—	139	62
Tomatlán									
Coyotes	4	3	—	—	—	—	—	—	—
Spaniards	34	21	—	—	—	—	—	—	—
Indians	10	9	—	—	—	—	—	—	—
Mestizos	55	35	—	—	—	—	—	—	—
Mulattoes	1	1	—	—	—	—	—	—	—
Total	104	69	—	—	—	—	—	—	—
Xochimilco									
Unknown	—	—	—	3	14	9	—	10	6
Spaniards	—	—	—	20	29	35	—	10	1
Indians	414	248	—	175	330	201	—	81	73
Mestizos	—	—	—	1	4	1	—	—	—
No data	—	82	395	200	59	161	424	321	313
"De razón" (non-Indians)	—	—	—	1	—	2	—	—	—
Total	414	330	395	400	436	409	424	422	393

Sources:

Libro de bautismos número 26, de la parroquia de Ameca

Libro de bautismos números 20 y 21, de Arandas

Libro de bautismos número 52, del sagrario de Guadalajara

Libros primero, segundo, tercero y cuarto de bautismos de la misión y villa del Pitic

Libros números 2 y 3 de bautismos de españoles, del sagrario de México

Libros números 10 y 11 de bautismos de expositos e hijos de padros no conocidos, del sagrario de México

Libro número 3 de bautismos de indios de Tecpan. Libro número 4 de bautismos, de Tecpan

Libro número 4 de bautismos de Tomatlan

Libro número 51 de bautismos de indios, de Xochimilco. Libros de bautismos de todos los feligreses, numeros 52, 53 y 54, de Xochimilco

TABLE II, SECTION B

Marriages by Race in Various Parishes, 1821–1832

Parish and Race*	1821	1822	1823	1824	1825	1826	1827	1828	1829	1830	1831	1832
Ameca												
Africans	1	—	—	—	—	—	—	—	—	—	—	—
"Citizens"	2	16	—	—	—	—	—	—	—	—	—	—
Coyotes	1	—	—	—	—	—	—	—	—	—	—	—
Coyote-Indian	1	—	—	—	—	—	—	—	—	—	—	—
Coyote-Mestizo	1	—	—	—	—	—	—	—	—	—	—	—
Spaniards	37	1	—	—	—	—	—	—	—	—	—	—
Spaniard-Indian	1	1	—	—	—	—	—	—	—	—	—	—
Spaniard-Mestizo	1	—	—	—	—	—	—	—	—	—	—	—
Indians	16	1	—	—	—	—	—	—	—	—	—	—
Indian-Coyote	1	—	—	—	—	—	—	—	—	—	—	—
Indian-Spaniard	9	1	—	—	—	—	—	—	—	—	—	—
Indian-Mestizo	9	1	—	—	—	—	—	—	—	—	—	—
Indian-Mulatto	3	—	—	—	—	—	—	—	—	—	—	—
Mestizos	6	1	—	—	—	—	—	—	—	—	—	—
Mestizo-Indian	1	—	—	—	—	—	—	—	—	—	—	—
Mestizo-Mulatto	2	—	—	—	—	—	—	—	—	—	—	—
Mulattoes	9	—	—	—	—	—	—	—	—	—	—	—
Mulatto-Spaniard	3	—	—	—	—	—	—	—	—	—	—	—
Mulatto-Indian	8	—	—	—	—	—	—	—	—	—	—	—
Mulatto-Mestizo	2	—	—	—	—	—	—	—	—	—	—	—

	C1	C2	C3	C4	C5	C6	C7	C8	C9
No data	—	—	—	—	—	—	—	29	1
Total	—	—	—	—	—	—	—	51	115
Guadalajara (Sagrario)									
"Citizens"	—	—	—	—	—	—	—	27	—
Spaniards	—	—	—	—	—	—	—	39	78
Spaniard-Indian	—	—	—	—	—	—	—	5	4
Spaniard-Mestizo	—	—	—	—	—	—	—	—	2
Spaniard-Mulatto	—	—	—	—	—	—	—	—	1
Indians	—	—	—	—	—	—	—	14	29
Indian-Spaniard	—	—	—	—	—	—	—	2	5
Indian-Mestizo	—	—	—	—	—	—	—	1	5
Indian-Mulatto	—	—	—	—	—	—	—	1	1
Mestizos	—	—	—	—	—	—	—	1	2
Mestizo-Spaniard	—	—	—	—	—	—	—	2	2
Mestizo-Indian	—	—	—	—	—	—	—	—	1
Mulattoes	—	—	—	—	—	—	—	—	1
Mulatto-Spaniard	—	—	—	—	—	—	—	1	—
Mulatto-Indian	—	—	—	—	—	—	—	—	2
Mulatto-Mestizo	—	—	—	—	—	—	—	1	—
No data	—	—	—	—	—	—	—	11	3
Total	—	—	—	—	—	—	—	105	136
Hermosillo									
"Citizens"	—	—	8	—	5	4	—	—	—
Spaniards	—	—	—	—	1	—	—	—	2
Cocori Indian	—	—	1	—	—	—	—	—	—

* Double listings indicate mixed pairs, male listed first.

[163]

TABLE II, SECTION B (*Continued*)

Marriages by Race in Various Parishes, 1821–1832

Parish and Race*	1821	1822	1823	1824	1825	1826	1827	1828	1829	1830	1831	1832
Hermosillo (*continued*)												
No data	—	—	—	8	8	1	3	—	10	37	1	7
Opatas	—	—	4	—	—	—	2	—	—	—	—	—
Peruvians	—	—	—	—	—	—	—	—	—	1	—	—
Pluma blanca	—	—	—	—	—	—	—	—	—	1	—	—
Pimas	—	—	—	1	—	—	1	—	—	—	—	—
Seris	—	—	—	—	—	—	1	—	—	—	—	—
"Vecinos"	—	4	2	—	—	1	—	—	—	—	—	4
Yaquis	2	2	—	1	—	1	3	—	—	—	1	4
Total	4	6	6	10	8	6	16	—	10	48	1	11
Mexico (Sagrario)												
Americans	—	2	—	—	—	—	—	—	—	—	—	—
German-Spaniard	—	1	—	—	—	—	—	—	—	—	—	—
Castizo-Spaniard (New Spain)	2	5	—	—	—	—	—	—	—	—	—	—
Castizo-Indian	—	2	—	—	—	—	—	—	—	—	—	—
Castizo-Mestizo	1	1	—	—	—	—	—	—	—	—	—	—
Colombian-Spaniard	1	2	—	—	—	—	—	—	—	—	—	—
Dominican-Spaniard	1	—	—	—	—	—	—	—	—	—	—	—
Frenchman-Spaniard	1	—	—	—	—	—	—	—	—	—	—	—

Spaniards (New Spain)	148	161	—
Spaniards (Spain)	43	36	—
Spaniard (New Spain)-Castizo	2	4	—
Spaniard (New Spain)-Indian	8	4	—
Spaniard (Spain)-Indian	—	2	—
Spaniard (New Spain)-Mestizo	5	6	—
Spaniard (Spain)-Mestizo	—	2	—
Indians	18	23	—
Indian-Castizo	1	2	—
Indian-Spaniard (New Spain)	15	11	—
Indian-Mestizo	6	5	—
Mestizos	3	7	—
Mestizo-Spaniard (New Spain)	6	8	—
Mestizo-Indian	3	2	—
Mulatto-Mestizo	—	1	—
No data	—	2	—
Venezuelan-Spaniard (New Spain)	—	1	—
Total	264	290	—

[165]

TABLE II, SECTION B *(Continued)*

Marriages by Race in Various Parishes, 1821–1832

Parish and Race*	1821	1822	1823	1824	1825	1826	1827	1828	1829	1830	1831	1832
Tecpan												
Indians	—	—	—	—	—	—	—	—	—	—	2	—
No data	—	—	—	—	—	—	—	—	—	—	10	—
Total	—	—	—	—	—	—	—	—	—	—	12	—
Tomatlán												
Coyotes	—	1	—	—	—	—	—	—	—	—	—	—
Coyote-Spaniard	—	1	—	—	—	—	—	—	—	—	—	—
Coyote-Indian	1	—	—	—	—	—	—	—	—	—	—	—
Coyote-Indian "de doctrina"	1	1	—	—	—	—	—	—	—	—	—	—
Spaniards	5	4	—	—	—	—	—	—	—	—	—	—
Spaniard-Coyote	1	—	—	—	—	—	—	—	—	—	—	—
Spaniard-Indian	—	1	—	—	—	—	—	—	—	—	—	—
Spaniard-Indian "laboria"	1	—	—	—	—	—	—	—	—	—	—	—
Spaniard-Mestizo	4	1	—	—	—	—	—	—	—	—	—	—
Indians "laborios"	1	1	—	—	—	—	—	—	—	—	—	—
Indians "de tabla"	—	2	—	—	—	—	—	—	—	—	—	—
Indian-Coyote	1	—	—	—	—	—	—	—	—	—	—	—
Indian "laborio"-Coyote	—	2	—	—	—	—	—	—	—	—	—	—

Indian "laborio"-Spaniard	—	—	—	—	—	—	—	—	—	1	—
Mestizos	—	—	—	—	—	—	—	—	—	3	3
Mestizo-Coyote	—	—	—	—	—	—	—	—	—	2	—
Mestizo-Spaniard	—	—	—	—	—	—	—	—	—	1	—
Mestizo-Indian	—	—	—	—	—	—	—	—	—	2	—
Mestizo-Indian "laboria"	—	—	—	—	—	—	—	—	—	1	—
Mulattoes	—	—	—	—	—	—	—	—	—	—	1
No data	—	—	—	—	—	—	—	—	—	—	5
Total	—	—	—	—	—	—	—	—	—	25	22
Tuito*											
Coyote-Indian "de tabla"	—	—	—	—	—	—	—	—	—	—	1
Spaniards	—	—	—	—	—	—	—	—	—	—	3
Spaniard-Mestizo	—	—	—	—	—	—	—	—	—	—	1
Indians "laborios"	—	—	—	—	—	—	—	—	—	—	1
Indians "de tabla"	—	—	—	—	—	—	—	—	—	—	2
Indian-Coyote	—	—	—	—	—	—	—	—	—	—	1
Indian "laborio"-Coyote	—	—	—	—	—	—	—	—	—	—	1
Indian-Mestizo	—	—	—	—	—	—	—	—	—	—	1
Indian "de tabla"-Indian	—	—	—	—	—	—	—	—	—	—	2
Total	—	—	—	—	—	—	—	—	—	—	13
Xochimilco											
Spaniards	—	—	—	—	—	1	2	—	—	9	5
Spaniard-Indian	—	—	—	—	—	—	—	—	—	—	1
Spaniard-Mestizo	—	—	—	—	—	—	—	—	—	1	1
Indians	—	1	1	1	—	3	12	—	—	69	129

* Covers the years 1821–1822.

TABLE II, SECTION B (*Continued*)

Marriages by Race in Various Parishes, 1821–1832

Parish and Race*	1821	1822	1823	1824	1825	1826	1827	1828	1829	1830	1831	1832
Xochimilco (*continued*)												
Indian-Spaniard	—	—	—	—	—	1	—	—	—	—	—	—
Mestizos	—	1	—	—	—	—	—	—	—	—	—	—
Mestizo-Spaniard	—	1	—	—	—	—	—	—	—	—	—	—
Mestizo-Indian	1	—	—	—	—	—	—	—	—	—	—	—
No data	—	37	66	111	87	125	253	69	61	59	47	—
Total	80	175	66	111	101	130	253	69	62	60	48	—

Sources:

Libro de casamientos número 7, de Ameca.

Libro de casamientos número 19, del Sagrario de Guadalajara.

Libro de casamientos, de Hermosillo.

Libros de matrimonios españoles, M1 y M2, del Sagrario de México.

Libro de casamientos (mayo de 1822–1847), de Tecpan.

Libro de matrimonios (julio 1810– . . .), de Tomatlán.

Libro de casamientos (1814–1837), de Tomatlán en ayuda de San Pedro del Tuito.

Libro de casamientos de indios número 29. Libro de matrimonios de españoles número 30, y libro de casamientos número 32, de Xochimilco.

No mixed marriages were celebrated in the churches of Hermosillo, and in Xochimilco the number was insignificant. In 1821, 79 per cent of the marriages performed in both Mexico City and Guadalajara were between people of the same race; in 1822 it was 75 per cent in Mexico and 50 per cent in Guadalajara. In Ameca in 1821 and in Tuito in 1822 it was 54 per cent. On the other hand, in Tomatlán, only 24 per cent in 1821 and 32 per cent in 1822 married within their own race. Therefore, the greatest proportion of mestizos (in the widest sense) was born in Tomatlán (58 per cent in 1821, 57 per cent in 1822) and in Tecpan (19 per cent in 1821 and 30 per cent in 1832). At the same time, the percentage is minimal in Mexico City (among the illegitimate 8 per cent in 1821 and 6 per cent in 1822; among the legitimate 6 and 4 per cent respectively) and in Guadalajara (4.7 per cent in 1821, 4.6 per cent in 1822).

These figures indicate that the Indian towns remained closed, that mestizaje was minimal in the large cities and the rule in the towns. This is especially true in towns to which Negroes were taken, such as Tecpan and, somewhat surprisingly, Ameca. "Spaniards" predominate in the large cities like Mexico City (where in 1821 they constituted 83 per cent of the legitimate population, 94 per cent in 1822; among the illegitimate these figures were 64 and 75 per cent respectively) and Guadalajara. In the final analysis, this small and somewhat arbitrary sampling is designed primarily to point out new avenues of investigation for the researcher.

CHAPTER 8

The Impact of Mid-Nineteenth
Century Economic Change Upon
the Indians of Middle America
Manning Nash

During the nineteenth century Latin America was swept into the international economy: the production of export crops on plantations or the mining of materials for European and North American industries became the major source of economic activity. Simultaneously, the belief in *laissez faire* and a crude version of Social Darwinism spread across the continent. Manning Nash, who teaches anthropology at the University of Chicago, maintains that the Indians of Middle America were either by-passed or overrun by this process of change. In the nuclear areas the Indian communities drew closer together in a defensive stance, organized a complex system for the exchange of goods, developed a hierarchical structure of political and spiritual power which bound the members of the community together, and elaborated a social-leveling mechanism to insure homogeneity. In the coastal regions the impact of economic change was even more devastating and one reaction to it was the elaboration of what is here called the "adjunct export economy." The author concludes that the Mexican Revolution "was a unique and unusually successful resolution of Mexico's problems," but that it is problematical whether a Mexican type solution is any longer "possible, probable, or productive."

In the twentieth century the Indians of Mexico and Guatemala present a striking phenomenon. Half of the population of Guatemala still remains Indian, still remains the most backward and poorest part of the Guatemalan nation, and about 13 per cent of the

THE IMPACT OF ECONOMIC CHANGE

Mexican population is visibly Indian and among the poorest, economically slowest-growing segments of the population.

On one level there is obviously no problem, not even a paradox. In the multiple societies characterizing Mexico and Guatemala during the nineteenth and early twentieth centuries, the Indians were the least prepared socially and culturally to benefit from the commercial and industrial changes in Mexico and Guatemala.[1] In any "foreign factor economy," the economically weakest go to the wall and find themselves at the bottom of the stratification order and in the least skilled and remunerative niches in the ethnic and occupational division of labor.[2] But at the level of social and cultural processes, the position of the Indian communities today is puzzling. How have people characterized as having a commercial libido, long used to markets and money, engaged in regional trade and settled in dense populations, come to be the unprivileged, the backward, and the economically most long suffering?[3]

Part of the answer lies in the way the social and economic changes of the nineteenth century worked on Indian communities; part, in the Indian's defensive response when the winds of change buffeted their societies; and part, in the whole climate of nineteenth-century liberalism. Certain aspects of the movement were especially important: its tenets of social competition, its emphasis on law and order, its enshrining of rationality as the guide to social policy, and its overtones of Social Darwinism as echoed in the philosophy of the "científicos" of the Díaz regime.

The pattern of national impact on the Indian communities of Middle America was first worked out in a now classic paper by La Farge, amplified for Guatemala by Goubaud Carrera, and brought up to date by Beals.[4] To see the nineteenth century in some

[1] Manning Nash, "The Multiple Society in Economic Development: Mexico and Guatemala," *American Anthropologist*, LIX (1957), 825–33.

[2] Jonathan Levin, *The Export Economies* (Cambridge, Mass., 1960).

[3] B. Malinowski and Julio de la Fuente, "La economía de un sistema de mercados en México," *Acta Anthropologica* (Mexico, 1957).

[4] Oliver La Farge, "Maya Ethnology: The Sequence of Cultures," *Maya and Their Neighbors* (New York, 1940), pp. 281–91; Antonio Goubaud Carrera, "Indian Adjustments to Modern National Culture," Sol Tax (ed.), *Acculturation in the Americas* (Chicago, 1951), pp. 244–48; Ralph Beals, "The History

[171]

historical perspective, a brief recapitulation of La Farge's stages is in order.

The Conquest in Middle America was a mixture of overthrowing the urbanized, class-structured, high civilization on the one hand, and the alliance of the tributary states with the Spanish conquerors, on the other. It decapitated native society, substituting at the top the Spanish for the Indian nobility: and, it introduced a host of new agricultural crops and techniques, new forms of social organization, especially in administration, and the dichotomies between ethnic and racial groups with differential civil and economic rights and obligations.

The first colonial period followed the Conquest. It was a time when a small minority of Spaniards administered and controlled vast Indian populations, a period of rapid and, in some cases, intensive acculturation. The religion of the conquerors spread rapidly during this period, even as did many of their domesticated plants and the use of metal implements. The institutions of administration were basically the *encomienda* and the religious reservation. These two types, of course, had differential effects on the Indian societies. The encomienda made Indians participants, at some level, in the whole economy of New Spain, whereas the religious reservation was, on the whole, isolating.

The second colonial period was ushered in by the abolition of the encomienda and the secularization of the religious organizations. During the previous phases, at least the upper strata of the Indian population had intermarried with the Spanish, but now this was replaced by a more rigid division into Spanish and Indian buttressed by the caste-like feature of enforced endogamy. Although the encomienda was abolished, its consequences continued. The colonial plantation economy developed side by side with the large cattle ranch. This is the period when acculturation slowed down, when Indian land began to be alienated, and when the Indian gave up whatever illusions he still had about any benefits accruing from continued acculturation.

The first and second republican periods, here called the National

of Acculturation in Mexico," *Homenaje al Doctor Alfonso Caso* (Mexico, 1951), pp. 73–82.

Period, gave the predominant cast to Indian life, and underlies the continuity of Indian culture and society in the forms visible until the Mexican Revolution and the post-World War II period with its emphasis on integration of Indians and equity for them. The first republican period involved Indians only marginally. As the *criollos* and mestizos threw off Spanish domination with the slogans and banners of the French Revolution, they neither considered nor involved Indians in their struggles. For the Indians it was a time of cultural and social consolidation, and erection of communication barriers between the two major ethnic groups.

The second republican period was the time of nation-building, of moderate industrialization, of commercial agricultural growth for the new countries of Mexico and Guatemala. The Indian was seen as anachronistic, an obstacle to the march of triumphant nationalism, on the then clear road to progress.

Against this schematic background of the major phases of social change in Middle America, the nineteenth century stands out as the era of greatest pressure on Indian communities. In sum, from the point of view of the Indian, it was a time of erosion of the land base for the community, together with a national ethos disprizing Indian culture. The Ley Lerdo in Mexico and the abolition of communal land by Barrios in Guatemala are economic signposts heralding the attack on Indian communities.

The elite's ideology in nineteenth-century Middle America was a curious blend of bizarre application of *laissez faire* principles in the economy and emulation of Europe in the realm of values and styles. For the Indian, the consequences were drastic. In the free competition for land, the communal landholdings of the Indians were turned over bit by bit to the growing hacienda economy. With land shortages came increasing specialization in the crafts and industrial specialties of Indian communities, and the growth of a rural proletariat. These adaptations to the external pressures generated by the national and international economy were paralleled by a social structure and cultural pattern evolved to keep intact, at whatever low levels of economic performance, the core of the Indian community. The strong "corporate" community reached its most definitive form under the twin goads of resource alienation from Indians and socal

[173]

policies designed to ignore or to crush evidences of Indian cultures.[5]

Economic growth in the national economics of Mexico and of Guatemala during the nineteenth century followed the same broad pattern. There developed an export, plantation agriculture, a hacienda and cattle complex, and industry and railroads based on foreign capital investments. The peasant in general, Indian or national, hardly shared in this general economic growth, and it is doubtful whether more than a small segment of the rich did benefit at all from rising national production.[6] For example, by 1910 over 80 per cent of Mexico's rural families were landless, while the Indians of Guatemala had such minifundia holdings that most of them came under the vagrancy laws requiring them to labor on the plantations of the export sector.

How the economic trends described above affected in detail the Indian communities is mainly a matter of reconstruction from fragmentary historical records. By the time of the republican or National Period, the dominant two-sector economic pattern had taken hold: a neglected rural sector of the minifundia dotted with Indian communities, and an export-industrial sector in which Indians participated as laborers on the plantations, the hacienda, and in the mines. The crop complex of European export commodities, sugar, and bananas, were already being produced, as were the European foodstuffs: wheat, barley, fruits, Spanish vegetables; and, the food and work animals were present. Indian communities in the nuclear areas of Mexico and Guatemala had developed the "solar marketing" system which still persists in those regions today. This solar marketing system may be characterized as follows:

Communities are linked into a system of rotating markets. In its most developed form the rotating markets look like a "solar system." A major marketing center is in daily operation. To it flow commodities produced throughout the region, goods from all over the nation, and even items from international trade. Around the major market are a series of market places which have their special days. Each of these

[5] Eric Wolf, "Types of Latin American Peasantry: A Preliminary Discussion," *American Anthropologist*, LVII (1955), 452–69.

[6] Raymond Vernon, *The Dilemma of Mexico's Development* (Cambridge, Mass., 1963).

market places tends to specialize in a given produce or commodity and to carry a reduced selection of the goods available in the central market. Goods, buyers, and sellers move around the solar system in terms of the days of the week when market activity centers in a particular market place. Such solar systems of regional interdependence are characteristic of the Western Highlands of Guatemala (where they are most highly developed), the Valley of Oaxaca, Central Mexico, Michoacán, Eastern Guatemala, and the Isthmus of Tehuantepec. Without the marked solar qualities, regional market interdependence is found in the highland of Chiapas among the Tzeltal and Tzotzil and in parts of the Alta Verapaz in Guatemala. The regional marketing system is "money organized in single households as both consumption and production units with a strongly developed market which tends to be perfectly competitive." [7]

This marketing system is only partially integrated by a single set of prices into the national and international economies, and in the nineteenth century, given the lesser development of the communication network, was probably less integrated. The predominant historical fact about the regional marketing system is the low level of capital employed in relation to the amount of labor involved in merchandising. Two things account for this. First, the Indian in the market place is the representative of a family or a household, not an agent of a firm or a business. Marketing, trading, and merchandising, however rational, price oriented, and economically opportunistic, is constrained by the absence of firms, credit mechanisms, capitalization, and a steady stream of ever more efficient inputs resulting from deliberate technical innovation. Second, the more modern processing industries, the capital intensive activities, and manufacture or even large scale agricultural activity get displaced from the Indian market place into the national market, which is a set of price making mechanisms, not a locus. [8]

The communities participating in this solar marketing operation in the nineteenth century were corporate; many of them still are.

[7] Sol Tax, *Penny Capitalism* (Smithsonian Inst., Inst. of Social Anthropology, Washington, D.C., 1953).

[8] David Kaplan, "The Mexican Marketplace Then and Now," *Essays in Economic Anthropology: Proceedings of the 1965 Annual Spring Meeting of the American Ethnological Society* (1965).

The corporate community has a social boundary: who is and who is not a member is clear. Moreover, it has temporal continuity so that despite the departure of some members, the structure persists. The "corporateness" of a community of Indians in Middle America has varied from time to time, and from place to place.

The political structure of corporate continuity was laid down in essence by the Spanish rules for the "Indian Republic," but the defensive, hostile posture of the corporate community toward the larger national society was an outgrowth of the economic facts of the nineteenth century, coupled with the ideology of elimination of the Indian, his cultures, and his local social organizations. The external pressures making for a corporate community consist of incessant attack by outsiders on community land and the presence of non-Indians in the same social space as the Indian. In this kind of interaction, the political and economic strength lies in the hands of the superordinate national populations, and Indians responded by developing modes of exclusion of outsiders, styles of dissimulation toward outsiders, and official communal representatives to deal with the political powers, thus minimizing direct contact and intervention by representatives of the national society. Of course, in some areas the pressure was so great on the Indians that they resorted to warfare and insurrection, but throughout the bulk of the nineteenth century, passive, defensive resistance was most common.

Beside the pressures of the hacienda (close at hand) and the plantation (migrant labor for part of the year, since plantations were coastal and most corporate communities were highland), the spread of new export crops in the nineteenth century brought the Mexican and Guatemalan national into close, face-to-face, continual contact with the Indians. In Guatemala, for example, the chief export crops were dye stuffs—indigo and cochineal. Indians along with *Ladinos* (as national Guatemalans of non-Indian societies are called) were participants in this export industry. It was the largest earner of foreign exchange in Guatemala until the development of the German chemical dye industries in the 1870s destroyed the natural dye industry. At about the same time, coffee was found to have good prospects in the highlands and the coffee growers began to move into Indian territory, and to use Indian labor. The vagrancy laws were in fact an outgrowth of the periodic manpower needs of the coffee producers. These needs brought recruiters into the highlands, and in their wake came the spread of the Ladino populations throughout the highlands, as store keepers, money lenders, and competitors for agricultural land.

The internal mechanisms of corporate community adaptation to the economic and social pressures of the nineteenth century were chiefly of two sorts: a political-religious structure which bound the members in a system of local services, on the one hand, and isolated the individuals from official contact with Ladinos and nationals on the other; and a cultural-economic system which depended upon the operation of a leveling mechanism for keeping internal economic and social homogeneity backed by a supernatural sanctioning system which killed or ostracized deviants. The political-religious system took the form of the civil-religious hierarchy. In simplified form, the hierarchy is a series of offices, some nominally religious and others nominally secular. These offices are ranked as to prestige and social honor. A man as representative of a family enters on the lowest rung of the hierarchy, and for the rest of his adult life alternates between posts on the civil ladder and posts on the religious ladder. Between offices, he gets longer or shorter "rest" periods. On completion of one of the top posts, he retires from community service and becomes an elder or a *principal*. The offices are unpaid, and, in fact, require outlays of cash and food by those holding them. In Indian parlance they are literally *cargos*, burdens. And to the community they are *servicios*, services necessary to daily life. Typically, as one ascends the ladder of ranked offices, the costs increase, the time devoted to the office approaches full time, and the prestige increases.

The ordinary operation of the civil-religious hierarchy defines the membership of a community. Only people eligible to serve in the hierarchy are members of the community. Even foreign Indians (those from a community other than the one in which they reside) do not have the qualifications to serve in the local hierarchy. The boundary-maintaining consequences of the hierarchy were probably much stronger in the nineteenth century than they are today. Local autonomy was greater, because of the weakness of the central governments vis-à-vis the countryside. The energy of the national government was concentrated in the urban capital and its immediate region, whereas the countryside was consigned to a series of local chieftains more or less loosely allied to and subordinated to the central regime. While the national populations exhibited the *patria chica* phenomenon of local loyalty, the Indian communities became entrenched and separatist. Even in the religious sphere, and the nineteenth-century church was in but light and intermittent contact with the corporate Indian communities, Indians proliferated local variations of folk Catholicism. Decrees exist barring the formation of new *cofradías* (religious brotherhoods) among Indians and deploring the amount of time and resources Indians were already pouring into religious observances.

The operation of the hierarchy gave the chief form to Indian social structure. It related all of the families of the community to each other through a single set of service and prestige. The hierarchy age-graded and prestige-ranked the community and at the same time discharged the more obvious tasks of community order, justice, physical upkeep, maintenance of the saint cult, cemetery, and church.

The fact that Indian communities had representatives who stood for the whole community vis-à-vis the two most important supra-local institutions, the church and state, provided a formalized and impersonal channel of communication between the Indian and the national society. Although the economic pressures of land aliena-tion and more or less forced labor cut the living standards of Indians in the nineteenth century, their cultures and social organizations became more and more tightly organized, defensive, and resistant to the encroachments of the national society.

One of the forces making for the smooth running of these corporate communities was the operation of the leveling mechanism. This leveling mechanism insured a high degree of social and economic homogeneity within the community and likewise insured that accumulated resources would be used for communal ends rather than for personal aggrandizement. When the leveling mechanism operates properly, the only socially relevant role distinctions are age, sex, community service, and access to the supernatural.

The leveling mechanism involves four interrelated aspects: 1) low level of technology and limited land (so that absolute wealth and accumulation is small in virtue of poor resources in relation to population and a technology which is labor intensive and not highly productive); 2) the fracture of estates by bilateral inheritance (whatever in fact is accumulated in capital goods is scrambled among sons and daughters in nearly equal shares. Almost everywhere in the region, bilateral inheritance prevails. The few places with patrilineal descent groups do not vest property right in a corporation but exhibit a pattern of division among the patrilineally related families); 3) forced expenditure of time and resources in communal office (that is, the *cargos* of the civil religious hierarchy); and 4) forced expenditure by the wealthy in ritual (those who have been skilled or lucky and have accumulated wealth must expend it for communal ends chiefly in feasting and drinking, so that wealth is consumed, not reinvested). The leveling mechanism keeps the fortunes of the various households nearly equivalent and serves to insure the shift of family fortunes from generation to generation. Classes, power groups, or special interest groups find inhospitable soil in the corporate Indian community.

The leveling mechanism is backed by a set of supernatural controls and sanctions. The chief form of internal social order in the corporate community was, and in many places still is, the accusation of witchcraft against those who became distinguished in some manner violating the homogeneous basis of social life. Along with the prevalance of witches there developed an ethos of *envidia*, of malicious envy of those who were rich but not generous, of those who stood out from the general level of the community.

And in the nineteenth century the execution or exiling of witches from the community were powerful sanctions, even as was the lash of envious gossip. The operation of the hierarchy put the direct brokers between man and the supernatural at the top of the social order and invested them not only with occult powers but also with secular offices allowing them to mete out punishments and settle disputes.

The nuclear areas of Middle America where the corporate communities flourished, where most Indians lived and still do, are but one of the indigenous adaptations to the economic and social currents of the nineteenth century. The Indians of the coastal regions or in the plantation economy responded in a different manner during the mid-nineteenth century. In many areas the first impact of the export economy, with Indians as plantation laborers, destroyed the Indian population, and they were replaced by Negro slave labor. But those that survived worked out an adjustment to the export economy which is best designated as the "adjunct export economy." This form of economic adjustment may be characterized as follows:

Communities produce chiefly for home and local consumption, but tend to have one or a few commodities produced for cash and market exchange. Specialization is rare, and from community to community the products, the skills, and economic organization is similar. The market and the marketplace is in the hands of non-Indians, and the Indians appear in the marketplace as small sellers of the primary, unprocessed products they have grown. This sort of economy can be seen among the coffee growers of Sayula, or the vanilla growers of the Totonac region around the major market of Papantala, and in the mixed coffee- melon- and citrus-growers of the Sierra Popoluca. Another variation of the export adjunct economy is toward paid labor on the plantation. In the nineteenth century this form approached debt peonage, and on the coffee *fincas* of Chiapas debt peonage was made legal by local legislation. The debt or debt labor on plantation may eventuate in what has been called a "rural proletariat." This was formed in the Yucatán peninsula on the *henequen* plantations, and is approximated in parts of the Vera Paz in Guatemala, and in the coastal regions where Indians are workers on coffee, sugar, rice, or banana plantations. In modern times the *colono* has replaced the *peón*, and the more modern the export enterprise, the more the sheer cash nexus replaces the patron-client relationship which habitually included a small subsistence plot and quasi-kinship responsibilities between patron and dependents.[9]

The adjunct export economy was just that—an addition, an accretion to the Indian's basic pursuit of milpa agriculture and near self-

[9] Manning Nash, "Indian Economies," *Handbook of Middle American Indians*, Vol. 6 (ed.) M. Nash, Austin, Texas, 1967, p. 88.

sufficiency. Cash cropping by Indians on their own land was virtually absent in the coastal regions and indeed is a feature of the twentieth century, where the waxing and waning of the international
demand for primary foodstuffs brings both Indian and national
into the export market. The export economy was, and continues to
be, an overlay on the basic life of the Indian community. But the
forced or voluntary export of labor for the international market
precludes the formation of the sort of corporate community found
in the highlands, and in fact the emergence of a rural proletariat
nearly precludes any community organization. The Indians of the
Yucatán peninsula are nearly a people within Mexico, and during
the nineteenth century were even more so. The War of the Castes
was in large part a nativistic reaction to the engulfing adjunct
economy.

In the adjunct sector, acculturation forces are stronger and more
persuasive than in the corporate, solar-marketing sector. Hence the
decline of Indian populations there was more drastic, and at the
same time the displaced Indian on the plantation became a feature
of the landscape.

The final form of Indian adaptation to the changes of the nineteenth century is found in the quasi-tribal economic system. The
quasi-tribal system is predicated upon meeting locally defined needs:

Economic effort is directed toward subsistence needs with handicrafts
for home use, and attention to the crops of the milpa. Indians with
this sort of economy tend to be in the remote, least accessible parts of
the national territory. The economic type is today represented by the
Cora and the Huichol, the Tarahumara, the Tepehuan and other groups
of Northwest Mexico.[10]

These were the groups that the nineteenth century saw in part
taken from the custodial, isolating care of the religious and placed
under either secular clergy or the direct rule of the nascent states.
They were, at the opening of the nineteenth century, much less
acculturated than the corporate Indian groups or the piedmont and
coastal Indians. And with Independence they were treated almost
like internal aliens. Sometimes the Mexican government waged

[10] *Ibid.*

wars against them, and sometimes they presented the anomaly of a nation making treaties with its own citizens. The forces of the nineteenth century affecting these Indians were more cultural and ideological and less direct or economic in character, for the hacienda-ranching pattern already had been worked out, and the mining industry, which was not booming, had little need for new Indian labor. The Indians were regarded as barbarians, to be either domesticated or exterminated. And with their greater mobility (because of less intensive agriculture) and their lesser density of population, they presented to Mexico a military problem rather than an economic resource or asset.

The mid-nineteenth century seems from this remove to have been nearly all of a piece in its generation of a series of economic pressures on Indian communities and tribal groups. The differential response and the still persisting differential patterns of Indian economic adaptation were, first of all, a function of the different basis from which the Indians developed. The three major types of adaptation are socially, culturally, economically, and ecologically distinct. The ecological and economic differences seem to have been legacies from the pre-Columbian past; although the social and cultural differences have roots in the pre-Conquest period, they seem more to have been shaped by the events of the nineteenth century.

Three important twentieth-century legacies have come from the pattern of interaction of the various Indian traditions of Middle America with the new states of Mexico and Guatemala. These legacies stem in large part from the economic structure of the complex society, the nation-state, and its ideology of ethnic relations. The nineteenth century, throughout the Euro-American world, was a time when the philosophy of *laissez faire* in the economy was in the ascendancy, when Social Darwinism was supposed to fit each person and each cultural variety into its natural niche, when progress was assured by the ordinary operation of the international market, when governments favored foreign investment and structured the arena so that the most entrepreneurial benefited the most, and the least entrepreneurial, the least.

In the context of Mexico and of Guatemala, the unfolding of the economic and social consequences of nineteenth-century practice and ideology can be seen clearly. On the economic side, a sectored economy, with the Indians at the bottom of the economic heap, unprovided with means to enter the narrow entrepreneurial sector of the export economy. On the social side, the Indians of the highlands in defensive corporate communities as bulwarks against the erosion of their cultures and societies; the coastal Indians as peons or in debt bondage to the plantations; and the tribal Indians as marauders on the periphery of the nation.

From the point of view of the nations as a whole, the nineteenth century wrought slow but massive economic and social changes. It laid the basis for the divided, weakly integrated national state, where local powers could and did compete with the central government. It produced an indigestible, culturally hostile core of corporate Indian communities. And it founded a virtually closed class system, with a landed oligarchy and foreign-backed industrialists as the pinnacle, a small urban based middle class, and a dispossessed peasantry.

The nineteenth century then left to the twentieth, in Mexico and Guatemala, these problems: 1) the making of an effective nation state; 2) the incorporation of the Indian into national life; 3) and the dismantling of a society and economy blocking sustained economic growth and modernization. These mid-nineteenth-century heritages have been resolved differently in Middle America. The Mexican Revolution from 1910 to 1940 was a unique and unusually successful resolution of Mexico's problems, although the decades of development in the twentieth century have raised others. Whether or not, in the twentieth century, in a nervous and volatile world of international relations, a Mexican type solution is possible, probable, or productive is an open and provocative question confronting all of Latin America.

CHAPTER 9

Official *Indigenismo*
in Peru in 1920: Origins,
Significance, and Socioeconomic Scope
François Chevalier

Just as the Mexican Revolution included in its program the protection
of Indian communities, the restoration of their corporate existence, and
the reversal of nineteenth-century liberal tendencies, so too in Peru a
movement in this direction found expression in the Constitution of
1920. French historian François Chevalier, director of the Casa Veláz-
quez in Madrid, shows that, paradoxically, the same economic forces
which led to the formation of urban groups opposed to the landed
oligarchy and thus interested in protecting the Indian also stimulated
the commercialization of highland products and increasing pressure
upon the Indian. Simultaneously, like some other Latin American
politicians, Peruvian Augusto Leguía played upon the interests of urban
merchants and intellectuals to gain power, but turned against them once
his position was assured. Thus the pro-Indian provisions of the Constitution remained almost a dead letter in Peru, although their enactment
inspired a reconsideration of the place of the Indian community within
the nation.

Under Spanish dominion, the society of Peru, as of other parts
of Spanish America, was doubly hierarchical. It was both a traditional society of the *ancien régime* and a colonial one. Thus, on
the one hand, it was composed not so much of individuals or citizens
as of closed racial groups, some in dominating, others in dominated
positions; at the same time, on another level it consisted of corpo-

[184]

rations with special statutes, ranging, for example, from simple guilds to the entire Catholic Church. Some racial groups, though not all, were also corporate bodies. Among them were the Indian communities, regarded as separate social or racial groups having their own peculiar organization and legislation, subject to tribute, and protected as minors under the tutelage of the Church and the Crown. Their property, held in mortmain, was inalienable. Indian communities functioned in legal separation from other social groups, not on a basis of racial segregation but essentially as a means of limiting their exploitation, indeed sometimes of preventing their destruction, by individuals better prepared economically or simply ready to take advantage of the weak. Aside from such moral considerations, the state for its own benefit evidently also wanted to preserve the capacity for labor and tribute represented by the Indians.

With Independence were abolished the legal prohibitions against whites, mestizos, "castas," and Negroes living among the Indians. Republican law no longer recognized protected communities, only individuals and citizens who were to be considered personal owners of their now disentailed lands. Under such circumstances, by use of some legal artifice it was not difficult to despoil the Indians of their property, especially after economic development and the commercialization of agriculture had made the possession of land still more desirable. Of this equality of conditions proclaimed by the law only a part of the mestizo population was able to take advantage, and for the Indians the effects were the inverse of what was intended.

This situation was almost the rule in Spanish America during the last half of the nineteenth and part of the twentieth centuries. During World War I, except in Mexico, which was still in the throes of the Revolution, a liberal-positivist approach to the Indian problem prevailed. These ideas (which might better be called utilitarian) were hostile to the Indian communities which were considered obstacles to economic development and the progress of the individual. Since the eighteenth century, enlightened men in France and Spain had thought the same way, although perhaps their opinions were rooted less in direct self-interest. For example, an eminent Peruvian jurist, Manuel Villarán, who was favorably disposed toward the

Indians, concluded a study in 1907 with the statement that "The Indian communities have no legal personality, and therefore cannot be a party in legal decisions." [1]

About this time a radical change of attitude occurred in Peru, before it did elsewhere. A sudden break with the secular tradition that had prevailed throughout the continent represented, in a way, a return to the colonial system. This change can be seen in the Constitution promulgated on January 18, 1920, by the new President, Augusto Leguía, which declared: "The State will protect the indigenous race and will enact special laws for its development and culture. . . . The Nation recognizes the legal existence of the Indian communities, and the law will proclaim the rights which pertain to them." Furthermore, the communal properties were made part of the state domain and thus became inalienable and imprescriptible (Title V, Arts. 58 and 41).

This important decision was complemented by a series of laws and initiatives, such as the creation on September 12, 1921, of a section of Indian Affairs in the Ministry of Development which was to supervise the implementation of measures enacted to protect the Indians. Since conflicts between the *hacendados* and the communities were becoming increasingly numerous and serious, a *Patronato de la raza indígena* (Foundation for the Protection of the Indians), with a central committee under the chairmanship of the Archbishop of Lima and several departmental and provincial committees, was established on May 29, 1922. Under a law enacted on March 18, 1920, the departmental courts were granted jurisdiction over cases involving Indian questions which previously had been in the purview of local judges dominated by political bosses and the great landowners (*gamonales*). Another series of laws (which were to remain more or less theoretical) also was promulgated. Somewhat later, after it had been recognized that defense of the communal lands was an essential aspect of the Indian problem, the government on July 24, 1925, ordered engineers of the Ministry of Development, under the supervision of the local committees of the Patronato de la raza indígena to make agricultural surveys of the communities. Finally, on August 28, 1925, the Ministry of Development opened

[1] Manuel Villarán, *Páginas escogidas* (Lima, n.d.).

a record office in which the Indian communities of Peru could be registered after examination of their applications. All these legal measures will be examined in greater detail below.[2]

Thus, President Leguía's attitude represented a frank departure from the previous policy, which had been tied to the liberal tradition (generous at first but later partially self-seeking), although for the moment, as we shall see, the new measures remained largely theoretical, restricted to the legal sphere. How, though, does one explain this change of attitude in Peru that, in fact, reflected a change in the mentality of the rulers?

On one hand, an active *indigenista* movement whose protests were taking new directions had developed in the country. On the other hand, a wave of unprecedented prosperity, a consequence of World War I, had favored the economic and political development of new middle groups, which seemingly were more sensitive than the old oligarchy to the misery of the highland Indians. It was precisely this new class, as we shall see, that had brought President Leguía to power.

Here, we cannot explore the origins of the Peruvian indigenista movement in detail. It first manifested itself in the indigenista literature of the late nineteenth century whose moralizing and romantic character at first made it parallel to the anti-slavery movement, which, appearing in Europe a hundred years before, had developed in America during the first half of the nineteenth century. Also, the disaster of the war with Chile led intellectuals such as Manuel González Prada to reflect on Peru's duties toward its oppressed Indians, who practically were segregated from the national community. Early in the twentieth century, Peruvian indigenismo began to consider the more concrete and practical aspects of the Indian question. After 1908 or 1910, these problems attracted the attention of a growing number of jurists, sociologists, and even politicians, who seem to have been influenced by certain European "Social Christians" or socialists, or simply by authors such as Joaquín Costa in Spain, who were interested in the problems of the countryside.

Though these indigenistas were to be found in Lima, Cuzco, and

[2] *Legislación indigenista del Perú* (Dirección General de Asuntos Indígenas, Lima, 1948). There are also other editions of these laws.

elsewhere, they appear to have been particularly prominent in Arequipa, where the "First Regional Congress of Normal School Graduates," which discussed education of the Indians and other problems, was held in 1911. In the following years some local jurists thought about the need for protecting the Indians and defending their lands, which increasingly were being attacked and monopolized, especially in the neighboring department of Puno by the shores of Lake Titicaca. Their conclusion was that such protection should be extended to the community rather than to the individual since the community was the framework of Indian life. In 1915 the Arequipa Bar (*Colegio de Abogados*) sponsored a contest for the preparation of "Indian tutelary legislation."

Shortly before, the deputy from Puno, M. Alto Zaa, had persuaded Parliament to appoint a commission for the study of protective legislation for the Indians. This commission produced several legislative proposals: by F. Gómez de la Torre in 1916, by J. A. Encinas in 1918, by Araníbar in 1920, to name a few. It also published other studies of still greater interest for us, such as Manuel Quiroga's investigation of the Indian and agrarian problems of Puno in 1915. Four years later a group of deputies with this orientation founded the "*Unión de labor nacionalista.*" [3]

Meanwhile, through general unrest in rural areas and numerous peasant uprisings in Puno which were little noticed in the capital, the attention of this small circle of intellectuals and politicians became focused on the urgency of solving the problem. Undoubtedly, Javier Prado y Ugarteche was influenced by the movement when, as President of the Preparatory Commission of the Constitution of 1920, he successfully advocated legal recognition of the Indian communities which, as he said, then never could lose their lands.

After 1920–1922, there was a proliferation of sociological studies of the communities with, among others, the publication of Valdés de la Torre's book on the evolution of the Indian communities, the

---

[3] Cf. Atilio Sivirichi, *Derecho indígena peruano* (Lima, 1946), pp. 140–55, in which the legal origins of the legislation enacted in 1919 and later are studied; Manuel Quiroga, *La evolución jurídica de la propiedad rural en Puna* (Diss. in Law, University of Arequipa, Arequipa, 1915); José Antonio Encinas, *Contribución a una legislación tutelar indígena* (Lima, 1918; 2d ed., 1920).

work of Frisancho, and, above all, *Nuestra comunidad indígena* (1924) by Hildebrando Castro Pozo, who had been head of the section for Indian Affairs in the Ministry of Development. Later, Maríategui and Haya de la Torre declared for similar pro-Indian and agrarianist principles, but against Leguía. The earlier writers, especially, sometimes idealized the possibilities of the community, some seeing in it the prototype of socialism, and all, the potential of small-scale, almost perfect democracy. These concepts did not fail to influence the ethnologists who later studied the Indians of Peru.

If we extend this circle of Peruvian ideological development, we must take note of the influence of Gorki and Russian agrarianist literature and also of socialism, both of which were reinforced by the success of the Soviet Revolution of 1917. Another influence on the Peruvian thinkers was the example of the Mexican Revolution and the Constitution of 1917. It must be borne in mind that in the wake of the *Plan de Ayala* of November, 1911, conceived by Zapata and completed in later years, Article Eleven of the Carranza Law (January 6, 1915), written by the distinguished jurist Lucio Cabrera, had recognized the rights of the Indian communities to hold property and reestablish the lost *ejidos*. This orientation was confirmed in the Mexican Constitution of 1917, although the policy was not translated into reality by the organization of peasant ejidos on an important scale until considerably later.

It should not be forgotten that Augusto Leguía's presidency coincided with an extraordinary and unprecedented wave of commercial and economic prosperity in Peru. After experiencing a slow increase beginning at the end of the nineteenth century, the value of exports, calculated in *soles*, tripled between 1913 and 1920. Although prices and the cost of living also rose sharply and nearly doubled, the balance nevertheless remained highly favorable. For the most part, foreign commerce continued at this level until the depression of 1929. The national budget, too, grew rapidly between 1917 and 1930. Thus, Leguía's regime corresponds exactly to this era of great prosperity that lasted from 1919 to 1930.

It is clear that this exceptional situation, which was to give a stronger base to the national economy, was connected closely to

[189]

two events of transcending importance. First, the opening of the Panama Canal enormously shortened the distance between Lima-Callao and the great centers of production and consumption in the United States and Europe. Second, the First World War stimulated the sale of Peruvian products, such as oil, copper, wool, and especially sugar and cotton, which enjoyed a boom of development along the coast, at very high prices in New York, which had already outstripped London as a market for Peruvian goods.

Although these economic conditions should be seen as a stimulus, and not, of course, the single cause, of a social process already in progress, the extraordinary commercial development and prosperity seem to have furthered the emergence of a new bourgeoisie of more modest origins than the old oligarchies, liberal or conservative, which had exercised power until then. Obviously, there will have to be further study of the economic and political advance of these new classes composed mainly of urban elements including some popular or working class representatives and most particularly the constantly growing number of government employees, teachers, and professors whose positions were made possible by the rapid increase in the size of the national budget.

Leguía himself came from a merchant family of moderate means in the North. Very sensitive to changes of public opinion, he skillfully flattered the new groups, presenting himself to them as a champion against the great families under whose aegis he had been President of the Republic earlier. With the help of his cousin, Professor Germán Leguía y Martínez (a disciple of the anti-clerical indigenista González Prada), J. A. Encinas, H. Castro Pozo, F. Roca, and others, he even managed to win the support of the students and young intellectuals of socialist tendencies associated with the newspaper *Germinal*. His ability to attract supporters was also used to advantage during the strikes that erupted in protest against the rising cost of living. Leguía's talk was of the need for reform and a new constitution to forge a "new fatherland." Finally, he was carried to power by a small revolution backed by certain elements of the army in the capital.[4]

[4] Jorge Basadre, *Historia de la República del Perú* (6th ed.; 10 vols. Lima, 1965), VIII, 3903–3910, 3931, 3955, ff. M. Basadre has also kindly provided us

Thus, in 1919–1920 Leguía received the support of the younger generation and of the rising new middle groups, and not only in Lima and the coastal region. In certain parts of the highlands too, where a class structure was beginning to replace the old pyramidal pattern of the landholding oligarchy and its familial clientele, a similar phenomenon could be noted. Here, the power of the oligarchy was being challenged by groups with some involvement in the new commercial prosperity and the subsequent increase of the public budget. An example in point is the case of a young and brilliant lawyer, Celestino Manchego Muñoz, who came from a very modest family with a Quechua-speaking mother in Huancavelica. With the support of mestizo artisans, merchants, employees, teachers, and small functionaries, he battled the great landowning families which, finding it difficult to adapt to the new economic conditions, began to emigrate to the coast. Finally, Manchego Muñoz became both Minister of Justice and the personal friend of President Leguía.[5] The rise of such "new men" seems to be an example of Magnus Mörner's contention that the vigorous expansion of the mestizo middle class has influenced social attitudes toward the Indians.[6]

Yet, Leguía and many of his associates, seduced by power and money, were to forget their promises. Once they had acquired large economic interests or great landholdings, they would find themselves in conflict with certain of the new groups that originally had supported the President. Leguía thus destroyed the good relations he had enjoyed, and the young indigenista intellectuals in 1923 opposed his re-election and urged the adoption of energetic measures in the highlands. As a result, Germán Leguía, Encinas, Castro Pozo, Roca, Doig, Alberto Solís, and others, soon to be followed by Haya de la

with additional information in the course of conversations. We should notice that Germán Leguía y Martínez, as distinguished from other indigenistas, does not seem to have been favorably disposed to the community as such. He believed it ought to disappear. Cf. Ricardo Bustamante Cisneros, *Condición jurídica de las comunidades de indígenas en el Perú* (Lima, 1918), p. 86.

[5] Cf. Henri Favre, "L'évolution et la situation des haciendas dans la region de Huancavélica, Pérou" (paper presented at the International Colloquium on "Les Problèmes agraires des Amériques Latines" in Paris, Oct., 1965; published by the Institute des Hautes Études de l'Amérique Latine in 1967).

[6] M. Mörner, "Race and Social Class in Twentieth Century Latin America," *Cahiers d'Histoire Mondiale*, VIII (Paris, 1964), 302.

Torre and Mariátegui, were exiled, imprisoned, or persecuted. Nevertheless, Leguía remained in power throughout the eleven prosperous years from 1919 to 1930, when the depression, which had ruined or panicked the merchants and many others, caused his fall. The historian Jorge Basadre properly notes that Leguía's rise and fall partially paralleled those of other South American presidents, Alessandri and Ibáñez in Chile, Irigoyen in Argentina, Siles in Bolivia, for example, who were also impelled up and down by the middle classes.

As always, the economic phenomena mentioned here are not the only factors by which a historical situation that was extremely complex can be explained. Rather, they were elements that speeded the slow, multifaceted social process that has been described above.

It has been pointed out earlier that the years immediately after World War I (between 1918 and 1925 or 1930) seem marked by increasing despoliation of many Indian communities. For example, in the department of Ayacucho, the communities of Puquio lost much of their pasture lands and *punas* to *misti* (non-Indians) and landowners of the area, who then monopolized and enclosed them, as the ethnologist-writer José María Argüedas shows so well in his work *Yawar Fiesta*. In the department of Puno there occurred similar developments, recorded not only by some Arequipeños in 1915 but also in the annual reports of the presidents of law tribunals after the war. Furthermore, in the years 1921 to 1923 a series of peasant uprisings, provoked by the same causes, broke out in the province of Azángaro on the shores of Lake Titicaca and other parts of the highlands such as the provinces of Canas, Espinar, Grau, and Aymaraes in the department of Apurimac.[7] This is the era generally denounced in the numerous indigenista and agrarianist novels that were published a few years later not only in Peru but also in the neighboring countries of Bolivia and particularly Ecuador.

[7] F. Chevalier, "L'expansion de la grande propriété dans le Haut-Pérou au XXᵉ siecle," *Annales: Economies, Sociétés, Civilisations*, XXI (1966), 815–31. Based on a paper read at the XXXVI International Congress of Americanists in which the novel *Yawar Fiesta* by J. M. Argüedas was analyzed with the help of such other sources as the *Memorias* of the Presidents of the Departmental Court of Puno. See especially that of Indalecio Díaz of March 18, 1924, included in *Memoria que el Ministro de Justicia . . . presenta al Congreso Ordinario de 1924* (Lima, 1925).

Paradoxically, the same forces that had occasioned the rise of a new middle class sensitive to the ideas of indigenismo also worked against the movement's goals by commercializing such products of the highlands as wool, leather, and cattle, which came into great demand in the capital, the coastal region, and abroad. The parallel commercialization of land then encouraged entrepreneurs and hacendados to new aggressions against the Indians. Meanwhile, the first legal obstacles to this despoliation instituted by the Leguía regime were too weak to control the forces at work. In fact, in 1920 the President had instituted a so-called road conscription (*conscripción vial*) which made it mandatory for all Peruvians to help build the roads and highways increasingly needed for continued economic progress. In practice, however, this obligation came to fall exclusively upon the shoulders of the Indians, who were put to work under the control of local political bosses or landowners (*gamonales*). This program entailed a new and very heavy burden indeed for the Indian communities.

Yet, at the same time, the application of laws designed to protect the Indians were delayed. To the astute Leguía these measures represented, above all, a means, not even the most important one, of placating and flattering a new sector of public opinion (in the capital and elsewhere) that had helped him gain power. The so-called *Patronato de la raza indígena* apparently did not function in all the departments and provinces. Of all the laws and measures favorable to the Indians, only a few were implemented even partially by the President. Above all, despite the enactment of the most important principle of legal recognition and protection for the communities, nothing was done for several years toward determining which groups within the native population in fact constituted legal communities. Only in 1925 was an official registry for these communities opened, and even then the administrative proceedings and formalities of recognition were performed sufficiently slowly to ensure that the situation of the communities remained for all practical purposes almost as before. That this is precisely what happened is shown by an analysis of the number of communities recognized yearly after 1925, a good indicator also of the practical, and not merely theoretical, indigenismo of the various Peruvian

[193]

governments. Thus, at the time of his fall in 1930, Leguía had recognized only 291 of the thousands of communities which actually existed. Nevertheless, this number compares favorably with the negative results of the years of government by military junta which followed. Only after 1935 did the number of recognized communities again reach a normal annual level. This level was maintained for about twelve years. Around 1948 the figures once again drop sharply under the government of General Odría and the second term of Manuel Prado. With the exception of 1956, when seventy communities were recognized, the downward trend continued until 1963,[8] when President Belaúnde Terry showed renewed interest in the problems of the highland Indian.

Returning to President Leguía, we find that by 1923 he had eliminated the most active group of indigenistas and intellectuals. Nevertheless, thanks to prosperity and, especially, the ever-larger national budget,[9] he was able to retain power in spite of growing discontent and disappointment displayed by students and other groups which formerly had supported him. Nonetheless, when his regime, unable to withstand the depression of 1929–1930, fell, popular feeling was such that even perfectly honest, courageous men, for example, Castro Pozo, who since 1923 had been persecuted, were made to suffer for their earlier collaboration with him.

Likewise, Leguía's indigenista legislation also was forgotten, even by Dora Mayer de Zulen, who since 1909 had been one of the principal promoters of the *Asociación Pro-Indígena*. In writing the highly critical *El oncenio de Leguía* about 1932, she neglects even to mention this aspect of the President's work.[10] In a sense Dora Mayer was right, for in reality Leguía's regime had not improved the condition of the Indian very much. On the contrary, their situation seems to have worsened during his presidency. Under the suc-

---

[8] *Padrón general de comunidades indígenas reconocidas oficialmente al 30 de junio de 1961* (Ministerio de Trabajo y Asuntos Indígenas, Lima, n.d.).

[9] See table below; for the relation between military costs and the national budget see Víctor Villanueva, *El militarismo en Perú* (Lima, 1962), p. 298. The Peruvian debt as given here is in accordance with figures given by M. Irigoyen Puente, quoted by Dora Mayer de Zulen, *El oncenio de Leguía*, 2 vols. (Lima, 1932?).

[10] Mayer de Zulen, *ibid.*

ceeding governments, too, change was very slow, despite the constitution and the many laws which always remained on the books,
as has been demonstrated in citing the number of communities
attaining recognition and protection.

It must be said, however, that the injuries inflicted upon the
Indian were, in great part, a consequence of the brutal penetration
of a modern economy into the rural world of the highlands. Who

ANNALES

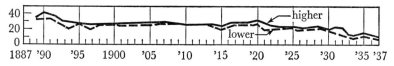

Millions of soles

COMERCIO EXTERIOR DEL PERU (1887-1937)
FOREIGN COMMERCE OF PERU

——— Exportacion-Export
— — — Importacion-Import

1887 '90   '95   1900   '05   '10   '15   '20   '25   '30   '35 '37

GOVERNMENT OF A. LEGUIA
Indigenous Legislation
Recognizing the Community

THE PERUVIAN SOL IN RELATION TO THE POUND STERLING
Peniques por sol
Pence per Peruvian sol

40
20
0
1887 '90   '95   1900   '05   '10   '15   '20   '25   '30   '35 '37

higher
lower

Source: *Commercial, Economic, and Financial Bulletin of Peru,* Ministry of Foreign
Relations, Commercial Department, Lima, II, 9, 1938, p. 224, 228, 240.

[195]

really could have found a remedy in such a short space of time? Only a few years after Mexico (which was engaged in a Revolution), and many years before the rest of Latin America, Leguía's Peru found the courage to break freely with the old secular tradition to which the others remained attached either through misinformation or, above all, self-interest in maintaining it. Peru had proclaimed a great principle when it extended legal recognition to the community. By giving it a special place in the nation, the government proposed to effect its progressive adaptation to the modern world. But, first and foremost, its purpose was to protect and defend the indigenous peasants from the despoliation of their lands. The 1,560 Indian communities recognized and organized by 1960 [11] resemble, to a certain extent, the peasant *ejidos* of regions of Mexico formerly inhabited by indigenous peoples. Perhaps the greatest difference derives from the continued presence in Peru of haciendas around the ejidos, whereas in Mexico most of these have been eliminated.

The concept of the protected community, represented by these principles, was not extended to the rest of the hemisphere (with the exception of the Mexican ejido and a few timid legal initiatives on the eve of World War II) until 1940. At that time in Pátzcuaro, Mexico, the First Inter-American Congress of *Indigenistas* proclaimed the ideal of "constructive protection" for all indigenous groups of the Americas. Of course, this does not mean that these principles have been converted rapidly into realities everywhere. Yet they have inspired positive initiatives with such practical results as the establishment in Mexico of the *Instituto Nacional Indigenista* under the direction of Dr. Alfonso Caso, with its schools and local centers. Further, they have guided the policies of several governments, more or less slowly, toward the improvement of conditions for their "native" populations.[12] For these reasons the importance of the Peruvian indigenista legislation of 1920 should not be underestimated.

---

[11] Today their number has increased.

[12] Cf. Alejandro Lipschütz, *La comunidad indígena en América y en Chile* (Santiago de Chile, 1956). See also the series of *Legislación indigenista* (plus country) published in Mexico by the Instituto Indigenista Interamericano.

PART IV

The Present State of Knowledge
and the Interdisciplinary Tasks Ahead

CHAPTER 10

Historical Research
on Race Relations in Latin
America During the National Period
Magnus Mörner

Despite the increasing interest of historians and other scholars in questions of race relations, slavery, and immigration, much still remains
to be done. Dr. Magnus Mörner of the Institute of Ibero-American
Studies, Stockholm, Sweden, here surveys the current historical literature
and points to particular aspects of the past which require investigation
on a priority basis. He sees six broad areas as most important: first, the
quantification of demographic aspects of race and class; second, the political role of ethnic groups during and after the wars of independence;
third, the relationship between the so-called Indian communities and the
larger socioeconomic contexts; fourth, the nature of Negro slavery and
the position of Negroes after the abolition of slavery; fifth, the place of
the immigrant; and, finally, the idea of race in Latin America as a problem in intellectual history. This study, it should be remembered, was
written in 1965 before the publication of some more recent studies, including Dr. Mörner's own *Race Mixture in the History of Latin America*.[1]

During the colonial period in Latin America the ethnic condition
of the individual determined his legal status and social position
within a hierarchical estate system of social stratification. The intimate correlation between "race" and social position cannot possibly

[1] Magnus Mörner, *Race Mixture in the History of Latin America* (Boston,
1967).

be overlooked in studying this period. In the course of the national period when the class system was being established and the legal boundaries between the ethnic groups already had ceased or almost ceased to exist, it becomes much more difficult to assess the importance of the ethnic factor. It even becomes quite difficult to identify the Negroes in post-abolition source materials, although during the last decades of slavery their presence was conspicuous. Mestizaje and interethnic relations as such no longer can be clearly traced in the administrative records of the national period. Nevertheless, historians are bound to take note of results of contemporary social science research, which shows both the continuing importance today of ethnic prejudice and of even milder forms of ethnic discrimination throughout Latin America as well as the existence of a caste-like "indigenous" sector at the bottom of the social ladder in all the "Indo-American" countries. Thus, in the words of Charles Gibson, the social historian has to face the fact that the "most serious single deficiency in historical knowledge pertains to the period 1810 to 1890—the former date marking the approximate point at which colonial documentation ceases; the latter, the point at which the memory of living Indians begins." [2]

The Establishment of Legal Equality and the Problems of Quantitative Study

The historian who works on the basis of written records analyzed with heuristic methods necessarily faces a difficult challenge when approaching the topic of "race" and "class" during the national period of Latin American history, and serious studies in this field have been few. Even the mere consultation of preserved records often will present considerable problems. As a rule, in Latin American archives the documentation corresponding to the national period is less well catalogued and attended to than is material relating to the colonial era. And much less of the source material relating to the social history of the national period has been made available in print. Nevertheless, the historian, I think, has to devote more atten-

[2] Charles Gibson, "The Transformation of the Indian Community in New Spain, 1500–1800," *Cahiers d'Histoire Mondiale,* II (Paris, 1955), 602–03.

tion to this task, which although formidable is not only of vital concern to his fellow sociologists and anthropologists but also deals with one of the most important and subtle undercurrents in the historical evolution of Latin American societies.

The first national constitutions abolished the legal and administrative use of such socioethnic terms as Indian, Mestizo, Pardo, and other "Castas." Socioethnic classification in the parish records was also discontinued. The Indians' lack of integration into the national society soon gave rise, however, to the administrative sanction of another designation: *indígena*. Their traditional headtax, tribute, was revived in 1826 under another name, *contribución de indígenas*, in the countries liberated by Bolívar. In Peru this discriminatory tax was abolished only in 1854. Thanks to the source material related to this tax, George Kubler has been able to present his extraordinarily interesting analysis of Peruvian ethnic divisions and demographical evolution during the national period. Among other things, he shows that, at least in certain districts, the rate of integration of the indígenas actually slowed during the early national period as compared to the late colonial era.[3] More research could be carried out along these same lines, with regard to Ecuador, for instance. Of course, it should be kept in mind that no conclusions about the purely racial composition of the population can be drawn on the basis of fiscal material. All historical source material relating to "Indians," "mestizos," "pardos," and other groups at least from the time of the eighteenth century has reflected the existence of social rather than racial categories. The censuses, which since the late nineteenth century have been taken from time to time in the different countries of Latin America, occasionally have included a breakdown into ethnic groups. The criteria employed have differed from census to census, but it is obvious that cultural and social characteristics by and large have played a much greater role than the phenotype of the individuals.

This limitation in the nature of the source material involving ethnic classification is perhaps not too serious from the historian's point of view. He is not overly concerned with the changes in the

[3] George Kubler, *The Indian Caste of Peru, 1795–1940: A Study Based Upon Tax Records and Census Reports* (Washington, D.C., 1952).

genetic composition of the populations. What is interesting to him rather is the evolution of the ethnic groups as modified by changing concepts and criteria. There are revealing examples of the continuing ambiguity of administrative ethnic divisions in the countries that suddenly had abolished the colonial "Régimen de Castas," and equalized citizens regardless of their ethnic condition. In 1876 President Barrios of Guatemala decreed that "for all legal purposes, the indígenas of the afore-said San Pedro de Sacatepéquez, of both sexes, are declared to be *ladinos*, supposing that, from next year onwards, they use the dress corresponding to the ladinos." This decree was suspended only in 1935. Probably a more exhaustive study of the administrative documentation in countries with a strong indigenous population also would uncover many cases of "neo-colonial" administrative sanctions of social attitudes and prejudices toward ethnic groups, especially the indígenas.[4] According to George Kubler, "The colonial attitude toward passage from Indian to non-Indian caste may be described as more relaxed and more permissive than since Independence. . . . The governing factors in the process are probably economic and ideological and in no case biological."[5] But as yet we have barely reached the threshold to some knowledge based on research in this truly fascinating matter.

To summarize our position regarding the possibilities of a quantitative study of the relationship between "race" and "class" during the national period: we do not think it will be possible to trace the evolution of any biologically-defined, relatively large group or of the process of miscegenation as such during this period. On the other hand, fiscal records and certain census figures make it possible to follow the evolution of the indígena population as compared with the rest of the populace. It must then be kept in mind

[4] Jorge Skinner-Klée (ed.), *Legislación indigenista de Guatemala* (Mexico City, 1954), pp. 33, 117–18. According to Moisés González Navarro some Mexican agencies of the Porfiriato were still classifying "Mexicans" and "Indians" separately in official documents; *La colonización en México, 1877–1910* (Mexico City, 1960), p. 97. See also, for example, Richard N. Adams, *A Community in the Andes: Problems and Progress in Muquiyauyo* (Seattle, 1959), p. 84, and David Bushnell, *The Santander Regime in Gran Colombia* (Newark, Del., 1954), p. 182.

[5] Kubler, *The Indian Caste of Peru*, p. 65. See also the article by Moisés González Navarro in the present volume.

that such changes as can be noticed may reflect a change in the rate of acculturation rather than the vegetative decrease or increase of one of the two sectors of the population.

Whereas the historical demography of the colonial period has at least received some attention, even in its interethnic aspect, the national period has been almost neglected by research. The most remarkable exception is the study by Kubler just quoted. Angel Rosenblat and Rodolfo Barón Castro, the latter in his pioneer book on El Salvador, provide abundant material but without submitting it to a strict analysis.[6]

The Ethnic Factor in the Wars of Emancipation and National Politics

The enormous extent of historiography devoted to the Wars of Emancipation notwithstanding, much still remains to be done on the social aspects of these wars. There can be no doubt that these conflicts had the character of civil wars; thus the social aspects become particularly important. Nevertheless, the pioneering articles and preliminary conclusions of Charles Griffin have been supplemented only to a small extent by results of more recent research.[7] Although to a certain degree they provoke a useful revision of traditionalist, patriotically-biased historiography, recent Marxist interpretations seem to convey somewhat anachronistic ideas about the socioeconomic structure of the revolutionary era. For example, they tend to disregard the role of interethnic conflict and to stress instead the struggles of economic classes. The Marxist view of Latin American

[6] Angel Rosenblat, La población indígena y el mestizaje en América (2nd ed., 2 vols., Buenos Aires, 1954); Rodolfo Barón Castro, La población de El Salvador: Estudio acerca de su desenvolvimiento desde la epoca prehispánica hasta nuestros días (Madrid, 1952).

[7] Charles C. Griffin, "Economic and Social Aspects of the Era of Spanish American Independence," The Hispanic American Historical Review (hereinafter abbreviated HAHR), XXIX (1949), 170–87; and Los temas sociales y económicos en la época de la Independencia (Caracas, 1962). See also his "Aspectos económico-sociales de la época de la Emancipacion hispanoamericana: una bibliografía selecta de la historiografía reciente, 1949–1959," El Movimiento Emancipador de Hispano-América. Actas y Ponencias, I (Academia Nacional de la Historia, Caracas, 1961), 347–60.

colonial history also discerns, of course, a pattern of class exploitation and conflict within the so-called Caste Society.[8] Other students
(including the present author) prefer to interpret Latin American
colonial society mainly in terms of the hierarchical estate-based society that in part persisted in Europe until the French revolution,[9]
for indeed it came into being mainly as the result of the transfer of
this kind of society to a multiracial colonial situation. Without
denying that a system of social classes was gradually taking shape
even before Emancipation, particularly in the rural sector, we maintain that the misnamed "Caste Society" continued to exist as the
basis of social attitudes, legal and social discrimination, and social
status until the very end of the colonial era. That is, the struggle
between the different strata of the population that occurred in the
course of the Wars of Emancipation may not necessarily be explained only in terms of class exploitation and conflict. It may also
derive from frustration engendered by the ethnic discrimination imposed by the "Caste Society."

The most dramatic examples of social conflict with ethnic overtones in the course of the Wars of Emancipation were the revolutions
of Hidalgo and Morelos in Mexico and the struggle in Venezuela in
1813 and 1814. In both cases the real issues have escaped the apolo-
getic-traditionalist historical school. In the view of the traditionalists,
Boves, the royalist leader of the Venezuelan cowboys (*Llaneros*),
is a personification of evil. On the other hand, some leftist writers
have tried to assign to this warrior the role of popular redeemer.
Germán Carrera Damas, a Marxist historian, in a recent work
calmly demonstrates the lack of documentary basis for either view.
Sacking and pillage were normal means of war financing.[10] In any
case, examples of hatred between "Indians" and "whites," "pardos"
and "criollos," abound in both Mexico and Venezuela, and it is also
clear that for a moment contemporaries thought a "racial war" ab-

[8] See, for example, Sergio Bagú, *Estructura social de la Colonia: Ensayo de
historia comparada de América Latina* (Buenos Aires, 1952).

[9] See, for example, Lyle McAlister, "Social Structure and Social Change in
New Spain," HAHR, XLIII (1963), 349–70.

[10] Germán Carrera Damas, *Sobre el significado socioeconómico de la acción
histórica de Boves* (Caracas, 1964). See also his *Tres temas de historia venezolana* (Caracas, 1961).

solutely imminent. Why did a struggle clearly fought along ethnic lines never take place in these two regions at least? My own impressions derived from published sources are that, in fact, the "white" leadership on both sides feared such tendencies and made what proved to be a joint effort to curb them. Such action would provide the context in which to place Bolívar's ruthless executions of a Piar and a Padilla. However, it also seems to me that a thorough study of the ethnic aspects of the struggle for Emancipation still remains to be done, as does also an unbiased study of the ethnic attitudes of the principal protagonists. Surprisingly enough, it seems that not even Bolívar's somewhat contradictory views on race ever have been submitted to a systematic and objective analysis.[11] Also, during the post-emancipation era ethnic tensions seem to have expressed themselves occasionally in Latin American politics, as during the Federal War of Venezuela and in the revolutions of northeastern Brazil between 1832 and 1848. They are, however, difficult to assess.[12]

The tendencies toward a struggle along ethnic lines during the Wars of Emancipation and later should be clearly distinguished from the participation of dark-skinned elements in the wars. During the Wars of Emancipation it is evident that although on both sides Indians, Negroes, and "Castas" usually provided the bulk of the fighting forces, their role was only a "passive" one, completely subordinated to aims dictated by the "white" leadership. Their neglected

---

[11] A brief account appears in my *Race Mixture in the History of Latin America* (Boston, Mass., 1967), 86–88.

[12] Carlos Rama, "Os movimentos sociais na América Latina durante o século XIX," *Revista de História*, VIII (São Paulo, 1957), 344, polemizes against V. I. Ermelaev. For bibliographical references on these conflicts see Stanley Stein, "The Historiography of Brazil, 1808–1889," HAHR, XL (1960), 245–51; Robert L. Gilmore, *Caudillism and Militarism in Venezuela, 1810–1910* (Athens, Ohio, 1964), pp. 40–41; Randall O. Hudson, "The Status of the Negro in Northern South America, 1820–1860," *The Journal of Negro History*, XLIX (1964), 236–39. R. F. Smith ("Twentieth Century Cuban Historiography," HAHR, XLIV [1964], 73) observed with regard to Cuba that the "problem of the Negro and the currents of racial antagonism which produced the Race War of 1912" would deserve an investigation. Finally, J. Icaza Tigerino, "Factores étnicos de la anarquía hispanoamericana," *Revista de Estudios Políticos*, XC (Madrid, 1956), 249–91, should be taken *cum grano salis*.

history should be written in these terms.[13] It is, for instance, surprising to find how little mention is made in literature of the fact that about a third of San Martín's army at Maipú and Chacabuco were Negroes. In the case of Negro slaves, recruitment provided the way to freedom—but the casualties they suffered were also heavy. The rapid decrease of the percentage of slaves and the corresponding increase of that of free Negroes and also the absolute diminution of the African element in continental Spanish America in the early nineteenth century must be seen against this background, as, for instance, José Luis Masini and Ildefonso Pereda Valdés have recognized.[14]

The wars provided opportunity for a considerable number of dark-skinned individuals to climb the social ladder by virtue of their military merits. This fact is verified easily in the biographies of such men as Santa Cruz or Agustín Gamarra. An even better example, on a more modest level, is that of the Chilean mulatto José Romero (1794–1858), called Sargento Mayor, described by Guillermo Felíu Cruz.[15] A more systematic study of the function performed by the wars as a promoter of upward social mobility (and ethnical passing) would probably be difficult but rewarding. Of course, this phenomenon is not restricted to the period of Emancipation but is a continuing and positive side effect of Latin American militarism. Neither have any serious studies been undertaken as yet with regard to the rest of the nineteenth century.[16]

The study of the abolition of the legal framework of "Caste Society" does not seem to present great problems. A succinct account of this process in Argentina has been presented recently by Orlando

[13] Alipio Valencia Vega's *El indio en la Independencia* (La Paz, 1962), does not meet scholarly requirements.

[14] José Luis Masini, *La esclavitud negra en Mendoza: época independiente* (Mendoza, 1962); Ildefonso Pereda Valdés, *Negros esclavos y negros libres: Esquema de una sociedad esclavista y aporte del negro en nuestra formación nacional* (Montevideo, 1941).

[15] Guillermo Felíu Cruz, *La abolición de la esclavitud en Chile* (Santiago, 1942), pp. 183–225.

[16] The aspect is only touched upon in Gilmore, *Caudillism and Militarism*. The books on militarism by J. Johnson and E. Lieuwen also give very little in this regard.

Carracedo.[17] The texts of the laws and constitutions are usually clear enough; also, the legislative debates preceding them in part have been made available in modern editions. Apart from the constitutions enacted in Latin America, the Cadiz constitution of 1812 is also worthy of attention in this connection because of the participation of so many Spanish American deputies in its elaboration. Furthermore, the ethnic composition of the overseas population became a hotly debated issue in Cadiz in respect to how popularly the representative system of the new Spanish constitutional monarchy would be constructed. The excellent study by James F. King sheds light on this topic.[18]

The era of Emancipation introduces a new kind of source material for the social history of Latin America: travelogues written by non-Iberian foreign visitors, be they merchants, scientists, diplomatic agents, or mercenary soldiers. Even the few earlier examples of this genre, by Alexander Von Humboldt and others, are sufficiently close to the time of Emancipation to serve as sources to some extent. Although the observations of foreign travelers—especially Anglo-Saxon ones—are often quoted, their works should be submitted to a more critical analysis than hitherto they have received. When the background, experiences, and particular attitudes of the authors are better known, and their evidence, with regard, for instance, to ethnic conditions, duly compared, they will probably prove a better source for knowledge.

The Evolution of the "Indigenous" Sector and Its Relation to the National Society

The necessity of defining the so-called Indians who constitute the population of parts of Meso-America and the South American Andes in social rather than racial terms has been stressed already. Since many—but not all—scholars today are aware of this circumstance, confusing statements abound. As we have already indicated,

[17] Orlando Carracedo, "El régimen de castas, el trabajo y la Revolución de Mayo," *Anuario del Instituto de Investigaciones Históricas,* IV (Rosario, 1960), 157–86.

[18] James F. King, "The Colored Castes and American Representation in the Cortes of Cadiz," HAHR, XXXIII (1953), 526–37.

this confusion is not a recent development. It is evident that by the eighteenth century both "Indio" and "mestizo" had become social rather than racial terms. Whereas even more or less "pure" Indians who had settled on the haciendas often rapidly lost their Indian identity (even in the legal-fiscal sense), those with similar Indian ancestry who remained in the landowning villages—with their peculiar Indo-Spanish municipal structure—remained true "Indians."

Emancipation did not really alter this situation in spite of the Liberators' intentions to establish equality among the Indian and mestizo inhabitants of the countryside and to dissolve the "comunidades." The frontal attack, that is, the efforts of the liberals best exemplified by the Lerdo Law in Mexico in 1856, did not begin until more than three decades after independence. It is obvious that political chronology, with its sharp division between the colonial and national periods, does not provide a very satisfactory framework for the study of the evolution of the rural sector, including interethnic relations. The middle of the eighteenth century seems to provide a better starting point for the study of these phenomena than does 1810.[19] Of course, it should be kept in mind that the basis had been laid earlier. The rise of the latifundium was essentially a product of the seventeenth century. The nineteenth century, on the other hand, witnessed no sudden change in the relations of the "Indian" to the outside world. It is obvious, however, that the profound change of the Latin American economy as a result of the world-wide technological and commercial revolution of the mid-nineteenth century also affected to a considerable degree the relationship of the Indian to national society. The last period of change, of course, was introduced by the Mexican Revolution of 1910. However slowly it proceeded, one cannot doubt the existence of this process of change.

The extant bibliography does not conform very well to the schema of evolution that we have just suggested. Often an excellent account has been cut short at 1810, as is the case of Charles Gibson's invaluble work, *The Aztecs Under Spanish Rule* (Stanford, 1964), or Mario Góngora's excellent study of the origins of the Chilean

[19] See, for example, Stanley Stein's remarks in his article on historiography in *Social Science Research in Latin America,* ed. Charles Wagley (New York and London, 1964), p. 89.

Inquilinos.[20] In other instances, conditions during the colonial period have been sketched only as a kind of introduction to modern developments. In such works, conditions during early colonial times usually have received more attention than the situation during the last decades of Spanish domination. In fact, historians of the national period largely have abandoned this field of study to their colleagues in sociology and social anthropology. Often the historian only gives the Indians passing attention in connection with some rebellion or legislative measure.[21] Among the most noteworthy contributions from the historical point of view is the study of the "comunidades" of Boyacá, Colombia, written by a sociologist, Orlando Fals Borda; indeed, all studies dealing with the history of the relationship between "Indians" and ladinos in Guatemala as far as I know have been written by anthropologists.[22] Even if some of these studies have gathered considerable source material (Fals Borda also has been using unpublished sources), their approach naturally has not been that of the historian. In this area the historian should have certain advantages: he is more familiar with unpublished records; he is capable of a more critical heuristic analysis; he possesses more knowledge of the general historical context in which the subject matter should be viewed.[23] The natural sympathy of the anthropologist toward the

[20] Mario Góngora, *Origen de los inquilinos en Chile Central* (Santiago, 1960. On the other hand, the excellent *Métodos y resultados de la política indigenista en México* (Instituto Nacional Indigenista, Mexico City, 1954) covers both the colonial and the national period.

[21] This seems to be true, for example, in the case of the otherwise most comprehensive work of Jorge Basadre, *Historia de la República del Perú* (5th ed., 6 vols., Lima, 1961–1962). On the other hand, Daniel Cosío Villegas' (ed.) *Historia moderna de México* (6 vols., Mexico City, 1955–1963) gives considerable attention to the Indians.

[22] Orlando Fals Borda, *El hombre y la tierra en Boyacá: Bases sociológicas e históricas para una reforma agraria* (Bogotá, 1957). Among students of Meso-America I think of the important contributions by Eric Wolf and Richard N. Adams. Among other recent articles: Alain Y. Dessaint, "Effects of the Hacienda and Plantation Systems on Guatemala's Indians," *América Indígena*, XXII (Mexico City, 1962), 323–54; Arnold Strickom, "Hacienda and Plantation in Yucatán: An Historical-Ecological Consideration of the Folk-Urban Continuum in Yucatán," *América Indígena*, XXV (Mexico City, 1965), 35–63; Rodolfo Stavenhagen, "Clases, colonialismo y aculturación," *América Latina*, VI (Rio de Janeiro, 1963), 63–104.

[23] Having used regional records himself for his study on Muquiyauyo (see

"Indians" with whom he is, as a rule, mainly concerned, may also make it more difficult for him to take an objective view with regard to the historical evolution of interethnic relations. Let me hasten to add that it is also true that the sincere indignation of the student who has observed "Indian" misery in the field has provided stimulus for studies which probably otherwise never would have attracted the attention of the historian in his library. A study by the Colombian Juan Friede, an anthropologist later turned historian, is a case in point.[24] More monographs like this, describing the long, desperate struggle of "Indian" communities and Indian forest tribes for survival from colonial through national times, certainly are needed.[25] As it is, the brilliant literary interpretation of this struggle in the Peruvian Andes by Ciro Alegría has no counterpart in scholarly bibliography, although materials would not be lacking. "Indian" rebellions, such as the Caste War of Yucatan, have attracted some attention from historians, but this subject is by no means exhausted.[26]

Two closely connected aspects of the relationship of the "In-

---

fn. 4), R. Adams says of his fellow anthropologists (p. 219) "When [they] do resort to history, such research is usually carried out in the libraries of major cities, or is limited to birth, death, marriage, and court records of the community in which they are working."

[24] Juan Friede, *El indio en la lucha por la tierra: Historia de los resguardos del Macizo Central Colombiano* (Bogotá, 1944). His study *Los indios del Alto Magdalena: Vida, luchas y exterminio, 1609–1931* (Bogotá, 1943), is also of interest, while his book *Los andakí, 1538–1947: Historia de la aculturación de una tribu selvática* (Buenos Aires and Mexico City, 1953), deals almost entirely with the colonial period. Alejandro Lipschütz, *La comunidad indígena en América y en Chile* (Santiago, 1956), deals with the struggle since 1813 of Chilean comunidades for their survival.

[25] Charles Hale (as quoted), "Research Opportunities in Modern Latin America," *The Americas*, XVIII (Washington, 1962), 357, suggests that "historians might be attracted to the purely historical side of recent anthropological community studies—if source material could be found."

[26] A recent work is Nelson Reed, *The Caste War of Yucatán* (Stanford, 1964). See also several contributions on the Caste War by H. F. Cline and the account by Moisés González Navarro in *Historia Moderna de México: El Porfiriato; Vida social*, ed. D. Cosio Villegas (Mexico City, 1957), 239–59. Another interesting item on Mexico is Jack Autrey Dabbs's "The Indian Policy of the Second Empire," in Thomas E. Cotner and C. E. Castañeda, *Essays in Mexican History* (Austin, Tex., 1958), pp. 113–26.

dians" with the outer world deserve particular attention from the historical point of view: land tenure and labor systems. In fact, it is surprising that despite the increasing importance of the land tenure question in Latin American politics, comparatively little scholarly effort has been made to trace its historical background. The penetrating study by Mario Góngora (historian) and Jean Borde (geographer) of the evolution of rural property in a district in Central Chile is perhaps the most remarkable exception.[27] Another is the survey (already mentioned) by Orlando Fals Borda of the evolution of the rural structure in Boyacá, Colombia. However, we need many more investigations of this quality before we can make generalizations on a more stable basis about the general and peculiar trends in the development of rural Latin America.

In regard to the labor systems (including the different forms of tenant labor) the extraordinary variety of terminologies in use makes a comparative study especially difficult. The twentieth-century situation seems to be rather well mapped, but we know very little about the historical background.[28] Góngora's study of the *inquilino* is an exception, and it does not cover the national period. It is obvious that systems that seem almost identical today may have had very different origins (also with regard to the ethnic groups of the laborers). On the other hand, a common historical background, as for example, the rural *mita/repartimento/cuatequil*, labor draft systems of colonial times, may have been antecedent to systems that are nowadays quite distinct.

Thanks to the initiative of the Inter-American Indigenista Institute, a great part of the legislative documents dealing with the "In-

---

[27] Jean Borde and Mario Góngora, *Evolución de la propiedad rural en el valle del Puangue* (2 vols., Santiago, 1956). Among other recent works, Francisco González de Cossío's *Historia de la tenencia y explotación del campo desde la época precortesiana hasta las leyes del 6 de enero de 1915* (2 vols., Mexico City, 1957), deserves to be mentioned.

[28] As to modern conditions, *Indigenous Peoples: Living and Working Conditions of Aboriginal Populations in Independent Countries* (Geneva, 1953), pp. 368–85, and other publications of the International Labour Office seem to be the best sources. Despite its title, Piedad de P. Costales's "El huasipungo y su evolucíon histórica," *Anales de la Universidad Central*, XCI (Quito, 1962), 16–36, has almost nothing to say on the history of this interesting labor institution.

dians" issued during the national period have become easily available in print.[29] These laws deal with land tenure, labor questions, and other aspects of "Indian" life. They convey an excellent image of the evolution of the "Indigenista" policies of the respective governments. But as sources for our knowledge of existing social conditions, they must be used with utmost caution, even as is the case with the Royal Cédulas of the colonial period. The gap between legal theory on one side and administrative practice and social reality on the other has remained as enormous in this sphere as it ever was. The only thing that can be said with any certainty is that the abuses which were prohibited must have existed. If the prohibition is repeated, this is an indication of their having continued to exist.

Anthropologists and sociologists of today seem inclined to emphasize more than scholars of the previous generation the contacts between the "Indians" and their communities and the outer world and the impact on them of external events. It is easy for the historian to share in their criticism of the concept of the complete isolation of the "Indian" communities. The technological and commercial revolution of the mid-nineteenth century as well as the industrialization of our own era must have exercised a profound, if often indirect, impact on "Indian" communities, augmenting outer pressure and exploitation and widening the gap between them and the more dynamic national society. As I see it, future historical investigation must try to investigate the impact of the mid-nineteenth century techno-commercial revolution on the "Indian" world of the Meso-American and Andean areas. As a matter of fact, despite the stimulating presentation by Sanford Mosk many years ago, far too little is known about the general effects of this universal change that oc-

---

[29] This series, appearing under the title *Legislación indigenista* plus the name of the respective country, covers Chile (Alvaro Jara), Colombia (Antonio García), Ecuador (G. Rubio Orbe), Guatemala (J. Skinner-Klée), Mexico (F. González de Cossío), Honduras, and Costa Rica. For other countries: *Legislación indigenista del Perú* (Dirección General de Indígenas, Lima, 1948); Jose Flores Moncayo (ed.), *Legislación boliviana del indio: recopilacíon de resoluciones, órdenes, decretos, leyes, decretos supremos y otras disposiciones legales, 1825–1953* (La Paz, 1953); Miguel Bonifaz, *Legislación agrario-indigenal* (Cochabamba, 1953); *Fuero indígena venezolano*, II, ed. by C. de Armellada (Caracas, 1954).

[212]

curred a hundred years ago in Latin America.[30] And how did the political instability, the financial chaos, and depressed foreign trade of the preceding decades affect the "Indian" world? Was it precisely the sequence of depression at first and then prosperity in the national sector that helped to slow down the process of acculturation and assimilation and to produce the ethnic dualism that is so characteristic of modern Mexico, Guatemala, Ecuador, Peru, and Bolivia? [31]

Nineteenth-Century Negro Slavery and Post-Abolition Conditions of the Negroes

During the period from the 1820s to 1888, slavery was abolished in country after country in Latin America. Abolition was preceded by suppression of the slave trade. Naturally, both steps were taken sooner in countries where slaves were few and slavery of little economic importance, such as Central America, than in countries where it constituted a basic element within the economy, as in Cuba and Brazil. both the suppression of the slave trade and abolition have received considerable attention from historians. James F. King's article on Great Britain and the suppression of the slave trade in the Spanish American countries and Alan Manchester's treatment of the same matter with regard to Brazil are especially noteworthy. A brief comment by Edison Carneiro interprets the suppression of the slave trade in Brazil as favorable to the slaveholders themselves because they got rid of their debts to the slave dealers.[32]

---

[30] S. A. Mosk, "Latin America and the World Economy, 1850–1914," *Inter-American Economic Affairs*, II (Washington, D.C., 1948), 53–82. In his article "Indigenous Economy in Latin America," *Ibid.*, VIII (Washington, D.C., 1954), 3–26, Mosk refers to Guatemala. He briefly shows the impact of the Depression on the Indian economy.

[31] The expression "ethnic dualism" may be discussed in the exceptional case of the areas in the South American Andes where the "cholo" has long constituted a transitional group between "Indian" and "mestizo." Unfortunately, José Varallanos's *El Cholo y el Peru: Introducción al estudio sociológico de un hombre y an pueblo mestizo y su destino cultural* (Buenos Aires, 1962), does not clarify this intriguing phenomenon.

[32] J. F. King, "The Latin American Republics and the Suppression of the Slave Trade," HAHR, XXIV (1944), 387–411; Alan Manchester, *British Pre-*

THE PRESENT STATE OF KNOWLEDGE

With regard to the process of abolition itself, monographs are numerous, if often of a rather poor quality. As far as Spanish America is concerned, the best studies are by Guillermo Feliú Cruz on Chile and by Harold Bierck on Gran Colombia. The principal legislative texts also have been made available, for instance in the bulky compilation on Colombia by Ernesto Posada and Carlos Restrepo Canal. With regard to Brazil, the literature is rather abundant. Monographs on abolition in the different Brazilian states also have appeared.[33] However, only the recent contributions by the São Paulo sociologists Florestan Fernandes, Octavio Ianni, and Fernando Henrique Cardoso have tried seriously to present more than a superficial compilation of abolitionist speeches and laws.[34]

As far as Spanish America is concerned, historians seem to lose

---

eminence in Brazil; Its Rise and Decline (Chapel Hill, N.C., 1933); Edison Caneiro, *Ladinos e crioulos: Estudos sobre o negro no Brasil* (Rio de Janeiro, 1964), pp. 91–94.

[33] Feliú Cruz, *La abolición de la esclavitud en Chile*; Harold A. Bierck, "The Struggle for Abolition in Gran Columbia," *The Hispanic American Historical Review*, XXXIII (1953), 365–86. Other contributions: L. M. Díaz Soler, *Historia de la esclavitud negra en Puerto Rico, 1493–1890* (Madrid, 1953); J. M. Núñez Ponte, *Ensayo histórico acerca de la esclavitud y de su abolición en Venezuela* (2nd ed., Caracas, 1954); P. A. Martin, "Slavery and Abolition in Brazil," HAHR, XIII (1933), 151–96; Carlos Martínez Durán and Daniel Contreras, "La abolición de la esclavitud en Centro América," *Journal of Inter-American Studies*, IV (Gainesville, Fla., 1962), 223–32; Ernesto Posada and Carlos Restrepo Canal, *La esclavitud en Colombia: Leyes de manumisión* (Bogotá, 1933); Carlos Restrepo Canal, *La libertad de los esclavos en Colombia o leyes de manumisión* (Bogotá, 1938); Julio Tobar Donoso, "La abolición de la esclavitud en al Ecuador," *Boletín de la Academia Nacional de Historia*, XXXIX (Quito, 1959), 5–30; the book by J. Oiliam on abolition in Minas Gerais (1962) has not been available for consultation; that by R. Girão on Ceará (1956) is hardly scholarly. Nícia Villela Luz, "A administração provincial de São Paulo em face de movimento abolicionista," *Revista de Administração*, II (São Paulo, 1948), 80–100, has not been available for consultation. How slavery occasionally reappeared is illustrated by Luis Chávez Orozco's *Maximiliano y la restitución de la esclavitud en México, 1865–1866* (Mexico City, 1961).

[34] See in the first place the recent, monumental work by Florestan Fernandes, *A integração do negro à sociedade de classes* (São Paulo, 1965). See also Octavio Ianni, *As metamorfoses do escravo: apogeu e crise da escravatura no Brasil Meridional* (São Paulo, 1962); Fernando Henrique Cardoso and Octavio Ianni, *Côr e mobilidade social en Florianópolis* (São Paulo, 1960); Fernando Henrique Cardoso, *Capitalismo e escravidão no Brasil Meridional* (São Paulo, 1962).

all interest in the Negro as soon as abolition is accomplished. In any case, he disappears almost completely from historical literature. In the case of Brazil, the famous sociologist (or social historian) Gilberto Freyre has followed up to some extent his interpretation of plantation slavery from *Casa Grande Senzala* (Masters and Slaves) with ideas on post-abolition conditions. But only the São Paulo group of sociologists already mentioned has really attacked the complex problem of how the Negro fared after he was freed. Historian Stanley Stein's short concluding remarks in his excellent book on the coffee plantations in Vassouras (Paraíba Valley) are also enlightening.[35]

The gradual process of abolition during the nineteenth century is already the subject of a vast if uneven bibliography. In many cases, monographs of a higher quality are needed, but the lacunae are not conspicuous by any means. A much more controversial and poorly known subject is the nature of slavery itself in Spanish and Portuguese America. Here the very boundary between the colonial and national periods is of little import although the chronological factor should always be kept in mind.

Gilberto Freyre first expressed the now widely diffused view that slavery in Ibero-America was different from and milder than its counterpart in Anglo-America. For explanation he referred to the ethnic variety of the Iberian background and the supposed lack of ethnic prejudice on the part of the Iberian conquistadores and settlers. Frank Tannenbaum, sharing the same view, supported it mainly by references to legal differences between Luso/Spanish, French,

---

[35] The article already mentioned by R. O. Hudson on the Negro in northern South America is a pioneering effort but its conclusions are vague and not too well supported. Another item, of greater value, is Ricardo Rodríguez Molas, "Los negros libres rioplatenses," *Buenos Aires: Revista de Humanidades*, I (1961), 99–126; Gilberto Freyre, *Introdução à história da sociedade patriarcal no Brasil; Sobrados e mucambos: Decadencia do patriarcado rural e desenvolvimento do urbano* (2nd ed., 3 vols., Rio de Janeiro and São Paulo, 1951); and *Ordem e progresso: Processo de desintegração das sociedades patriarcal e semipatriarcal no Brasil sob o regime de trabalho livre* . . . (2 vols., Rio de Janeiro, 1959). Cf. Thomas Skidmore, "Gilberto Freyre and the Early Brazilian Republic: Some Notes on Methodology," *Comparative Studies in Society and History*, VI (The Hague, 1963–1964), 490–505. See also Stanley J. Stein, *Vassouras: A Brazilian Coffee County, 1850–1900* (Cambridge, Mass., 1957).

[215]

and Anglo-America. Stanley Elkins has followed the same path.[36] But the documentary basis for these hypotheses has obviously been weak. The reconstruction of social reality on the basis of legal documents is notoriously dangerous and never more so than in the case of slave codes limiting the rights of an owner of human property. The "humane" Spanish slave code of 1789 which played an important role in Tannenbaum's argumentation has proved to be a rather complex issue; it was inspired by the French *Code Noir* of 1685.[37]

The frequency of voluntary manumissions among the Spaniards and Portuguese has often been used as an argument for the humane nature of slavery in Latin America. That at times these acts should be explained by the economic convenience of the ex-owners has been demonstrated by Federico Brito Figueroa.[38] The whole problem of the extent and nature of manumissions deserves a special investigation. It is quite obvious that it was easier for some categories of slaves to purchase their liberty than for others.

This leads us to the opponents of the Freyre-Tannenbaum school who prefer to explain the nature of slavery on the basis of the economic function of the enslaved manpower. Whereas slaves working in a profitable enterprise will be harshly exploited, slaves held at least partly for noneconomic motives (servants and others) are likely to receive more lenient treatment. They will also be able to purchase their freedom more easily. The degree of rentability of

[36] Frank Tannenbaum, *Slave and Citizen: The Negro in the Americas* (New York, 1947); Stanley Elkins, *Slavery: A Problem in American Institutional and Intellectual Life* (Chicago, 1959). See also, for example, M. W. Williams, "The Treatment of Negro Slaves in the Brazilian Empire: A Comparison with the United States of America," *Journal of Negro History*, XV (1930), 315–36. The evidence presented by Manuel Cardozo, "Slavery in Brazil as Described by Americans, 1822–1888," *The Americas*, XVII (1961), 241–60, also lends some support for a positive evaluation.

[37] Fernando Ortiz, *Hampa afro-cubana; los negros esclavos: Estudio sociológico y de derecho público* (Havana, 1916), p. 363; José Torre Revello, "Origen y aplicación del código negrero en la *América española* (1788–1794)," *Boletín del Instituto de Investigaciones Históricas*, XV (Buenos Aires, 1832), 42–50; Javier Malagón, "Un documento del siglo XVIII para la historia de la esclavitud en las Antillas," *Miscelánea de estudios dedicados a Fernando Ortiz*, II (Havana, 1956), 951–68.

[38] Federico Brito Figueroa, *Ensayos de historia social venezolana* (Caracas, 1960), pp. 108–14.

slave labor rather than the nationality of the slaveholder or the character of the legislation then will be held responsible for the character of slavery. This view, first formulated in a convincing way by Eric Williams of Trinidad, seems for instance to harmonize with the evidence presented for the Caribbean by Sidney Mintz. Also it may very well be that the gloomy picture that Stanley Stein presents of slavery on the coffee plantations of the Paraíba Valley and the much brighter picture given by Freyre with regard to the sugar *fazendas* of Recife reflect the contrast between a profitable, capitalistic enterprise and a more old-fashioned, decaying economy.[39] The contributions of the São Paulo group of sociologists on slavery in the South of Brazil also fit into this briefly summarized theory. It should be kept in mind that slavery more than anything else is an *economic* institution, whereas the juridical aspect, so stressed by Tannenbaum and others, is of a much more secondary character. There is a risk, however, that a strictly Marxist interpretation of the functional theory will lead to an over-simplification of historical reality.

The new approach to the character of slavery in the New World means that comparisons will be meaningful only insofar as the whole economic context is brought into the picture and similar categories of slaves are compared. But it is doubtful that even such comparisons will shed much light on the post-abolition development of interethnic relations in Latin and Anglo America, since slavery by definition was an inhumane institution everywhere.[40] It seems more rewarding to look into the question of the quantitative relation between free Negroes on the one side and mulattoes and slaves on the

[39] Eric Williams, *Capitalism and Slavery* (Chapel Hill, N.C., 1944); Sidney Mintz, "Labor and Sugar in Puerto Rico and in Jamaica, 1800–1850," *Comparative Studies in Society and History*, I (The Hague, 1959), 273–81; Mintz's review of Elkins' book in *American Anthropologist*, LXIII (1961), 579–87; Richard M. Morse, "Negro-White Relations in Latin America," *Reports and Speeches of the Ninth Yale Conference of the Teaching of the Social Sciences, April 3–4, 1964* (New Haven, Conn., 1964).

[40] The same Gilberto Freyre illustrates this very well in his *O escravo nos anúncios de jornais brasileiros do século XIX. Tentativa de intepretação antropológica através de anuncios de jornais, de características de personalidade e de deformação de corpo de negros* . . . (Recife, 1963), p. 220. See also Stein, "The Historiography of Brazil," HAHR, XL (1960), 259.

other, as well as the relationship between these freedmen and the "poor whites" during the period that preceded abolition. Marvin Harris suggests that the vast sector of "poor whites" in the North American South had no counterpart, for instance, in Brazil. Instead of competing with the "poor whites," the freedmen of the slave era filled a virtual vacuum in society.[41] Probably the Caribbean, because of its national heterogeneity, will prove especially rewarding for such studies and comparisons.[42]

Apart from the recent work by Florestan Fernandes and others of the São Paulo group, the post-abolition conditions of the Negro in Latin America remain little known. Emancipation in Latin America usually came step by step, as in Brazil. Furthermore, it came about peacefully. Thus, it is natural that the consequences were less dramatic in Brazil than in the United States or in Jamaica for instance. Less interethnic tension was provoked in Latin America than in Anglo America by the very fact of abolition. Even so, the studies of the São Paulo group have shown that the growth of ethnic prejudice in the wake of abolition was a natural phenomenon, because of the need to substitute racial inequality for the former legal inequality. Probably it also is possible to discern a correlation between the development of prejudice and the competition for jobs. The study of the absorption of the Negro into society in the periods of mass manumissions during the decline of slavery and in the post-abolition era must, of course, be pursued against the background of the respective economic structures. By and large, the lack of other job or subsistence alternatives rapidly restored the plantation economy on a wage-earner or share-cropper basis, but where other alternatives existed the Negro abandoned the plantation, causing alterations to the economy. It will be the task of future research, especially in the case of some countries in Spanish America where slavery played a

[41] Marvin Harris, *Patterns of Race in the Americas* (New York, 1964), pp. 83–89. The extent of the continuing supply of slaves should, of course, also be brought into the picture. Celso Furtado in *A formação econômica do Brasil* (Rio de Janeiro, 1959), pp. 141–43, makes a daring observation in this regard.

[42] To compare Northeastern Brazil with the Guianas with regard to both slavery and interethnic relations as such is also rewarding; see Rudolf Van Lier, *Samenleving in een grensgebied H. Een social-historische studie van de maatschappij in Suriname* (The Hague, 1949).

more important role, such as Venezuela and Peru, to try to reconstruct the details of this process. This also might reveal the existence of other important factors in the process of absorption.

The historian working with the subject of interethnic relations in the post-abolition era, especially if he is trying to compare developments in different parts of the Americas, will necessarily face subtle problems—probably of crucial importance—that are beyond his reach. The study of racial attitudes lies properly within the domain of the sociologist or social psychologist.[43] Even so, it also might be useful for him to fix his attention more on the mulatto and his position in society instead of concentrating on the Negro, as he has until now.[44] It is well known that the contrast between Brazilian and Anglo-American interethnic relations rests more on the Brazilians' acceptance of the existence of miscegenation and of the mulatto than on the respective attitude toward the Negro.

Nineteenth- and Twentieth-Century Immigration and the New Mestizaje

The European immigration to Latin America during the latter half of the nineteenth century and the first decades of the twentieth brought a profound change in the ethnic composition of southern Brazil, Uruguay, Argentina, southern Chile, and Cuba, whereas the other countries were affected only slightly. Post-Second World War immigration has added Venezuela to the list of countries strongly influenced by this factor. The Caucasoid predominance in previously Mestizo southern South America is thus a product of the last hundred years.

[43] The importance of the white elite's own "somatic norm image" is, for example, stressed by Harry Hoetink in *The Two Variants in Caribbean Race Relations* (London, 1967).

[44] Richard Morse, for example, criticizes O. Ianni for not having distinguished clearly between the free Negro and the free mulatto in his "As metamorfoses do negro," review in *American Anthropologist*, LXVI (1964), 179. Psychological factors probably account for the paradox indicated by Thomas Matthews: As long as slavery lasted, continuous import of slaves into the Caribbean was needed to prevent diminution of the Negroes. After abolition, their numbers increased, although nobody was any longer interested in their increase. *El mestizaje en la historia de Ibero-América* (Instituto Panamericano de Geografía e Historia, Mexico City, 1961), p. 94.

THE PRESENT STATE OF KNOWLEDGE

This important process has been mapped only in part by serious research by geographers and historians. Little is known about relations in general and intermarriage between the newcomers and the national populations. As in the case of sixteenth-century Iberian immigrants, the sex ratio has been the major determinant of "mestizaje." For instance, since Germans in Brazil immigrated with their families, there was less need for intermarriage with other ethnic groups.[45] Within other groups, male predominance was a fact which necessarily led to a higher rate of intermarriage. The process of acculturation started by immigration was evidently a two-way phenomenon. Although the "Europeanizing" effect is obvious and often has been stressed, many immigrants (especially in rural sectors) also underwent a profound transformation under the impact of the environment and competition with native labor.[46] To what extent a different religion and different concepts of the family and morals have affected relations between the immigrants from non-Latin countries and the native Latin Americans is a subject about which we know little for the pre-1930 period. The more recent colonies founded by such religious sects as the Mennonites and the Hutterians in Paraguay are better known in this regard.

In São Paulo poor Italian immigrants already had begun to replace African labor on the coffee fazendas prior to the abolition of slavery. To the plantation owner, the color of his labor was a matter of little consequence, and the Italian newcomers were treated almost as harshly as the Africans. This caused the Italian government to suspend emigration to that region in 1902. Here then is a good example of how the pattern of forced labor and harsh attitudes characteristic of the plantation system of the time continued even after abolition. It also exemplifies the international complications that because of such conditions arose with the mother countries of non-

---

[45] See E. Willems, *A aculturação dos alemães no Brasil: Estudo antropológico dos imigrantes alemães e seus descendentes no Brasil* (São Paulo, 1946), pp. 451–62, and Jean Roche, *La colonisation allemande et le Rio Grande do Sul* (Paris, 1959), pp. 455–72.

[46] This latter phenomenon is stressed by Leo Waibel in his *Die europäische Kolonisation Südbrasiliens* (Bonn, 1955).

African immigrants.[47] "Coolie" immigration is another case in point. The 114,000 Chinese imported to Cuba between 1847 and 1867, as well as their 80,000 compatriots who went to Peru between 1849 and 1874, were to be substitutes for Negro slaves, and their treatment was shockingly brutal. Watt Stewart's monograph on "Chinese Bondage in Peru" is most enlightening, also with regard to the diplomatic aspect of this matter. Other Asiatics were sent to European territories in the Caribbean and the Guianas. The whole phenomenon of the Coolies waits for comprehensive treatment by a scholar or a team of scholars familiar with the Asiatic background of the Coolie migration.[48] It is obvious that this migration was overwhelmingly male so that homosexuality became a frequent phenomenon among the Coolies, which, in turn, was likely to increase the prejudice against them. When the immigrants from China and India finally were released from their position of pseudo-slavery, they seem to have improved their socioeconomic situation rapidly, but not even Stewart's study tells us much about that. Nor do we know very much about the character of intermarriage that occurred. The Japanese immigration to Latin America took place later—from around 1900 onwards—and had a very different character. Well organized, as a rule, from the home land, it aimed at the establishment of agricultural colonies. After some time, at least, the sex ratio among the Japanese became fairly normal and enabled them to pursue an endogamic family pattern. Almost 200,000 Japanese went to Brazil before Pearl Harbor, and a great many also found their way to Peru. This latter emigration has been described by the Japanese historian Toraji Irie. Many of these Japanese came from the Ryukyu Islands,

[47] Roger Bastide and Florestan Fernandes, *Brancos e negros em São Paulo: Ensaio sociológico sobre aspectos da formação, manifestações atuais e efeitos do preconceito de côr na sociedade paulistana* (2nd ed., São Paulo, 1959), pp. 78–79.

[48] Watt Stewart, *Chinese Bondage in Peru* (Durham, N.C., 1951); Eugenio Chang Rodríguez's "Chinese Labor Migration into Latin America in the Nineteenth Century," *Revista de Historia de América*, XLVI (Mexico City, 1958), 375–99, is very sketchy. As to the East Indians, see Dwarka Nath's *A History of the Indians in British Guiana* (London, 1950). See, finally, Sidney Mintz, "The Role of Forced Labor in Nineteenth Century Puerto Rico," *Caribbean Historical Review*, II (1951).

such as Okinawa. After the Second World War people from these islands, now under United States control, have continued to migrate to Latin America. Their emigration has been studied in detail by J. L. Tigner.[49]

Although Asiatic immigration has received some attention from a few historians and other students, there is only a general treatment, a survey by Anita Bradley published in 1942, that is very brief and now out-of-date.[50] Latin American reactions against the Asiatics soon were reflected in discriminatory legislation, sometimes subtle, other times more outspoken. In one country after another, the doors of entry were closed to these immigrants. A special study would be worthwhile. Isolated outbursts of aggression against the Asiatics also occurred, similar in character to the persecutions of the Chinese in California. Charles Cumberland has given an interesting account of one of these tragic outbursts in Mexico during the Revolution.[51]

Although their phenotype and strong cultural traditions, which extended even to the poorest strata, tended to make the assimilation of immigrants from the Far East problematical, no comparable difficulties seem to have affected the many immigrants from the Near East. The immigration of the "Turcos" and "Syrio-Lebanese" into Latin America is a subject awaiting research. Individuals of this ethnic background even appear in contemporary national politics, a domain which otherwise seems closed to non-European immigrants and their descendants.[52]

[49] Toraji Irie, "History of Japanese Migration to Peru," HAHR, XXXI (1951), 437–52, 648–64; XXXIII (1952), 73–82; James L. Tigner, "The Ryukyuans in Bolivia," XLIII (1963), 206–29; *The Okinawans in Latin America* (Washington, D.C., 1954, multigr., Pacific Science Board, National Research Council). An interesting aspect of Japanese immigration is dealt with by Tigner in "Shindo Remmei: Japanese Nationalism in Brazil," HAHR, XLI (1961), 515–32. See, finally, Hiroshi Saito, *O japonês no Brasil: Estudo de mobilidade e fixação* (São Paulo, 1961), and Y. Fuji and T. L. Smith, *The acculturation of Japanese immigrants in Brazil* (Gainesville, Fla., 1959).

[50] Anita Bradley, *Trans-Pacific Relations of Latin America: An Introductory Essay and Selected Bibliography* (New York, 1942).

[51] Charles C. Cumberland, "The Sonora Chinese and the Mexican Revolution," HAHR, XL (1960), 191–223. On the Chinese in Mexico prior to 1910, see Moisés González Navarro in *Historia moderna . . . El Porfiriato: Vida social*, ed., D. Cosío Villegas, pp. 166–72.

[52] T. J. Bastani, *O líbano e os libaneses no Brasil* (Rio de Janeiro, 1945), has not been available for consultation. See the short note by Donald W. Bray,

The subject of the changes that the ethnic map of Latin America has suffered in the course of the last hundred years is not exhausted by any means with reference to immigration from Europe and Asia. In the wake of the techno-commercial revolution of the mid-nineteenth century, the need for labor both for plantations and other purposes (such as the digging of the Panama Canal) often caused considerable migrations within Latin America itself. In the Caribbean, the sturdy Negroes of Jamaica were attracted in great numbers to the Central American and Mexican coasts. Haitian migrant labor went to Cuba and the Dominican Republic.[53] Highland Indians settled down as workers on the plantations along the Caribbean as well as along the Pacific. We know much less about the history of these migrations than we do about immigration from outside.

Finally, it should be kept in mind that the contemporary processes of migration from the countryside and urbanization are bringing about other changes in the ethnic composition of Latin American populations. The real impact of this phenomenon is perhaps recent enough to escape historical perspective, but the antecedents may deserve the attention of the historian.

In summary, let us state that the European and Asiatic immigration has been studied in a considerable number of scattered monographs, but that many lacunae remain. Often the subject has not been placed in a proper historical context and the aspect of inter-ethnic relations (and intermarriage) has received rather little attention. There is a need for comprehensive studies. With regard to the history of internal Latin American migrations that are of ethnic interest, almost everything remains to be done.

Ideological Aspects: Indigenismo and Re-evaluation of Mestizaje

The history of ideas in Latin America during the national period has been dealt with rather often in the Spanish and Portuguese lan-

---

"The Political Emergence of Arab-Chileans, 1952–1958," *Journal of Inter-American Studies*, IV (Gainesville, Fla., 1962), no. 4.

[53] See, for example, Victor C. Dahl, "Alien Labor on the Gulf of Mexico, 1880–1900," *The Americas*, XVII (Washington, D.C., 1960/1961), 21–35.

guages. On the other hand, this aspect on the whole has been neglected by foreign students. The ideological aspect of the race and class problem is obviously very important. The attitudes and programs related to ethnic conditions in contemporary Latin America reflect the impact of new ideas.

Whereas the Indian and to some extent the Negro now and then provided writers of the Romantic era with a theme, early Liberal thought gave them little attention.[54] To the more comprehensive Positivist and Social Darwinist school of the latter part of the nineteenth century, the abundance of Indian and Negro "blood" in Latin America became a source of serious concern, particularly under the impact of European racist ideas as conceived by Count Gobineau, Houston Chamberlain, Vacher de Lapouge, and others. It has to be kept in mind that the anthropological science of their time rested partly on racist assumptions. The existence of "inferior" races and mixtures was hardly questioned.[55]

In this light, it is really surprising to notice that some Latin American positivists evidently escaped the pitfalls of racism, stressing instead the role of education as a redeemer of the dark-skinned masses from their inferior status. On the other hand, Latin America also produced a number of extreme racists. It is perhaps symptomatic, though, that some influential racist writers such as Carlos Octavio Bunge and José Ingenieros, both Argentines, were of immigrant background. On the other hand, in countries where the majority of the inhabitants remained more or less dark-skinned, racism lead either to extreme pessimism or adopted more subtle and artificial forms. In Chile it was able to merge with the nationalist feelings of a successful nation by pointing to the "Gothic" background of the Chilean conquistadores. The mestizaje between them and Indians of the quality of the Araucanos had to produce a better

---

[54] Interesting points of view are presented by Charles Hale in "José María Luis Mora and the Structure of Mexican Liberalism," HAHR, XLV (1965), 213–18.

[55] See two interesting studies by Martin B. Stabb, "Martí and the Racists," *Hispania*, XL (Baltimore, Md., 1957), 434–39, and "Indigenism and Racism in Mexican Thought, 1857–1911," *Journal of Inter-American Studies*, I (1959), 405–23; also Fernando Ortiz, "Martí y las razas de librería," *Cuadernos Americanos*, XXI (Mexico City, 1945), 185–98.

breed than in other parts of Latin America! Racism also could serve the interests of an oligarchy by classifying the "white" elite as vastly superior to mixed or dark plebeians. This was the original European version of racism, even more easily applied in the multiracial environment of Latin America.[56]

Although one or another of the Latin American racist writers, a category that has lingered on until very recent days, has attracted the critical attention of modern students (Martin Stabb for example), a comprehensive study of this interesting aspect of Latin American "*Geistesgeschichte*" remains to be written. Of course, a calm and objective study would be more revealing than a polemical approach.

It is truly remarkable that *Indigenismo*, as both a cultural movement and social action program, grew out of an environment that was imbued with racism. A program of study and advancement of the Indians was approved by Porfirio Díaz of Mexico prior to his being overthrown, and another program of protection of the long-neglected forest tribes of Brazil was started at the same time (1910) thanks to the efforts of a positivist, General Rondon. The Luso-Africanist school regards as its founder Nina Rodrigues of Bahia, himself a racist convinced of the inferiority of the Negroids. The author of the first real "Indigenista" novel, the Bolivian Alcides Arguedas, was racist in his concept of the effects of miscegenation. This paradox has been observed in recent studies but is far from being well known.[57]

On the other hand, the later development of "indigenista" thought and social action in Mexico has been the subject of extensive writings. Appearing in such journals as *America Indígena*, these articles

[56] Charles Griffin, "Francisco Encina and Revisionism in Chilean History," HAHR, XXXVII (1957), 7–8, 26; Frederick Pike, *Chile and the United States: The Emergence of Chile's Social Crisis and the Challenge to United States Diplomacy* (South Bend, Ind., 1963), 36, 289–92, 444–45 (bibliogr.).

[57] Juan Comas, *Ensayos sobre el indigenismo* (Mexico City, 1953), p. 70; Mathias Kiemen, "The Status of the Indian in Brazil after 1820," *The Americas*, XXI (Washington, D.C., 1965), 263–73. In my own article, "Race and Social Class in Twentieth Century Latin America," *Cahiers d'Histoire Mondiale*, VIII (1964), 302, I neglected the relationship between Positivism, Spencerism, and even Racism and the birth of the *indigenismo*.

have been written mostly by leaders of the movement itself. Among outside observations, the thoughtful analysis of Luis Villoro deserves to be mentioned. In the Andean region, Indigenismo forms an ingredient within the eclectic body of Aprista thought, which perhaps has been interpreted as a more systematic ideology than it really is by Harry Kantor.[58] The basic contradiction inherent in Indigenismo (that is, the aim of incorporating the "Indian" into society coupled with the concern for preserving the positive assets of his traditional culture), has been confronted in different ways by Indigenista theoreticians. Some (Gamio and others) have stressed the need for preserving the spiritual values of native culture. Leaving this aspect aside, a Mexican authority, Luis Mendieta y Núñez, asserts that the transformation of the Indian into a citizen is really more necessary from the point of view of national society than from the point of view of the Indian himself. In any case, Indigenistas are still walking a tightrope between the "colonialist" ideal of preserving the Indian through isolation and special protection, and imposed assimilation likely to produce "pochismo," that is, a kind of Lumpenproletariat. The achievements of the movement in political and social action must be assessed in this context.[59]

Notwithstanding the remarkable similarity between indigenista social action and Spanish colonial policy, indigenismo as a way of cultural expression forms a dialectical opposite to Hispanidad—that is, the stress on the Spanish tradition in Latin American culture. This conflict has coincided with political tendencies of the extreme left and the extreme right, especially since the 1930s. Although the conflict was stimulating to a certain point, the extremism of many participants has caused sterility in certain cases and propagandist turns that restrict the purely literary and artistic values of the works

[58] Luis Villoro, *Los grandes momentos del indigenismo en México* (Mexico City, 1950); Harry Kantor, *The Ideology and Program of the Peruvian Aprista Movement* (Berkeley and Los Angeles, 1953).

[59] A critical note is struck by Beate Salz in "Indianismo," *Social Research*, XI (1944), 441-69. See also Víctor Alba, *Las ideas sociales contemporáneas en México* (Mexico City, 1960), pp. 345-56. On the achievements of indigenismo as social action see Juan Comas, *La antropología social aplicada en México: Trayectoria y antología* (Mexico City, 1964).

produced. Of course, when raised to the status of official cultural expression, indigenismo, like every other cultural movement, is in particularly grave danger of losing its spiritual values. The risk of becoming an inverted racism also is always present in the case of indigenismo. But even so, it seems that the vitality of the indigenista movement has no counterpart on the side of Hispanidad, whose artificial character has become more and more obvious. Nevertheless, its evolution and inspiration deserve an unbiased analysis. The short study by Bailey Diffie is now out-of-date.[60]

Africanism in the Caribbean and Brazil is a phenomenon parallel to indigenismo; but it is considerably weaker since it lacks a significant program of social action. To a great extent Africanist intellectuals have devoted themselves to the study or use of Negro folklore in the New World. The growth of the movement was impressive during the 1930s. In Brazil, thanks to the initiative of Gilberto Freyre, two Afro-Brazilian Congresses took place. The later books and statements of the enthusiastic and increasingly influential spokesman Freyre show a curious trend toward the idealization of the plantation past and an ethnocentric concern with so-called Luso-Tropicology and supposed Portuguese lack of prejudice. Instead of stimulating and supplementing a program of well-needed social action in favor of the obviously depressed Negro strata of society, the Freyre interpretation runs the risk of being used as an argument in favor of existing social conditions.[61] In the 1940s Brazil witnessed the growth of another movement born among certain Negro and mulatto intellectuals who rallied around the so-called *Teatro Experimental do Negro*. Criticizing other Africanist intellectuals—mostly whites—for dealing with the Negro as an exotic being, this group stressed that the Negro was Brazilian and should be studied as such. And not only studied. The Negro should be encouraged to

[60] B. V. Diffie, "The Ideology of Hispanidad," *The Hispanic American Historical Review*, XXIII (1943), 457–82.

[61] Gilberto Freyre, *New World in the Tropics* (New York, 1959). Stanley Stein, "Freyre's Brazil Revisited," HAHR, XLI (1961), 113, icily comments: "The perfervid regionalist who once exhumed the colonial past seems now enamored of a corpse."

improve his situation in society.[62] This effort seems to have had little impact, however. The vagueness and subtle character of prejudice and race concepts in Brazil's multiracial environment cannot easily be turned into a struggle along caste lines, as in the United States, a fact that probably few Brazilians regret.

Whereas Freyre has been stressing solidarity with Portugal and its colonialism *sui generis*, a Brazilian historian, José Honório Rodrigues, has recently dared to express exactly the opposite view. While the historical basis he suggests for Afro-Brazilian friendship and alliance seems somewhat strange (the slave trade), common underdevelopment and nationalist bitterness born of previous exploitation may seem more realistic.[63] In any case, Rodrigues's theorizing sheds an interesting light on the alternatives to the Latin Americans' traditional adherence to occidental values. His work was an intellectual counterpart to the independent approach to international politics taken by Jânio Quadros.

Both indigenismo and africanismo have helped to stimulate a reevaluation of mestizaje. Modern genetics has confirmed the fact that miscegenation as such has no evil effects. The marginality of so many mixed-bloods can be ascribed only to the effects of prejudice and an unhealthy social environment characterized by promiscuity and illegitimacy. But in the eagerness of defending mestizaje, some Latin American intellectuals have gone too far. The phenomenon has been idealized and sublimized in order to serve as a national symbol. The loose, rhetorical use of a term that only implies the mixture of human races is responsible for more than scholarly confusion. Thus used, mestizaje, in common with both indigenismo and Hispanidad, stresses the biological aspect of human history, as Angel Rosenblat has keenly observed.[64] It will seem that in fact the three concepts of indigenismo, Hispanidad, and mestizaje are but three expressions of the same desire of the inhabitants of the New World. The three concepts are needed in order to prolong the historical

[62] An account by a partisan of this group in A. Guerreiro Ramos, *Introdução crítica à sociologia brasileira* (Rio de Janeiro, 1957). Compare with Charles Wagley (ed.), *Race and Class in Brazil* (Paris, 1952), pp. 50–151.

[63] J. H. Rodrigues, *Brasil e Africa: outro horizonte* (Rio de Janeiro, 1961).

[64] Rosenblat, *Población* . . . , II, 187–88.

perspective, be it by looking at the Indian, the Iberian, or the Ibero-American past.[65] One or another is being used to build up nationalism in the Latin American countries. The enhancement of mestizaje may be chosen as a better alternative to the old-fashioned Hispanidad approach. However, what serves as a link with the past may not serve as a means of understanding the existing reality or as a guide for the future. The ideological stress on "race"—for all the sublimization of the term—finds itself in strange contrast to contemporary society in Latin America, where race mixture has become an almost imperceptible process and somatic and genealogical differences are losing much of their previous importance, even among the higher social strata. Though ethnic divisions are still strong in the Indo-American highlands and racial prejudice by no means absent, the basic problems of modern and future Latin America had best be spelled in nonracial terms.

This statement may be criticized for anticipating the results of more extensive research into the nature of recent intellectual trends in Latin America. My purpose is, however, to show the need of looking into the possible interrelation and affinity of ideas which seem superficially at least completely opposite. Indeed, the historian is needed for the analysis of ideas that draw all their strength from a real or, more often, idealized historical past.

Summary of Suggestions for Future Research

As we have seen, the questions related to *Race and Class in Latin America during the National Period* only to some extent have been touched by historical research. The topics and aspects that might prove rewarding for the historian abound. Let me list only a few that seem particularly urgent:

1. Post-emancipation ethnic conditions as reflected in administrative practice. How was the abolition of ethnic terms carried out or interpreted on different administrative levels?

2. To the extent that available records allow, more studies of the demographic evolution of ethnic groups, similar to George Kubler's

[65] Harold B. Davis, "Trends in Social Thought in Twentieth-Century Latin America," *Journal of Inter-American Studies*, I (1959), 64-65.

The Indian Caste of Peru. As far as slave-holding countries are concerned, special attention should be given to the evolution of the ratio between slaves, freedmen, and non-African low and middle groups.

3. A critical analysis and survey of travelogues and other descriptive sources for the history of different ethnic groups during the national period.

4. A study of the concept of race in the intellectual history of the Era of Emancipation.

5. Investigations into the role of the Wars of Independence and of later militarism as promoters of ethnosocial upward mobility.

6. The evolution of the rural sector offers an almost boundless area for historical investigations. Monographs are very much needed on regional developments, both with regard to land tenure and labor systems. Historical studies of the survival or destruction of representative "indigenous" communities are also needed. An investigation of the impact of the mid-nineteenth century economic change on selected indigenous communities seems to be most urgently required.

7. Investigations of the nature and extent of manumissions of slaves during the national era in both Spanish and Portuguese America would fill a great void.

8. The economic and social effects of abolition and the absorption of the emancipated Negroes into society deserve monographs in the case of such countries as Peru and Venezuela.

9. A comprehensive survey of Asiatic immigration into Latin America during the past hundred years. The evolution of discriminatory legislation also should be especially studied.

10. A study of the ethnic aspect of internal migrations in Latin America during the last hundred years.

11. An inquiry into the impact of European racism on Latin American thought. The possible importance of domestic traditions (from the colonial "Sociedad de Castas") in this connection, of course, should not be overlooked.

12. A study of the evolution of ideas selected to "Hispanidad" in Latin America and their relationship to the re-evaluation of mestizaje.

[230]

CHAPTER 11

The Concepts of Race and Class

and the Explanation of

Latin American Politics

Charles W. Anderson

The sudden renewal of interest in Latin America during the last decade
has resulted in the growth of a new generation of political scientists
anxious to re-examine the "conventional wisdom" regarding that area
of the world. Professor Charles W. Anderson of the University of
Wisconsin here demonstrates this interest as he surveys the literature
in the field and notes how uncritically it has usually treated class and
race as political phenomena. Although the concepts of race and class—
especially class—have been widely used as organizational and explanatory
devices both in textbooks and in studies of particular political problems,
very few have attempted either to define or to measure the political
characteristics of racial and class groups. Professor Anderson questions
the utility of class and race as central factors for the explanation of
Latin American politics and suggests empirical studies that could now
begin to test the current theory.

The study of Latin American politics[1] is characterized by hetero-

[1] I have defined the discipline of political science quite narrowly, basing these
observations only on the published writings of two groups: 1) professional
political scientists in the United States recognized as specialists in the Latin
American region; 2) a group of North American historians who have spe-
cialized in contemporary Latin American political history. As to sociologists,
and economists, I have included their contributions under the rubric "materials
borrowed from other fields."
I have restricted my comments to North Americans for a number of rea-

geneity of style and method. Political scientists have been tardy in systematizing their approach to this region of the world. In an excellent essay summarizing the achievements of political science in Latin American studies, Merle Kling points out the predominance of "traditional" studies, highly descriptive in nature and stressing constitutional structure, contemporary history, and comprehensive, encyclopedic reporting on individual nations. Up until the late 1950s, little effort was made to define sharp-edged problems for investigation or to specify the major variables to be taken into consideration in political analysis.[2]

Such studies presupposed little in the way of common assumptions or unifying theory. Even recent efforts to "modernize" the study of Latin American politics probably have served more to increase diversity of approach to the subject than to create agreement on common propositions, concepts, and research objectives. Thus, although both Kling and Kalman Silvert have suggested general frameworks for studying certain problems in Latin American politics,[3] neither has succeeded in setting a "trend" for research in the field. Other scholars have attempted to apply general models or theories to Latin America. Thus, Robert Scott and George Blanksten attempted to

---

sons. First, only a rudimentary counterpart to the discipline of political science as practiced in the United States exists in Latin America. Second, the lines between political sociology and political science, between political analysis and action-oriented political writing, are much more difficult to define in Latin America. For similar reasons, I have excluded a number of well-known commentators on Latin American political affairs, among them those whose primary professional identification is with journalism. Thus, the community of scholars considered is in fact quite small. There were only 114 members of the American Political Science association who in 1960 indicated a special interest either in Latin American politics or inter-American affairs.

[2] Merle Kling, "The State of Research on Latin America; Political Science," in Charles Wagley (ed.), *Social Science Research on Latin America* (New York, 1964), pp. 168–213. For a related critique of the "state of the discipline," see Kalman H. Silvert, "American Academic Ethics and Social Research Abroad," *American Universities Field Staff Reports, West Coast South America Series*, XII (July, 1965).

[3] Kling, "Toward a Theory of Power and Political Instability in Latin America," *Western Political Quarterly*, IX (March, 1956), 21–35; Silvert, *The Conflict Society; Reaction and Revolution in Latin America* (New Orleans, 1961).

adapt interest group theory[4] and also to use the structural-functional approach borrowed from anthropology in interpreting the politics of the region—Blanksten in an essay in the pioneering work of Gabriel Almond on the politics of developing nations[5] and Scott in a treatment of the political culture of Mexico.[6] A similar effort to apply theories and concepts derived from the theoretical literature of political development to Latin America is to be found in Silvert's work on political modernization and national integration.[7] At present, one detects a new enthusiasm for the use of rigorous, quantitative, "behavioral" techniques. This interest, however, is so recent that, although a variety of research projects are currently underway, little has as yet been incorporated into the existent literature of the field.[8]

Given such diversity of interest and technique, it is almost surprising to find a great similarity in the assumptions and judgments made about the political systems of Latin America. There are, in fact, very large areas of implicit agreement among students of the subject regarding the most important factors which should be taken into account in the course of analyzing any Latin American political phenomenon. Furthermore, there is a marked consistency within the literature on the political qualities or characteristics that are to be imputed to these units of analysis. Thus, whether we are reading political science *circa* 1950 or 1965, we will find compatible judgments on the political properties of basic governmental institutions, political parties, major industrial and commercial groups, labor organizations, the army, the Church, the landholding system, the urbanization process, and, most important for our purposes here, social

---

[4] Robert Scott, *Mexican Government in Transition* (Urbana, 1959); George Blanksten, "Political Groups in Latin America," *American Political Science Review*, LIII (1959), 106–27.

[5] Blanksten, "The Politics of Latin America," in Gabriel Almond and James Coleman (eds.) *The Politics of Developing Areas* (Princeton, 1960).

[6] Scott, "Mexico: The Established Revolution," in Lucian W. Pye and Sidney Verba, *Political Culture and Political Development* (Princeton, 1965).

[7] Silvert, "National Values, Development, and Leaders and Followers," *International Social Science Journal*, XV (1963), 560–70.

[8] See below, notes 49–53. [ed.: as of 1966.]

classes and racial groups. The changes that occur over time in the interpretation of these fundamental building blocks for analysis and explanation probably owe more to changes in the data, to the emergence of new political movements and forces within Latin America, than to the development of new interpretive schemes or methods of analysis.

Whether the style be "traditional" or "modern," we will find considerable uniformity of emphasis and interpretation regarding such matters as executive dominance over the legislature, the basic taxonomies to be employed in describing political party systems, and the fundamental cleavages in such institutions as the military and the Church. Such social correlates as "Indianism" and "political disengagement" and "middle class" and "nationalism" are also highly consistent.

We may find satisfaction in the fact that, although political scientists may differ over method and approach, they agree on many of the political characteristics and problems of Latin American politics. It may be that after all we do have a theory of Latin American politics, even though as yet not satisfactorily synthesized, and that despite highly heterodox methods and analytic concerns, political scientists have arrived at similar perceptions and conclusions concerning the nature of the beast which they are studying. We should, however, be wary of such a conclusion. It may also be that we have developed a "conventional wisdom" regarding Latin American politics. It may be that we have not been sufficiently critical of our highly conventionalized assumptions and judgments. It may be that progress in the study of Latin American politics has been in some measure a matter of incorporating unexamined propositions into new analytic schemes rather than of questioning the adequacy or validity of the propositions themselves.

It is within this context that I would describe the use of class and race as explanatory variables in the study of Latin American politics. *Use* is the controlling word. As we shall see, there has been little research by political scientists *into* the political properties of class and racial groups. Class and race are generally independent variables in political science research. Characteristically, they are factors to be taken into account in the explanation of something else. Seldom have the political properties of class and racial groups been the explicit targets of research.[9]

Most political scientists would agree that class and race are fundamental political cleavages in the Latin America area. Most use quite similar classificatory schemes in considering such phenomena, though few find them adequate. Statements about the political characteristics of class and racial groups are always highly qualified. There has developed a movement away from one-track class taxonomies (upper, middle, and lower) and toward two-track schemes (new and old upper, middle, and lower classes). Today, many political scientists would accept Silvert's distinction between the "traditional" agrarian and clerical and the "modern" industrial and secular upper class, the older service and commercial and the new professional and white collar middle class, and the agrarian and urban-industrial lower class.[10] Other characteristic classificatory schemes include Scott's consideration of Mexico in terms of unintegrated Indians, the lower class, small town middle class, and the urban middle and upper classes,[11] and Alexander Edelmann's discussion of the old landed aristocracy, the new managerial elite, the middle sectors, and the rural and urban lower classes.[12]

Race is handled either as a correlate of class (as in the classical association of white and upper class, mestizo and middle class, Indian and lower class) or as a pattern of cleavage parallel to class, as, for example, a white-Indian dichotomy is superimposed on and related to a taxonomy of social class. The white-Indian or white-Indian mestizo scheme is the only racial taxonomy really used for explanatory purposes by political scientists, although other racial patterns are often described. I know of no political study where the white-negro dichotomy is considered a basic political problem.

[9] I know of only one non-Marxian theoretical framework for the study of Latin American politics which directly focuses on class factors, and this seems relatively unimpressive: Robert L. Peterson, "Social Structure and the Political Process in Latin America: A Methodological Reexamination," *Western Political Quarterly*, XVI (1963), 885–96.

[10] Silvert, *The Conflict Society*.

[11] Scott, *Mexican Government in Transition*, Ch. 3.

[12] Alexander Edelmann, *Latin American Government and Politics* (New York, 1965), Ch. 3.

Class and race are often used to differentiate and distinguish the various political systems of Latin America. A good part of the conventional wisdom of Latin American politics concerns such matters as the relationship between democratic practice and the predominance of the middle class in such nations as Uruguay and Costa Rica, and the distinctiveness of such political systems from those of the "Indian" nations, including Bolivia, Ecuador, Guatemala, and Peru, where the political process is confined to the white upper and middle classes.

In using race and class to interpret the dynamics of Latin American politics, most studies adopt as a point of departure some notion of an hierarchical and relatively rigid social structure which is assumed to be more or less symmetric with the conditions of political power and influence in society. Thus, the "upper classes" are invested with the property of "power" based apparently on traditional status, control of economic resources, and access to governmental institutions. The "power" of the upper classes is "challenged" by the middle sectors, who possess the skills and attitudes appropriate to the operation of modern, Western political and economic institutions. They are nationalistic and seek certain basic social and economic reforms. Their chosen instruments of political action are the political party and the associational interest group. The lower classes are presumed to be more the objects or subjects of political action than participants in the political process. Although the organized urban lower class may have some share of influence and power, both urban and rural lower classes tend to be politically ineffectual and indifferent, though most analyses include a vague and ominous warning that such conditions are not likely to continue. In nations where the observation is appropriate, the Indians are distinguished from the lower class. Although subject to the "power" of the upper class, they are essentially unassimilated and apart from the political processes of the nation.[13]

As we shall see, considerable uncertainty, ambiguity, and frustration attend the application of this rudimentary class model to the analysis of Latin American politics. No one is very clear as to the precise meaning of the "power" of the upper class, for example.

[13] Blanksten, "Political Groups in Latin America."

Few political scientists are willing to accept the concept of the "middle sectors" as defining a meaningful, cohesive political group. Judgments on the political attitudes, behaviors, and political potential of the urban lower class are often so highly qualified as to be virtually meaningless.

Most of the political characteristics that political scientists impute to class and racial groups in Latin America are borrowed from the research of colleagues in other disciplines. Although students of Latin American politics frequently accuse their fellow Latin Americanists of not asking appropriate political questions, most judgments in the literature on the political characteristics of Indian groups are based on the work of anthropologists, while our concept of the political behavior of the middle class derives from studies by historians and sociologists. Our very rudimentary notions concerning the political attributes of the traditional upper class may come from economists or even from novelists. It is interesting that the bibliography for the chapter on social class in Edelmann's textbook on Latin American politics contains references to works of four anthropologists, seven sociologists, two economists, two historians, one geographer, one Latin American social commentator, and one political scientist.[14] The bibliography to William Stokes's chapter on social classes in the contemporary period includes references to works of seventeen anthropologists, three economists, fifteen sociologists, three historians, two geographers, and three political scientists. Twenty-three of the authors cited by Stokes could not be identified with any specific social science discipline.[15]

In surveying the treatment of class and race in the study of Latin American politics, we will first consider the use of these concepts as organizational and explanatory devices in textbooks on Latin American politics and in studies of the total political systems of individual Latin American nations. Then we shall discuss the use of race and class as explanatory variables in the study of particular problems or phenomena of Latin American politics. Next, we will consider political studies that actually have attempted to define or measure the political characteristics of class or racial groups. We

[14] Edelmann, *Latin American Government and Politics*, pp. 83–84.
[15] W. S. Stokes, *Latin American Politics* (New York, 1959), pp. 25–32.

will conclude with some questions about the applicability of the concepts of race and class in the study of Latin American politics and some suggestions for research in this field.

Race and Class in Latin American Politics Textbooks

The extent to which political scientists are concerned with the factors of race and class and the way they use these factors in explaining Latin American politics as a whole are perhaps best revealed through examination of textbooks in the field. There are two basic ways of organizing textbooks on Latin American politics. In the 1950s and early 1960s the "topical" method of organization, in which separate chapters are devoted to critical factors of politics in the region as a whole, appeared to be more popular than the nation-by-nation approach.

Of the nine major textbooks using a topical approach which have been published in the past generation, race and class appear as critical organizing variables in only two. William Stokes's 1959 volume includes the most extensive and detailed treatment of such concepts. The first two chapters of Stokes's text are devoted to consideration of social classes; racial groups are looked upon as correlates of class status. Independent consideration is given to the class-race system in the colonial and contemporary periods. Furthermore, Stokes's text differs from all other texts in the field by treating race and class as key explanatory themes for an entire theory of Latin American politics. For Stokes, the failure of constitutional democracy and liberal economic practice in Latin America is directly attributable to the rigidities of class lines and the tendency to authoritarianism implicit in a hierarchically organized society.

Class and race are also critical organizing variables in Alexander Edelmann's recent text.[16] These concepts are described as "social fountainheads of political action." The separate chapter devoted to these factors uses a goodly amount of contemporary sociological and anthropological material. The concepts developed in this chapter, however, do not really carry through the book in a systematic explanation of Latin American politics.

[16] Edelmann, *Latin American Government and Politics.*

THE CONCEPTS OF RACE AND CLASS

Three other topical textbooks give some attention to the political qualities of race and class, but the consideration is less central and less critical to the total treatment than that of the Stokes and Edelmann books. Karl M. Schmitt and David Burks[17] consider race and class among other factors that set the stage for consideration of the dynamics of Latin American politics, giving approximately equal emphasis to these factors and the Latin American political *Weltanschauung*, "economic considerations" (including inflation, foreign investment, population problems, as well as such class-related problems as agrarian reform), interest groups, and political parties. Martin C. Needler, in his shorter volume, *Latin American Politics in Perspective* (Princeton, 1963), considers race and class along with "The Colonial Heritage" and "Issues in the Evolution of Latin American Politics" in an introductory chapter on political culture. Asher N. Christensen, in an older book,[18] adopts something like a shotgun approach toward the "conditioning factors" of Latin American politics, including attention to race and class along with the colonial system, geography, demography, religion, and economics. In none of these books, it should be noted, are observations on race and class systematically related to the remainder of the materials covered. With the exception of Stokes, all topically organized texts giving priority attention to race and class use the concepts more as an organizational device, a central focus in one of a series of more or less independent chapters, rather than as an integrating theme for the entire book.

The four remaining textbooks treating of Latin American politics from a topical approach give only passing notice to the phenomena of race and class. William Pierson and Federico Gil[19] adopt basically a historical and institutional approach, and although they note the importance of class cleavage in their introductory chapter, they dispose of the topic in less than a page. The influential text edited

---

[17] Karl M. Schmitt and David D. Burks, *Evolution or Chaos: Dynamics of Latin American Government and Politics* (New York, 1963).

[18] Asher N. Christensen, *The Evolution of Latin American Government* (New York, 1951).

[19] William W. Pierson and Federico G. Gil, *Governments of Latin America* (New York, 1957).

by Harold E. Davis[20] gives only passing mention to race and class as a variable in the chapter entitled "A Changing Society and Economy," although the concepts are used as explanatory devices in the consideration of some other subjects, particularly in George Blanksten's use of the notion of rigid class structure to explain revolution in Latin America. R. A. Gomez's short text[21] adopts a highly institutional approach, in which there is no theory of class or race beyond a highly rudimentary treatment of the role of the "oligarchs." In Miguel Jorrín's text, class and racial cleavage is not explicitly considered but is to some extent assumed in consideration of such topics as "labor and the state" and "government and business." [22]

Three Latin American politics textbooks adopt a nation-by-nation approach. Austin F. MacDonald's classic textbook[23] deals primarily with contemporary history and governmental institutions. Race and class do not loom large in the explanation of the politics of any of the Latin American nations. In an introductory chapter, MacDonald considers the "failure of democracy" in Latin America in terms of five factors: the colonial heritage, lack of education, "the tradition of force and fraud," *caudillismo,* and the influence of the church. Though several of these could be considered as class-related factors, they are not explicitly so treated by MacDonald. James Busey's short text[24] introduces a nation-by-nation treatment of Latin America with emphasis on the "cleavages" that prevent "an agreement on the rules of the political game." The "Heritage of Feudalism" is the central theme of the introductory chapter. This initial emphasis on class conflict, however, is developed through consideration of the individual nations only to a limited extent. Finally, in the nation-by-nation text edited by Martin Needler,[25] the "social and economic

[20] Harold E. Davis (ed.), *Government and Politics in Latin America* (New York, 1958).

[21] R. A. Gomez, *Government and Politics in Latin America* (New York, 1960).

[22] Miguel Jorrín, *Governments of Latin America* (New York, 1953).

[23] Austin F. MacDonald, *Latin American Politics and Government* (New York, 1954).

[24] James Busey, *Latin America: Political Institutions and Processes* (New York, 1964).

[25] Martin C. Needler (ed.), *Latin American Political Systems* (Princeton, 1964).

system" is one of five topics considered by each author, and rudimentary analyses of class and racial systems are characteristic of most of the essays.

If textbooks represent a distillation of research in the field, if they indicate what the profession would have North Americans know about the general characteristics of Latin American politics, a consideration of the available volumes would seem to suggest that certain ideas about class and race are considered important to an understanding of Latin American politics. Most texts, however, fail to demonstrate the significance of such concepts. Although discussed under various rubrics, race and class are generally treated as "background" material, as "setting" or "context" for consideration of institutions and processes more particularly political. With the possible exception of the Stokes text, nowhere do we find that the propositions advanced about race and class have much to do with the explanation of political processes and institutions.

Race and Class in Studies of Individual Nations

Apart from textbooks, the most characteristic genre of North American writing on Latin American politics has been the "nation-study," the comprehensive treatment of the political system of a particular Latin American country, or the consideration of a particular regime within an individual nation. Again, some notion of the extent to which political scientists are concerned with the problems of race and class, and the use they make of these concepts, may be gained by a consideration of this literature.

Out of sixteen of the most important nation-studies central to the literature in English on Latin American politics, race and class appear as major explanatory principles in only eight. The treatment of the problem of race and class varies widely. George Blanksten's work on the Perón regime in Argentina[26] deals with a political movement in which class appeal played a major role. The same may be said of the work of Robert Alexander, who is not a political scientist, on Bolivia and Venezuela,[27] as well as of Harry Kantor's

[26] Blanksten, *Perón's Argentina* (Chicago, 1953).
[27] Robert Alexander, *The Bolivian National Revolution* (New Brunswick, 1958) and *The Venezuelan Democratic Revolution* (New Brunswick, 1964).

studies of Peru and Costa Rica.[28] Kalman Silvert's discussion of Guatemala includes the most extensive discussion of the relationship between governmental institutions and the culture of Indian groups.[29] There is, however, also considerable discussion of this theme in Blanksten's book on Ecuador.[30] Only Robert Scott, in his work on Mexico, really provides a rigorous taxonomy of social classes.[31]

Among nation-studies that do not use race and class as central themes, William Stokes's study of Honduras considers the problem, but dismisses class and race as having little political significance.[32] In the remaining works, class and race are hardly considered at all.[33]

The Use of Race and Class in Explaining Latin American Politics

A consideration of texts and nation-studies gives us some impression of the extent to which political scientists have been concerned with the problems of race and class in Latin America. What is more significant, however, and at the same time problematic, is the way in which students of Latin American politics have used the concepts of race and class to explain the distinctive characteristics of political life in this region.

The problem that has most concerned political scientists dealing with Latin America has been that of explaining why democratic political practices and institutions have not been characteristic of

[28] Harry Kantor, *The Ideology and Politics of the Peruvian Aprista Movement* (Berkeley, 1953) and *The Costa Rican Election of 1953* (Gainesville, 1958).

[29] Silvert, *Guatemala: An Area Study in Government* (New Orleans, 1954).

[30] Blanksten, *Ecuador: Constitutions and Caudillos* (Berkeley, 1951).

[31] Scott, *Mexican Government in Transition*.

[32] Stokes, *Honduras: An Area Study in Government* (Madison, 1950).

[33] Russell H. Fitzgibbon, *Uruguay: Portrait of a Democracy* (New Brunswick, 1954); Philip B. Taylor, Jr., *Government and Politics of Uruguay* (New Orleans, 1962); James L. Busey, *Notes on Costa Rican Democracy* (Boulder, 1962); John Martz, *Central America: The Crisis and the Challenge* (Chapel Hill, 1954) and *Colombia: A Contemporary Political Survey* (Chapel Hill, 1962); Ronald Schneider, *Communism in Guatemala: 1944–1954* (New York, 1959); William Tucker, *The Mexican Government Today* (Minneapolis, 1957).

many nations in the region, and related to this, why political instability, dictatorship, and the use of violence in politics have been so endemic to the Latin American area.

In explaining Latin America's frequent deviations from Anglo-American norms of political conduct, political scientists almost universally adopt two related lines of interpretation. In general the distinctive characteristics of Latin American politics are looked upon as being due either to the heritage of Hispanic political culture or to the social structures present in the region. The two are, of course, interrelated. It is generally assumed that the Hispanic colonial legacy has a great deal to do with the class system of the region. The two arguments are remarkably persistent. For example, Martin Needler begins a discussion of the explanation of Latin American politics by criticizing both:

Explanations along these lines, however, while plausible enough so long as one considers only the American republics themselves, lose their force when one tries to apply them on a wider scale. Poverty and illiteracy have after all been the rule in human societies, in the stable and orderly ones, too; while on the other hand a politics of violence, a "Latin American" type of politics, is becoming visible in countries that have never known Spanish or Portuguese rule.[34]

Needler proposes the concept of the "legitimacy vacuum"—lack of a consensus on authority and the rules of the game of politics—as an alternative explanatory factor. When he comes to consider *why* such a legitimacy vacuum exists in Latin America, however, his discussion rests largely upon the character of the Hispanic colonial system and the rigidities and cleavages inherent in the social structure.

Perhaps the most complete statement of the conventional wisdom used in assessing the failure of democracy in Latin America is that contained in the symposium "The Pathology of Democracy in Latin America" published in the *American Political Science Review* for March, 1950. A consideration of the causes of democratic failure presented by the three contributors to this symposium reveals the relationship between class and race-related explanatory propositions

[34] Needler, *Latin American Politics in Perspective*, p. 33.

[243]

and other factors conventionally used in discussing the peculiar phenomena of Latin American politics. Thus, W. Rex Crawford, expressing the "sociologist's viewpoint," stresses the nonassimilation of Indians, individualism, family loyalty, corruption, the lack of a middle class with appropriate values, and the absence of a tradition of self-government at local levels as key factors contributing to the "pathology" of democracy in the region. Sanford Mosk, speaking as an economist, stresses the lack of freedom implicit in the landholding system, instability generated by severe economic fluctuations, low standards of living fostering political oligarchy, and foreign economic intervention in politics. Russell Fitzgibbon, expressing the political scientist's point of view, deals with the lack of a tradition of self-government, excessive individualism, the "authoritarian" influence of Catholicism, the lack of political integration, class inequality, U.S. foreign policy, the presence of unassimilated Indian populations, illiteracy, the prevalence of a negative attitude toward politics, the lack of a free press, the imperfections of political parties and elections, negative attitudes toward social legislation, and the influence of the military.

The language of political science has changed over the years, yet the assumptions made about the detrimental effect which the prevalent Latin American class system has on democratic practice remain remarkably consistent. Although the argument may be expressed in different ways, although different writers may emphasize different facets of the problem, there is, nonetheless, a high level of agreement among political scientists on the subject. Thus, Russell Fitzgibbon, in the article cited above, states that: "If loyalty to a class, whether a proletariat in the professional sense or an elite group, supersedes the common loyalty then democracy suffers accordingly." [35] In more modern language, such a failure of political community, the sense that those things that divide us are more important than those that unite us, is, of course, central to Needler's concept of the "legitimacy vacuum," as it is to the close correspondence between "national integration" and democratic practice in many recent studies.

[35] Fitzgibbon, "The Pathology of Democracy in Latin America: A Symposium," *American Political Science Review*, XLIV (1950), 124.

A slightly different perspective on the problem is that provided by William Stokes. He stresses the "belief system," the incompatibility between the hierarchic assumptions on which the Latin American social structure is founded and the egalitarian tenets of democratic theory. For Stokes, when dignity and power are monopolized by one class, political privilege and favoritism are no more than expectable. Furthermore, the hierarchical nature of the class system leads to the conviction that "authority" must impose solutions, rather than to the presumption that the individual will assume responsibility for the quality of political and social life.[36] To stress such "psychocultural variables" is completely consistent with Silvert's discussions of the implications of "traditional" and "modern" orientations toward political life.[37]

Fundamentally, however, the restrictive effect of the class and race system on political participation is presumed to inhibit democratic development and so explains the disparity between political practice in Latin America and the democratic norm. For most students of Latin American politics, class and racial barriers are fundamental factors in restricting the "scope" of the effective political process. Thus, George Blanksten writes of Ecuador:

The "national life" of Ecuador has continued to be dominated by a small ruling class. These "whites" constitute approximately twenty per cent of the population of the republic. The Ecuadorian political process rests on a brand of anarchy or chaos within the ruling class. This condition is occasionally referred to by Ecuadorians as "democracy in the Greek sense"; a considerable degree of liberty and equality has developed within the "white" group as far as intra-class behavior is concerned. The nation's rigid class system imposes an impressively strong barrier between the "whites" and the overwhelming mass of the people of the country.[38]

Although not totally sanguine about the direct correspondence between popular participation and democratic practice, Kalman

[36] Stokes, *Latin American Politics*, pp. 24–25.

[37] Silvert, *The Conflict Society*, and more particularly, "National Values, Development, and Leaders, and Followers," *International Social Science Journal*, and (with Frank Bonilla) "Education and the Social Meaning of Development: A Preliminary Statement," American Universities Field Staff (Mimeo., 1961).

[38] Blanksten, *Ecuador*, pp. 169–70.

Silvert's comparison of the class and race-related characteristics of political life in the different Latin American nations is an expression of propositions that most political scientists would endorse:

Caste-like racial distinctions and a sharp cultural cut between the city and the country make popular sovereignty and the dispersion of political power at best a very limited possibility in such countries as Guatemala. The homogeneity of Argentina speeds communications, distributes aspirational goals almost universally, and promotes mass participation in politics for good or evil.[39]

Most political scientists have stressed the close relationship between the strength of the middle class and the viability of those institutions, processes, and attitudes characteristic of modern democratic practice. Given the fact that such an observation is little more than a bromide of political analysis generally, it is somewhat surprising that the factor should be so stressed in the explanation of Latin American politics. Perhaps it is only because conventional wisdom so long underlined the hierarchical character of the Latin American class systems that John Johnson's thesis that political change in Latin America had something to do with the "emergence of the middle sectors" could appear as a new departure in the analysis of Latin American politics.[40] Johnson imputes to the middle sectors the political characteristics of urbanization, belief in universal public education, belief that the future of their nations is tied to industrialization, nationalism, a desire for state intervention in the economy, and support for political parties. Despite the imprecision and circular reasoning of much "middle sectors" theorizing (for example, Schmitt and Burks's statement: "The middle class has been the most nationalistic of all classes. . . . This national consciousness may be attributed mainly to the fact that most intellectuals belong to the middle class"),[41] mention of the middle sectors theory is

[39] Silvert, *The Conflict Society*, p. 18.
[40] John J. Johnson, *Political Change in Latin America: The Emergence of the Middle Sectors* (Stanford, 1958).
[41] Schmitt and Burks, *Evolution or Chaos*, p. 49.

virtually obligatory in many types of contemporary political analysis, particularly in the study of political parties.[42]

Some applications of the middle sectors theory describe symbiotic relationships between these middle groups and other classes and political institutions. Hence, urban migration may involve a transfer of the *patrón* loyalty to the new party or union organizer.[43] Several studies have stressed the prevalence of middle-class orientations among the "reforming" elements of the armed forces.

Certain propositions about race and class have been widely used by political scientists in explaining both the incidence and the absence of democratic practice in Latin America. It is not surprising that these same propositions, in reverse, find widespread use in explanations of such political phenomena as violence, political instability, and dictatorship. William Stokes, in his classic study of violence as a power factor in Latin American politics, lists some of the explanations offered by Latin Americans for the high incidence of violence in Latin American political life.[44] Race and class-related propositions are very much in evidence. Stokes's catalogue of explanations includes: social pressures building up for generations; Marxist theories of class conflict; violence as essential to enforce *latifundia*-type land and labor relationships; ethnic, geographic, or climatological factors (that is, "hot blood," "warm climate"); the political infirmity of governments characterized by brutality and corruption; the use of violence to bring about democracy in the face of dictatorship; the "world militarist epidemic"; cultural conditioning (the *hidalgo* tradition—a man expresses his manhood through violence); and the adoption of Communist or anarcho-syndicalist ideologies.

In an insightful and imaginative article,[45] Merle Kling offers an

---

[42] See Federico G. Gil, *Genesis and Modernization of Political Parties in Chile* (Gainesville, 1963). I also have used the "middle sector" approach in studying political parties; see Charles W. Anderson, "Central American Political Parties: A Functional Approach," *Western Political Quarterly*, XV (March, 1962), 125–39.

[43] Schmitt and Burks, *Evolution or Chaos*, p. 53.

[44] Stokes, *Latin American Politics*, pp. 325–28.

[45] Kling, "Toward a Theory of Latin American Politics," *Western Political Quarterly*, IX (1956), 21–35.

explanation for instability in Latin America based on the assumption that "rigidities" of the social and economic structure are "static" elements of power in Latin America, whereas government offers a "shifting base" of economic power to those who have no satisfying place in the traditional class and race system, yet are ambitious and upwardly mobile. Government becomes "a special transformer through which pass the currents of economic ambition."

Implicit in many theories of Latin American politics is the assumption of massive class conflict, impending or actual. Characteristic of the genre is Vernon Fluharty's statement concerning Colombia:

The gaps between the classes in Colombia are so great and so rigid that in a time of social ferment violence is always potentially present. Even when social and economic resentments merely simmer below the surface, the stream of national life may give a deceptive appearance of placidity that belies the facts and misleads the observer.[46]

The political implications of the "revolution of rising expectations" have become an almost obligatory part of any analysis of Latin American politics:

For the first time, broad and important segments of society are profoundly conscious of the differentials in urban-rural, upper-class–lower-class, and Latin American-North American standards of living. . . . The change in attitudes,—preceding as it does substantial and rapid economic growth—has produced demands that cannot be immediately satisfied, and thus threatens the existing social, economic, and political structures.[47]

The assumption of the "coming revolution in Latin America" has become so fixed a part of the folklore of political interpretation that even when evidence is being presented to the contrary, it seems incumbent on the writer to add the ominous note of impending upheaval. For example:

The political activity of the slumdweller is at present minimal—he is apathetic and "alienated" from the political process—and today he is

[46] Vernon Fluharty, *Dance of the Millions* (Pittsburgh, 1957), p. 182.
[47] Schmitt and Burks, *Evolution of Chaos*, p. 45.

most logically considered as a social problem rather than a social force, as object, not as subject. This situation is unlikely to last indefinitely, however.[48]

In suggesting that we have accepted this doctrine of the "coming upheaval" somewhat uncritically, I do not mean to imply that I am opposed to basic reform in Latin America. Rather, I am merely suggesting that I find many such statements somewhat gratuitous. The arguments that appear in the literature in support of impending class conflict, and its related political repercussions, are highly conventionalized. Seldom do they reveal tough-minded investigation of basic presuppositions. Never have the various forms and consequences of social unrest been catalogued. The tendency is to foretell doom and drop the subject.

Political Characteristics of Class or Racial Groups

Finally, in considering the use of race and class in the explanations of Latin American politics, we should discuss the use of these concepts as independent variables, or categories for measuring the incidence of political characteristics. An example would be a study to determine the proportion of each social class which affirms a specific political opinion or attitude. Actually, at the moment of writing, few of these "behavioral" studies of Latin American politics have yet been incorporated into the literature. One hears of substantial research projects in a number of countries, inquiries into political socialization (Scott, Hess, Silvert), alienation (Kenneth Johnson), and basic attitudinal research (Daniel Goodrich, the SENDES project in Venezuela), but only fragmentary findings and research designs are presently available in other than privately circulated mimeographed form.

Among available studies of this type are Gabriel Almond and Sidney Verba's *The Civic Culture*, which includes a wide range of materials on political attitudes in Mexico, some of which are correlated with class. Other notable pioneering ventures include Silvert and Bonilla's most extensive effort to correlate class, political participation, religiosity, and attitudes toward nationalism and development among selected groups in Chile, Brazil, Argentina, and

[48] Needler, *Latin American Politics in Perspective*, p. 64.

[249]

Mexico.[49] The results of this survey have not yet been published in final form. In a pilot project, Daniel Goodrich and Edward Scott compared political orientations among students at two Panamanian secondary schools, one drawing primarily from the upper, and one from the middle and lower classes. Although they found somewhat more political cynicism among the lower- and middle-class students, as well as a greater social awareness and a diminished concern for tradition, attitudinal differences between the two groups were not really very sharp.[50] A brief research report by Robert Hess on political socialization in Chile might suggest that formal schooling has a markedly greater impact on the initial political information of working-class than upon middle-class children, but the data are really too limited for any conclusions to be drawn.[51]

I would be the last to suggest that quantification cures all ills, but it does seem pertinent to note that analysts of Latin American politics have been more concerned with manipulating the imputed political characteristics of class and racial groups into satisfying patterns of explanation than in discovering to what extent significant political characteristics are, in fact, class- and race-related. Seldom have political scientists used either class or race as an explicit target of research. Despite our affirmations of the actual or potential importance of the unassimilated Indian populations in the political life of Latin America, very few political scientists have actually studied politics within Indian communities. The most important studies of this type are Kalman Silvert's considerations of the orientation of Guatemalan Indian groups to political community, and the character of local government in Guatemalan Indian communities, and a rather suggestive study of the processes of political change in Indian Guatemala by Roland H. Ebel.[52]

[49] Silvert and Bonilla, "Education and the Social Meaning of Development."
[50] Daniel Goodrich and Edward Scott, "Developing Political Orientations of Panamanian Students," *Journal of Politics*, XXIII (February, 1961).
[51] Robert Hess, "The Socialization of Attitudes Toward Political Authority: Some Cross-National Comparisons," *International Social Science Journal*, XV (1963), 542–49.
[52] Silvert, *The Conflict Society*, Ch. 5, and *Guatemala*; Roland H. Ebel, "Political Change in Guatemalan Indian Communities," *Journal of Inter-American Studies*, VI (1964), 91–104.

Conclusions

Several conclusions can be drawn from our survey of the use of concepts of race and class in studying Latin American politics. First, race and class systems have been widely used to explain many of the peculiar phenomena of Latin American politics. Second, most of these explanations follow from the assumption of a rigid, hierarchically organized class- and race-structure. The political implications of social stratification in Latin America are virtually universally accepted among students of Latin American politics. Third, social classes and racial groups have been invested with specific "political characteristics" of attitude, interest, political style, political resources (or power), and ideology.

These observations suggest certain possibilities for further research in this field. Although I am loath to suggest specific priority targets for the investment of research resources, I would mention certain questions that trouble me about the existing literature. I would classify these questions under two general headings. First, there are problems of theoretical development, of critical reexamination of even the most "obvious" assumptions made about the political implications of class and racial systems of Latin America. Second, there are questions of empirical research, of the rigorous testing of propositions contained in the "conventional wisdom" regarding class- and race-related political characteristics of Latin American politics.

I approach the subject of a theoretical reexamination of the political implications of social structure with a certain trepidation, for in some academic quarters such questions are virtually taboo. To many scholars of Latin America, the suggestion that the political problems of the region may lie elsewhere than in the inequities of the social system is inconceivable. To many, it would seem the obligation of the North American scholar to demonstrate, as forcefully as possible, the need for sweeping social reform in the region. To reserve judgment, even for a moment, on the direct relationship between social structure and the need for reform, may cause one to be classed as a reactionary by one's colleagues. Given our concentration on the problems of change and reform, there is

[251]

a tendency to affirm enthusiastically such propositions as "The slow pace of agrarian reform in Latin America is due to the power of the landowner," despite the fact that one can find little systematic evidence in support of such a proposition, and despite such alternative or supplementary theoretical possibilities as the lack of qualified personnel, the difficulties of implementing such programs among largely unassimilated populations, or the simple fact that any major policy departure takes time to fulfill in any society. (Compare the pace of civil rights policy in the United States with agrarian reform programs in Latin America.) In any event, I am persuaded that it is more illiberal to insist upon a perception of the problem that may not be totally adequate than to examine critically even the most basic postulates of the case for reform in Latin America.

There is certainly a basic fuzziness about our correlation of hierarchical class- and race-structures with the conditions of political power in Latin America. Either explicitly or implicitly (because in so many studies observations on class structure are not systematically related to political dynamics) we tend to presume a "power elite" which simultaneously controls political, economic, and social institutions. But are social, economic, and political power identical in Latin America? Kling[53] has made an equally plausible case that those who have contested and held political power in Latin America have characteristically been those who did *not* possess either social or economic power. Johnson argues that "political change" in Latin America may be described in terms of the "emergence" of a middle group which did not fit comfortably into the class system.[54] But is Johnson really perceiving a process of change or has the relationship of holders of political power to the rigidities of the class system been fundamentally the same throughout the independence period? Is the "power" of the landowner that of influencing public policy, or is it more a matter of the lack of power in the state to change the traditional *patrón-peón* relationships of the *hacienda* system?

The case could be made (and there is not space to develop it fully here) that the class- and race-system of Latin America is not

[53] Kling, "Toward a Theory of Power."
[54] Johnson, *Political Change in Latin America.*

"reflected" in the political system, but that throughout the independent history of the region the state has been set against the traditional class- and race-system. The essential problem of reform in Latin America may not be that the state has been *unwilling* to advance liberal programs because it has been controlled by elites who have a vested interest in the status quo, but that the Latin American state has been *unable* to effect the reforms that have been so consistently and persistently enacted in constitutional document and statutory law alike, that the powers and resources of the state have been simply inadequate to the task of modernizing a deeply traditional society.

However, our answer to the question of whether political, economic, and social power are better understood as complementary or competitive in Latin America depends a great deal on our clarification of the concept of "power" itself. To illustrate the character of the problem, let me make the following argument. It is perfectly sensible, in political science, to define "power" as the capacity to enforce one's will upon others. It is also a central part of the conventional wisdom of Latin American politics that the "Indian" is essentially powerless, that he is the last recipient of all the relationships of influence and control in the political system. It might also be argued, however, that the most salient political characteristic of the Indian peoples of Guatemala and Peru, for example, is their capacity to resist cultural assimilation into the Hispanic part of the society. Sequentially, they have maintained their cultural integrity against the efforts of the Spaniards, the Church, the governments of the independent nations, and the modern-day technical assistance experts. It is not the will of the Indian that has been frustrated in his confrontation with Western civilization. It is rather the "modernizing elites" who have been powerless to create the nationally integrated, economically developed, Westernized societies to which they have aspired. And the main stumbling block to their achievement of these desperately sought goals has been the "power" of the Indian to resist change. Is the argument absurd? If it is, refutation will depend upon a more compelling definition of "power" than we have available at the moment.

In reexamining the implication of concepts of race and class in the study of Latin American politics, we might also ask whether these are the most useful "units" of political analysis. Although most political scientists avoid such grotesque shortcuts to political explanation as "the middle sectors believe" and the "rural masses demand" by careful qualification, the very fact that political studies point up race and class as fundamental analytic factors probably encourages this type of superficial consideration of Latin American politics. Most political scientists are disturbed by the "grossness" of the race and class variables, but they have as yet been unable to find widely acceptable alternatives for them.

It may be that our reliance on race and class as categories for political explanation has something to do with the belated political modernization of Latin America itself. Political science is like economics in that it relies heavily upon the amount and quality of data churned up by the society itself for its analyses. As economists have difficulty in describing and analyzing societies where much of the population lives outside the money economy, where the characteristic indicators of gross national product, currency flows, and so on are imperfect or deceptive, so political scientists have problems with societies where the systems of representation imperfectly reflect the differentiation of interest in the polity. Hence, our summary statements about the interests and attitudes of the "peasantry" are a reflection of an ignorance shared by statesman and political analyst alike. We lump together such diverse groups as smallholders, sharecroppers, the middle class, and so on. But in contemporary Latin American politics, when is a landowner *really* a landowner? He is also apt to be an industrialist, a businessman, a senator. Is it not possible that at some times and on some issues he makes political choices as an estate owner, and at other times, in other policy contexts, he brings the values and perceptions of other socioeconomic roles to his political life? Similarly, one generalization for the "peasantry" will not fit both the *patrón-peón* relationship and the choice to join a guerrilla band. It might be interesting to assess the different political roles available within different social classes.

To raise such questions about the utility of class and race as central factors for the explanation of Latin American politics, however, is not to suggest that we abandon the conventional wisdom out of hand. Rather, the prevailing theoretical apparatus for the study of Latin American politics would seem to offer many opportunities for testing long-accepted propositions and assumptions. It would be interesting to learn whether some of the political characteristics long imputed to class and racial groups actually prevail. It would also be important to find out something about the extent to which important political characteristics, such as party identification, "national" identification, and the techniques of political socialization, are in fact class and race-related. Finally, some of the class and race "units" that appear in the conventional wisdom would, in themselves, make excellent targets for research. In this respect, despite our many assumptions and propositions, our knowledge of the political world of unassimilated Indian groups and of newcomers to the cities is particularly limited.

It is easy to criticize the conventional wisdom concerning the political characteristics of race and class in Latin America. However, our tone need not be exclusively critical. Equally as important as the defects of the present literature is the fact that students of Latin American politics do share a large number of ideas about the political implications of race and class. Within the study of Latin American politics, there does exist a body of generally understood assumptions which can serve as a point of departure both for the creative theorist and the dedicated and skeptical fact-finder. And, after all, any body of theory exists only to be transcended.

CHAPTER 12

Research on Race
Relations in Brazil
Octavio Ianni

Brazil has long been of special interest to those concerned with race relations, and it is therefore not surprising that in that country a vigorous new group of social scientists excited by these questions has come to the fore. Octavio Ianni, of the University of São Paulo, is one of these scholars. He here surveys the state of knowledge on this subject in his country, attacks the myth of Brazilian racial democracy, and relates race and class by arguing that both that myth and the prejudice that belie it serve the interests of one dominant class. He also discusses studies of the acculturation of the Indian and the European immigrant, the gradual absorption of the Negro into the proletarian class, the devastation of Indian civilization under the impact of "internal colonialism," and the role of racial prejudice in Brazil. He also analyzes the problems which confront the Brazilian social scientist when studying his own society. In Ianni's view, the ambiguities which Brazilian society presents both to itself and to other nations stem from its historical relationship with more developed civilizations. "As a nation, a culture, an economic structure, Brazil is the outgrowth of a capitalist civilization dominated from abroad."

An eminently practical reason—the effort to use scientific methods to clarify the relationship of the various ethnic and racial groups to the national society as a whole—first interested Brazilian social scientists in the structure of race relations. They had become aware that in some aspects the advance of Brazilian civilization depends upon the scientific study of the nature and direction of race relations. Indeed, they recognized that the better understanding of certain problems is vital; for example, why have some groups of German, Italian, and Polish "colonists" in southern Brazil prospered more than certain of their "Brazilian" neighbors? On the other hand, why have other communities of Germans, Italians, and Poles not only failed to make progress, but also become peasants of the Brazilian type? How important was the role of the Italian and Syrio-Lebanese and their descendants in the industrial expansion of São Paulo, whereas at the same time large groups of Italians (and their descendants) were becoming small farmers, workers, or artisans? Why does detribalization continue to be generally disastrous for the culture and person of Indians? To what extent has the experience of slavery determined the later relationship of Negroes and mulattoes to whites in urban zones, centers of industrialization, and agricultural regions? In what way is there developing an industrial and agricultural proletariat comprised of the descendants of Italians, Germans, Poles, Negroes, mulattoes, and Japanese? These are only a few of the innumerable problems that challenged social scientists as scientific thought began to be incorporated systematically into Brazilian society.

Along with such questions, however, other considerations related to the destruction of false social images among the different ethnic and racial groups, as well as within society as a whole, also stimulated the scientific study of race relations. The web of conceptual stereotypes woven by the positive and negative attributes of one group or another has tremendously complicated the development of an accurate and constructive interpretation of Brazilian society. Although many studies have been undertaken as a result of such considerations, other studies have been influenced by false conceptions still current today. The dominant myths of a society are always those which serve to maintain the prevailing structure of vested interests and social conventions.

The need to understand and destroy certain ideological misconceptions has, therefore, forced research on the structure of race relations in Brazil to acquire scientific stature. Consequently, studies in this field have always had two practical objectives: first, to understand the nature of the reality; second, to destroy the ideological framework on which the perpetuation of economic, social, and political distinctions is partially based. For these reasons, such studies constitute an important contribution to the development of democracy in Brazil. In a certain sense, they are basic to every consideration of the possibilities of a civilization in the tropics.

Undoubtedly, the Brazilian racial situation has always been characterized by great contradictions, among which the following stand out: the idealization of the Indian past and the real poverty of the Indian at present; the plastic exoticism of such religious cults as *candomblé, batuque, umbanda,* and *quimbanda,* and the classification of the Negro as an African, the descendant of slaves, or other characterizations of negative connotation; the myth of racial democracy and the doctrine of the inferiority of the mestiço. The works of Euclides da Cunha, Nina Rodrigues, Arthur Ramos, Oliveira Vianna, Gilberto Freyre, and Roger Bastide are not free from such ambivalences. To a certain degree, these contradictions are basic to research on the social reality of the country. To the extent that they express the difference between real and imaginary behavior, they represent challenges to the social scientist. Therefore, the scientific study of the structure of race relations in Brazil is a contribution to the ideological unmasking of patterns which block the progress of society toward democracy. The development of a democratic personality is necessarily dependent upon the existence of a democratic culture. This factor becomes even more important when the political order itself remains to some extent authoritarian.

It should not be considered, however, that the contributions of social scientists to an understanding of the Brazilian racial situation lack fallacies. In such studies ideological stereotypes rooted either in approach or interpretation continue to appear. In particular, since such studies are not immune to fascination with the exotic and the unusual, they often lose sight of important aspects of reality. Sometimes, too, the influence of the myth of racial democracy persists and colors considerations of ethnologists and sociologists. In other cases, the scientist's approach to the Indian is characterized strongly by romanticism. In some instances, he dramatizes the sufferings of the Negro and the mulatto. Such examples illustrate some of the difficulties which affect the full use of scientific method. In other words, Brazilian culture continues to present formidable barriers to a scientific interpretation of some of its secondary contradictions.

Nevertheless, these fallacies have not prevented researchers from treating fundamental themes; nor do they do so at present. In fact, studies of the Brazilian racial situation have evolved continuously in the direction first of clarifying and then of destroying these ambivalences. Even if a study by a social scientist contains implicit fallacies (of which, indeed, the scientist himself may not even be aware), somehow it manages to fit into the progression of predominant ideological emphases. In this area scientific method becomes a technique for developing a rational consciousness of the social reality. The incorporation of scientific method into Brazilian society is being carried out in an atmosphere characterized by a widespread general transformation of the structures of production, distribution, and political organization. It is destined to play a particularly important role in the creation of conditions for social progress and, consequently, in the destruction of myths which are of value only to the dominant group in an agrarian-export society.

The positive aspects of scientific activity in this civilizing process become clear when we examine the basic themes of studies concerned with race relations in Brazil. Among aspects of the situation which are of greatest interest to social scientists, if we can judge on the basis of published works, the following are noteworthy; the acculturation process in general; the nature and conditions of social mobility; manifestations of marginality; the process of proletarianization; concomitant situations of pauperism; manifestations of racial prejudice; and the relationship between the structure of race relations and politics.

Rather than undertaking to examine current opportunities for research on Brazilian society, let us survey some of the outstanding characteristics of the studies on different aspects of the racial situation in the country. In this way we shall review certain fundamental themes; at the same time, some suggestions for new research and interpretation will arise during the course of the discussion.

[259]

Acculturation

Brazilian studies of acculturation cover the Indians, Negroes, Germans, Italians, Japanese, Poles, Syrio-Lebanese, Jews, and Spaniards. Although scientific standards of description and interpretation show considerable unevenness, undeniably scholarly works on these groups are in abundance. The majority deals with the Indian and the *caboclo*, followed by works on the Negroes, Germans, Italians, Japanese, and other groups.

The sequence in which ethnologists became interested in cultural contact and change is very significant. One of the themes which first attracted attention was miscegenation. Population characteristics were studied on the basis of theories of nineteenth century physical and cultural anthropology. Among the works in this category are Euclides da Cunha's *Os Sertões*, Nina Rodrigues's *As Collectividades Anormães*, and Oliveira Vianna's *Raça e Assimilação*. Nor did Gilberto Freyre escape this preoccupation:

Of all Brazilian problems, there is none that disturbs me as much as miscegenation. Once, after more than three years' absence from Brazil, I saw a group of Brazilian sailors, mulattoes and *cafusos*, disembarking from either the "São Paulo" or the "Minas"—I can't remember which—in the soft snow of Brooklyn. They impressed me as being caricatures of men.[1]

The Brazilian social scientist sees himself reflected in the mirror of Europe and the United States and thinks in the terms of the social sciences formulated in those places. Consequently, he has not always been immune to European and North American values and problems, especially during the time when incorporation of scientific method into Brazilian society was still in its infancy. The weakness of a tradition of autonomous thought in the country facilitated then, as it does now, the naïve transposition of particular intervening issues with conceptual systems.

In other words, studies of miscegenation were related directly

[1] Gilberto Freyre, *Casa Grande e Senzala* (2 vols.; 7th ed.; Rio de Janeiro, 1952), I, 17.

to the "inferiority complex" which is prevalent throughout Brazilian culture, and which developed during the long period of Indian and Negro slavery and of dependence on the outside world. The problem of the inferiority of the mestizo became an important theme in the development of Brazilian civilization largely as a result of doctrines formulated in the last half of the nineteenth century, which was in itself an era of intense European imperialism on several continents. In a certain sense, the works of Gobineau, Lapouge, and others were very important to this stage in the "Europeanization" of the world.

Furthermore, the doctrine of the inferiority of the mestizo, Negro, and Indian suited the ruling classes in Brazil, since they were interested in maintaining the status quo, and has continued to play a very important role in the preservation of the archaic structures of control. Darcy Ribeiro sums up the situation: "Despite copious legislation concerning him, the Brazilian Indian is a citizen by omission before the law and has an ambiguous legal status which gives rise to a series of problems." [2] This ambiguity is not accidental; it functions to benefit those who control the organizations and instruments of power; it seeks to preserve established structures in order to hinder social change. In the case of the Negro,

the existing situation is born, in great part, of the fact that racial inequality is understood, interpreted, and accepted socially as a *natural, just and inevitable thing,* as if the competitive social order were not altering the traditional pattern of relations between the "Negro" and the "White." The only dynamic source, then, of uncontrollable corrective influence, has come to be the competitive social order.[3]

Thus, conceptual stereotypes clearly become techniques of domination—that is, of preservation of established structures which are generally archaic in character.

Research on religious acculturation has developed in like manner. From the time of Nina Rodrigues to that of René Ribeiro, many studies were made of manifestations of Afro-Brazilian religious

[2] Darcy Ribeiro, *A política indigenista brasileira* (Rio de Janeiro, 1962), p. 114.

[3] Florestan Fernandes, *A integração de negro à sociedade de classes* (São Paulo, 1964), p. 736.

[261]

syncretism, the most ambitious of which is *Les Religions Africaines au Brésil* by Roger Bastide. Some of these works reveal only a descriptive interest in Negro religious life, in *candomblé, umbanda, batuque,* and so forth. Other studies, however, attempt to grasp how an important segment of African culture has been preserved in Brazil, or seek to discover what role the religious life plays in determining the nature and evolution of contacts with other groups in the society at large. In yet other cases, manifestations of religious life are treated as a "sub-culture" of the lower classes in urban and rural Brazil.

Other scholars, such as Herbert Baldus, Egon Schaden, and Eduardo Galvão, have become interested in the religious life of the Indian and the *caboclo*. Some studies discuss the changes wrought in Catholicism by contact with caboclo culture:

The history of the development of contemporary caboclo religion, like that of the culture to which it belongs, is not a uniform and gradual process of the diffusion of the concepts of our Western civilization which would have passed from the great urban centers to regional centers and from there to villages and farms. On the contrary, interspersed with periods of accelerated transformation were others of relative stability or barely noticeable change. The modifications in regional culture were engendered largely by factors such as religious proselytizing, the enslavement of the Indian, the policy of colonialism and the rubber boom. The origins and structures of such factors were determined by forces outside the Amazon region; that is, in the Portuguese metropole, in Rio, and in the great international centers of commerce and industry. Nevertheless, the products of the interaction of these forces took on local characteristics, which emerged from the necessary process of adjusting the methods of exploitation to the particular geographical environment involved.[4]

In this case, interpretation of religious acculturation is based upon scientific understanding of the succession of historical events which gave it meaning.

The religious life of the Indian also was studied from other perspectives. Messianic movements among them attracted the attention of some ethnologists, who regarded these movements as a bridge to

[4] Eduardo Galvão, *Santos e visagens* (São Paulo, 1955), p. 185.

understanding the "invisible" structures beneath crises that resulted from contact with the national society. In this field, the work of Egon Schaden entitled *A Mitologia Heróica de Tribos Indígenas do Brasil* is outstanding. The study of heroic mythology affords a deeper understanding of both tribal culture and its response to contacts with the culture of the dominant society:

Tukuna millennialism cannot be explained without studying tribal mythology, but the mythology alone cannot explain this movement. It cannot be analyzed unless the condition of poverty or deprivation of the Indians is taken into account, but this is not sufficient cause in itself. It cannot be understood except in terms of [the Indian's] contact with civilization; but it is not the contact in itself that is responsible for the movement, [but rather] the socio-economic conditions arising from it, especially the domination and exploitation of the Indians by rubber planters who took away their tribal lands and tried to impose a highly exploitative commercial relationship on them. Tukuna millennialism is a *praxis* by which the Indians consciously or unconsciously seek to free themselves from domination by, dependence on, and subjection by "civilized" men. This goal is clearly understood by the rubber planters, who never fail to intervene, and to intervene by means of physical violence, threats, and appeals to the authorities.[5]

In interpretations such as this, the relationship among race, culture, and society is clarified by showing how they are related to the means of production. In this way, the wholeness of the object of study is retained in its entirety.

Other studies of acculturation concentrate on the area of technology and on changes in ecological organization, linguistic processes, and artistic expression. To a certain extent, Brazilian popular art—especially the theater, music, poetry, films, and the novel—reflects the widest application of acculturative processes among Negroes, Indians, Italians, and others.

Internal "Colonialism"

Studies of acculturation do not exhaust the problems treated by ethnologists and sociologists interested in the indigenous population.

[5] Maurício Vinhas de Queiroz, "Cargo Cult na Amazonia. Observações sobre o milenarismo Tukuna," *América Latina*, VI:4 (Rio de Janeiro), 58–59.

Along with research of the conventional variety on indigenous cultures, or changes produced in them by contact with other groups or with society as a whole, more ambitious research projects have also developed. Some recent studies and research still in progress indicate that, with regard to the scope of the problems treated and the scientific method employed, a positive development has occurred.

In general, these studies have begun with fairly serious criticism, open or veiled, of the *Serviço de Proteção aos Indios*. Analysis of the operation of this agency, related to the data gathered in direct contact with caboclo and indigenous groups, has caused ethnologists and sociologists to adopt a less romantic and more broadly scientific outlook. As a result, such important works as *A Política Indigenista Brasileira* by Darcy Ribeiro and *O Indio e o Mundo dos Brancos* by Roberto Cardoso de Oliveira have been published. In a similar vein, but enriched by an effort to capture the spirit of civilization in the tropics, is *Tristes Trópicos* by Lévi-Strauss.

From their ephemeral experience with civilization the Indians retained only Brazilian clothing, the hatchet, the knife, and the sewing needle. Everything else was lost on them. Houses had been constructed for them, but they slept in the open air. Attempts were made to establish them in villages, but they remained nomads. As for their beds, these they burned for firewood and they slept on the ground. The herds of cattle sent to them by the government wandered free because the Indians found their meat and milk repugnant. A common device in Brazil known as a *monjolo* consisting of wooden pylons, water-power operated by the alternate filling and emptying of a receptacle attached to a lever which operates pulverizers—imported by the Portuguese, perhaps from the Orient—rattled for lack of use, and hand grinding remained the general practice.[6]

This situation explodes into all its tragic dimensions in the pilgrimage of the Indian Uirá who vainly wandered in search of God.[7]

Little by little, the scientist adds "new" dimensions of reality to his research. He discovers that cultural processes do not occur in

[6] C. Lévi-Strauss, *Tristes Trópicos* (Transl., São Paulo, 1957), p. 60.
[7] Darcy Ribeiro, "Uirá vai ao encontro de Mairá," *Anhembi*, No. 76 (São Paulo, 1957), pp. 21–35.

the abstract. Rather, it is necessary to look for the means of production at the core of research on problems surrounding the contact of the Indian and the caboclo with the larger society.

To the Indian, the national society presents many different faces, depending upon whether it takes the form of an extractive pastoral, or agrarian economy for him. There are different interests involved in the use of the environment in each of these economies. Each is organized according to its own structural principles and exercises different types of pressures on the tribal groups which it confronts.[8]

We see, then, that as scientific experience is accumulated, the interpretative horizon of the ethnologist is widened. Likewise, as the integrity of the object of investigation is maintained in strictly scientific terms, the old fallacies are destroyed.

In this way, then, research on internal colonialism has developed. In fact, this colonialism was already an official doctrine when it began to be studied and denounced in scientific studies. Nevertheless, one of its tenets merits our attention:

The *Rumo ao Oeste* program is a renewal of the campaign initiated by the builders of the nation, the *bandeirantes* and the *sertanistas* but with modern cultural processes as a new component. We must encourage this forward thrust in every way and in all aspects so that we may fill the demographic vacuums of our territory and make our economic frontiers coincide with our political ones. This is our brand of imperialism. We do not covet one hand's breadth of territory that does not belong to us, but we have an expansionist policy, which is to grow within our own frontiers.[9]

Here, then, is the concept of the "Westward March" determined by the exigencies of the expansion of capitalist civilization. It was carried out, however, and is still being carried out, without the collaboration of the social sciences:

Despite the efforts of the Indian Protection Service and the religious missions to protect the Indian against exploiters and butchers, there are

[8] Darcy Ribeiro, "Culturas e línguas indígenas do Brasil," *Educação e Ciencias Sociais*, Year II, Vol. 2, No. 2 (Rio de Janeiro, 1957), 21–23.

[9] Getulio Vargas, *As diretrizes da nova política do Brasil* (Rio de Janeiro, 1942), p. 285.

still many isolated tribes in Brazil which are unprotected and threatened by extermination.[10]

The truth is that the employees of the Service are not adequate to the task:

Not having learned to overcome their own ethnocentric prejudices, they lock themselves within a superiority complex which at best makes them consider the Indians as "children," as do the missionaries. Thus the supervisor of a Post is unable to adjust to his environment, and unless he is led or motivated by some religious or scientific ideal, he easily comes to thirst for money or is driven to drink.[11]

Faced with this situation, ethnologists and sociologists have turned to other problems or redefined conventional themes. That is, they have attempted to recover the integrity of the object of their studies. They have given up conventional academic postures and have sought cooperation in the fields of political economics and other social sciences in order to broaden the horizons of scientific interpretation. Current works stemming from the study project on areas of interethnic friction can be placed in this line of development. Any study of the Brazilian Indians which purports to reveal their true situation cannot fail to emphasize the character of the pioneer movements that come into contact with them today, even in their remotest strongholds. The roles played by these fronts of national expansion vary according to the intensity and type of contact between the Indians and whites. Because of this, any data that may contribute to the formulation of a comprehensive view of the suitable types of civilized work and the means of employing regional Indian and non-Indian labor are especially important.[12]

Throughout its successive stages of development, the Indian-caboclo "question" has evolved in the direction of increasing inte-

[10] Herbert Baldus, "Métodos e resultados da ação indigenista no Brasil," *Revista de Antropologia*, X, No. 1/2 (São Paulo, 1962), 37.

[11] Herbert Baldus, "Tribos da Bacia do Araguaia e o Serviço de Proteção aos Indios," *Revista do Museu Paulista*, N.S., II (São Paulo, 1948), 167–68.

[12] Roberto Cardoso de Oliveira, *O índio e o mundo dos brancos* (São Paulo, 1964), 31. See also the project of research published as an appendix in the same work.

gration. Different aspects of the local reality come to be considered in the light of "external" determining factors derived from the national society. Concomitantly, the historical dimensions of the cultural, economic, and political relations between the indigenous world and capitalist civilization come to be better presented in these studies.

Racial Prejudice

The majority of works on race relations in Brazil have treated in varying degrees with the more important aspects of prejudice. Studies of the acculturation of Germans, Italians, Poles, Japanese, and others all contribute something to the description and interpretation of prejudice. Since such studies generally deal with acculturative processes in relation to the multiple manifestations and possibilities of social mobility, the problem of prejudice arises continually. Works concerning indigenous and caboclo groups also must handle this question.

The most systematic work on racial prejudice appears, however, in reference to relations between white and Negro. After having passed through various stages, studies of the Negro and the mulatto have begun to include fuller treatment of the mechanisms of social mobility and discrimination. At first, ethnologists and sociologists were concerned with issues related to miscegenation. Later, they turned to religion and the various manifestations of syncretism. It has been only since 1945 that social scientists have turned fully to the study of the conditions, manifestations, and implications of racial prejudice. Existing published works have made important contributions in regard to the nature of prejudice in such social situations as work, leisure activities, marriage, school, and so forth.

Such studies have been undertaken for various reasons. Of prime importance is the intolerable contradiction between the myth of racial democracy and the actual prevalence of discrimination against Negroes and mulattoes. Another type of prejudice is practiced against Indians and caboclos, Poles, Italians, and others. Therefore, it has become imperative for social scientists to investigate the reality of interracial contact as distinct from the prevailing myth proclaimed by the poets:

[267]

Here democracy means the absence of any prejudice against origin, creed or color; it is the social flower that has evolved. (Mélange, melting pot, *a tinga piranga*.) One is born here, once again, as in the Pentateuch.[13]

As a national consciousness—derived from a self-awareness based on scientific principles and the general progress of civilization—develops, it becomes the obligation of social scientists to disprove false conceptions. Advancement of knowledge about the social reality also depends upon the scientist's ability to approach critically the doctrines and conceptions which surround and emanate from the very existence of the situation itself.

In the second place, research on the condition of the Negro and mulatto was stimulated by the intellectual climate of the Second World War, which fostered the development of a more responsible attitude among the world's peoples toward racial antagonisms, discrimination, and hatred. Since severe ethnic and racial problems had been an important factor in the economic and political conflicts which produced the war, social scientists of various nations became openly interested in racial tensions. UNESCO originally initiated the broad, special research project on the structure of racial relations between Negroes and whites. Under the auspices of this program, several important works were published: among them are *Race and Class in Rural Brazil* by Charles Wagley, Marvin Harris, Harry W. Hutchinson, and Ben Zimmerman; *O Negro no Rio de Janeiro* by L. A. da Costa Pinto; and *As Elites de Côr* by Thales de Azevedo. These studies developed further in the work of sociologists associated with Florestan Fernandes and Roger Bastide in the research project known as *Racial Prejudice in São Paulo*. These efforts produced or inspired *Brancos e Negros em São Paulo* by Roger Bastide and Florestan Fernandes; *A Integração do Negro à Sociedade de Classes* by Florestan Fernandes; *As Metamorfoses do Escravo* by Octavio Ianni; *Capitalismo e Escravidão* by Fernando Henrique Cardoso; and *Côr e Mobilidade Social em Florianópolis* by F. H. Cardoso and O. Ianni.

[13] Cassiano Ricardo, "Carta de D. Pedro II a Gobineau," *Suplemento Literário: O Estado de São Paulo* (July 6, 1957), 3.

[268]

The completion of these studies concerning the structure of race relations in various parts of Brazil provided an invaluable source for information regarding the national reality, since they investigated various acculturative, social, economic, and demographic processes. Of particular importance are the contributions they make to a fuller understanding of racial prejudice, racial ideologies, and the structure of social consciousness itself. Using various approaches, all these works deal with the relationship between race and social class, an issue which already had been raised in Donald Pierson's pioneer study, *The Negro in Brazil*, which quite clearly attacks the old myths.

Taken as a whole, these studies of the relationship between Negroes and whites in Brazil contribute greatly toward the understanding of certain fundamental aspects of Brazilian civilization. Indeed, they represent a serious effort to grasp its uniqueness:

The progress of the social sciences in Brazil has been reflected amply and profoundly in the quantity and quality of the research they have produced on ethnic and race relations. Such a trend is quite natural because our nation is "a melting pot of races and cultures," as it has been called frequently. Although such studies purport to have empirical and theoretical bases—and up to the present all of them have been undertaken for the purpose of augmenting our understanding of various types of inter-ethnic or inter-racial contact in Brazilian society—they indirectly fulfill practical needs of wide general application. No one can ignore the extent to which cultural and racial heterogeneity have affected and will continue to affect, the possibilities of developing "Western civilization" in Brazil. From this standpoint, the pertinent questions involved constitute a national problem. This fact lends an undeniable practical interest to the various studies that have been completed or are still in progress.[14]

Thus, it can be seen that the study of race relations, motivated by practical and scientific considerations alike, has acquired considerable complexity and depth.

[14] Foreword by Florestan Fernandes in *Côr e mobilidade social em Florianópolis* by Fernando Henrique Cardoso and Octavio Ianni (São Paulo, 1960), xi.

Proletarianization

As scientific studies of Brazilian race relations increase in quality and number, the possibilities for research become proportionately richer, and the intellectual horizon of the scientist is broadened. In a country such as Brazil, which is engaged in the process of industrialization, social science research cannot ignore the role of the prevailing economic forces. Therefore, research on race relations must be concerned with social mobility in general, and the process of proletarianization in particular. As a matter of fact, the analysis and interpretation of this process primarily focused on and developed in studies of the Negro. Of course, it arises in connection with other groups as well.

In great part, the history of the Negro since the abolition of slavery in 1888 is the history of his proletarianization. Released from bondage, he found himself in a new and unfamiliar situation. Because of the historical conditions under which capitalism was developing in Brazil, the Negro could not be absorbed, immediately and fully, into the economic system. Decades passed before he could be sure of receiving a salary. It was necessary for him to pass through several phases before he began to be accepted and sought as a worker. Basically, the dilemma of the Negro since 1888 can be summarized as follows: he was not prepared to sell his labor nor was the entrepreneur ready to buy it.

During the development of capitalism in Brazil, the creation of the proletariat also was based upon the law of supply and demand, by which the stronger always seeks to reap the maximum advantage. Thus, according to economic principles as well as to cultural factors emanating from the heritage of slavery, the Negro found that the immigrant ranked far above him in the scale of preference. So it was the Negro who constituted the bulk of the idle and unemployed. Since the labor supply was larger than the demand—a situation created deliberately by both official and private immigration policies—the Negro remained on the fringes of productivity. To him, also, fell the lowest rank in the surplus labor market. In addition, the labor surplus tended to depress the levels of wages and disguised forms of income. Therefore, during an important period of the development of capitalism in Brazil, the pauperism of salaried workers was reinforced by the lawless condition of the unemployed:

Whenever high production levels, as reflected in the rate of economic growth and the division of labor, were achieved, real possibilities for the creation of an authentic labor market existed. In such areas, the former slaves had to compete against the so-called "national workers" who constituted a veritable reserve army which was kept out of productive work in the prosperous regions by the degradation of slave work. However the Negro's principal competition was the labor imported from Europe, which generally was better suited to the new labor system and to its economic and social implications.[15]

In the more industrialized centers of the country, this situation began to change after 1930, when the economy became more dynamic and differentiated. In other regions the movement did not begin until after 1945. And in a large part of the country, the process has just started.

Thus, upon becoming a citizen the Negro was introduced most brutally to the alienation that was part of his freedom. "Brazilian society left the Negro to his own fate, laying upon his own shoulders the responsibility for re-educating himself and for making the necessary adjustments to the new patterns and concepts created by the advent of free labor, the republican regime, and capitalism." [16] Thus, the study of race relations must proceed in steps from particular firsthand cases to consideration of general structures. Only in this manner can changes in the social position of Negroes and mulattoes be understood fully. Within this context, the process of proletarianization acquires special significance for the study of race relations. To understand the condition of the Negro and mulatto during the long period between abolition and industrialization, it is necessary to be familiar with changes which were occurring at this time in the organization of economic activities, the demographic structure, and so forth. In this process, scientific research should

[15] Florestan Fernandes, *A integração* . . . , p. 5.
[16] *Ibid.*, p. 8.

[271]

"consider proletarianization not as a decline, but rather, on the contrary, as a collective promotion." [17]

Likewise, with regard to the Indians and caboclos, ethnological studies have also begun to take into account such factors as the development of a class society and the mercantilization of the labor force. Many works related to internal colonialism and to the areas of interethnic friction also make an important contribution in this direction. In addition, books such as *Os Parceiros do Rio Bonito* by Antonio Cândido and *O Demônio no Catulé* by Carlo Castaldi, Eunice T. Ribeiro, and Carolina Martuscelli also comprise notable contributions to the description and interpretation of certain critical phases of the commercialization of the factors of production.

Culture and Politics

Inevitably, as investigation of race relations in Brazil has developed, the problems dealt with have multiplied. At the same time, the interpretative ability of social scientists has also increased. The development of scientific methods of research and the deliberate effort to make knowledge useful have led specialists to study basic issues. As a consequence, fallacies regarding race relations in Brazil have been gradually analyzed, abandoned, and destroyed.

The problem of the relationship between race, culture, and politics can be viewed in terms of this trend. In a certain sense, it has underlain most of the contributions in this area. It arises equally in discussions of the policies of the Indian Protection Service and in studies of Jewish youth. These works touch, to varying extents, upon the connection among political relations, cultural contact, and race relations.

With regard to the Negroes, Roger Bastide and Florestan Fernandes have carried out the most complete studies. They have examined carefully the Negro's political reaction to the racial situation which as a consequence of urbanization and industrialization has evolved since Abolition. They have also discussed the roles played by social and political movements among the Negroes. Roger Bastide has studied the role of the Negro press in São Paulo, grasping

[17] Roger Bastide, *Sociologie du Brésil* (Paris, n.d.), p. 19.

particularly well the manifestations of social mobility and self-awareness within Negro and mulatto groups. The general proletarianization of the Negro and mulatto and the incipient movement of both into the middle classes have facilitated the study of their integration into these social groups.

With regard to the Germans, Italians, Japanese, Poles, and others, the political issue must be placed in a different context. It is clear that the relationship between culture and social mobility is expressed through organizations and behavioral patterns of political importance. For example, associations and clubs with both recreational and political roles are founded. Such organizations often serve as electoral bases for the political candidates who represent "German," "Polish," "Italian," or "Syrian" groups.

In addition, immigrant groups have always received special attention from the governments and the economic, political, cultural, and religious organizations of their native countries. Generally speaking, such efforts have been directed toward "easing" conditions of acculturation. In practice, however, they have functioned as mechanisms to preserve loyalty to the countries of origin. In this sense they are actually anti-acculturational. Certain important questions related to the relationship between cultural change, race relations, and political behavior and organizations are raised in Constantino Ianni's *Homens sem Paz* and José Arthur Rios's *Aspectos Políticos da Assimilação do Italiano no Brasil*. Outstanding among nonscientific works that, nevertheless, have great documentary value are *A Ofensiva Japonesa no Brasil* by Carlos de Souza Moraes; *A Quinta Coluna no Brasil* by Aurelio da Silva Py; and *Hitler Guerreia o Brasil Há Dez Anos* by Mario Martins. These works discuss the nature of links between immigrant groups and their countries of origin. More specifically, they give important information on the relationship between race, culture, and politics:

Italian colonialism which was unsuccessful in Africa sought to establish economic and political bases in the communities developed abroad by Italian immigrants. Thus it is that in Brazil at least, the Italians (as compared to the Portuguese or Japanese) represent the only case of an expatriate community regarded by the government and certain economic groups in the home country in terms usually reserved for colonial pos-

[273]

sessions. There are basically three types of colonies: areas of settlement, of exploitation or of commercial activity. Certain dominating interests in Italy clearly have considered the Italian communities abroad as colonies of commercial activity (in that they provide new outlets for exports) or colonies of exploitation (with reference to remittances which differ little from the typical means of exploitation used by metropolitan powers in their overseas possessions). . . . At the same time these communities are also colonies of settlement which have helped alleviate Italy's internal demographic pressure.[18]

Such as the "external" variables of the acculturation process. This illustration shows specifically how race, culture, and politics can be dependent upon economic factors.

Guerra e Relações de Raça by Arthur Ramos, however, merits special attention here, for this work marks an important stage in the reformulation of the issues involved in the study of race relations in the Brazilian environment. Although its line of reasoning has not been developed further, the book represents a milestone in the broadening of scientists' horizons. Heavy emphasis is laid upon the need for ethnologists and sociologists to consider the relationship between culture and politics in their investigations of the structure of race relations. Inspired by the struggle against fascism in its various forms, Ramo's work sets important problems before the social scientist. In particular, it reminds him of his responsibilities as an intellectual and as a citizen. Better still, it points out that the study of race relations always involves structures of domination. The same problems are treated on a more strictly anthropological plane in *A Aculturação dos Alemães do Brasil* by Emílio Willems. As in the case of the Italians, research on the conditions and patterns of acculturation among the Germans, Poles, Japanese, and others should always include an analysis of the means by which the governments and organizations of the home countries both interfere and collaborate in the acculturation process.

Scientific Issues

In great part, the evolution of Brazilian research on race relations is related to the development of a scientific framework for the social

[18] Constantino Ianni, *Homens sem paz* (São Paulo, 1963), p. 27.

sciences. Further, the development of a scientific ethnology and sociology in the country has been based upon assimilation of the contributions made by different scientific schools of thought in France, the United States, England, and Germany. Brazilian studies, therefore, often deal with themes and problems that have no counterparts in the intellectual traditions or issues of Brazilian society. Nonetheless, such efforts are not always irrelevant. Rather, they often make an important contribution to either the reformulation of those problems or the theoretical manner of treating them. Some of the principal criticisms of the focus and theoretical tendencies of Brazilian ethnology and sociology were emphasized in *A Etnologia e a Sociologia no Brasil* edited by Florestan Fernandes. The articles and essays by Herbert Baldus, Egon Schaden, Charles Wagley, Marvin Harris, Thales de Azevedo, and others in this volume provide an adequate picture of the general development and special aspects of the ethnological and sociological research in Brazil. They also examine problems related to methodology, subject matter, and interpretation in research on race relations. Certain important aspects of the field remain to be discussed, however.

In part, research in this field still faces difficulties rising from the tenacity of the old fallacies about the character of race relations in Brazil. For example, the myth of racial democracy continues to act as an obstacle and threat to development of certain studies. Free discussion of some dramatic aspects of the life of the Indian, the caboclo, the Negro, the Pole often meets with veiled or open resistance. Society often considers such concerns unscientific. For example, criticism of the Indian Protection Service (SPI) has not been expressed fully and openly because of the obstacles this agency could place in the way of scientific research. Worse still, ethnologists and sociologists have been unable to obtain the cooperation of the SPI in scientific research on the Indian and caboclo world. Since the bureaucrats of this agency control the means of access to indigenous groups, criticism of its activities and orientation can never go beyond certain limits.[19]

On the theoretical level, the study of race relations suffers at

[19] This was written before the shocking news about abuses committed by SPI officials spread around the world in 1968 (ed. remark).

times from an unsatisfactory relationship with the true nature of the object of study. In many works there is a veritable "dehumanization" of the issues; that is, the important role of man as the creator of culture and as the object of his own cultural creations is often overlooked. In their zeal to attach definitions to subject matter, some scholars atomize reality, isolating culture, society, economics, and demography as if laboratory procedures were valid in the behavioral sciences. Consequently, the integrity of the subject matter, reduced to inanimate fragments, is lost.

For these reasons, many studies do not view race relations as meaningful structures, as processes. The effort to produce "objective" studies has even led to the total distortion of historical reality. Because of the bias of some specialists against employing knowledge gathered in other disciplines and to the generally inadequate understanding of "division of labor" in the social sciences, some works are devoid of a sense of history in regard to the cultural sphere.

Thus it can be seen that the social sciences have failed to deal adequately with certain important themes. Among problems still awaiting research and interpretation are: the relationship between social structure and personality structure; the marginality of the caboclo and the mulatto, seen perhaps as heuristic situations; race relations and the relationship of production in the primary, secondary, and tertiary sectors; race and social class in the urban industrial world and in the rural environment; the conditions of production and the characteristics of the Negro's social image; the unfavorable self-image of the Indian and the basis of the caboclo's fatalism. On another level, studies should be made of the relationship between messianic movements and the structures of interacting cultures, and regarding the forms assumed by syncretic religious movements in the face of capitalist civilization. Another set of issues stems from the social scientist's attempts to study the relationship of reality to the collective stereotypes and the current doctrines produced by these same phenomena. Thus, there is a need to study facial ideologies presented as "scientific" formulae as fundamental functions of processes basic to race relations.

A Tropical Civilization?

Several studies of Brazilian race relations have used the image of a civilization in the tropics. Charles Wagley, Roger Bastide, and Florestan Fernandes are among those who have shown interest in this idea. To varying extents, they have made important contributions toward the understanding of this problem. In addition, certain studies of race relations, as broadly defined here, have also made important contributions to the discussion.

From a different viewpoint, Euclides da Cunha, Oliveira Vianna, Gilberto Freyre, and Sérgio Buarque de Holanda have been concerned with this issue. Brazilian society, especially its intellectual sector, cannot escape the fascination of this theme. Many have sought to clarify the trends, possibilities, and character of Brazilian civilization, hoping to find the source of its essential unity.

Although this is not the place to raise the question again, one of its fundamental aspects seems relevant. Basically, the issue arises from the ambiguities which Brazilian society presents both to itself and to other nations. More especially, it is a result of the harmony, ties, and misunderstandings which exist between more developed civilizations and Brazil. Although the ultimate unity and autonomy of Brazilian society should be kept in sight, there exists today a significant discrepancy between the reality of that society and the way it perceives itself. The process by which the self-image of the Brazilian people is formed frustrates a clear understanding of national culture. One of the chief factors in this serious image-distortion is the powerful influence exercised by hurriedly assimilated currents of thought originating in the developed countries. Thus, an adequate interpretation of Brazilian culture often eludes the social scientist, who is not only unable to deal with the divorce between thought and reality but also is himself subject to the influence of these same distortions.

In truth, Brazil is an invention of European capitalism. Therefore, it cannot be understood except in the context of its relations with the United States, Germany, France, England, Italy, and Japan. As a nation, a culture, an economic structure, Brazil is the outgrowth of a capitalist civilization dominated from abroad. This fact gives rise to the strange struggle for self-confirmation, to the ambiguous national consciousness that seeks to develop itself as a civilization in the tropics. Finally, it is the source for the unhappy consciousness of a people seeking its future in a mirror of other peoples without itself possessing the means by which it could master its own destiny.

CHAPTER 13

A Geographer's View of
Race and Class in Latin America
Hilgard O'Reilly Sternberg

To appreciate the role of geography in an interdisciplinary approach to race and class phenomena, it should be borne in mind that in their studies of man and milieu, geographers like Professor Hilgard O'Reilly Sternberg of the University of California, Berkeley, are concerned with the total environment, not just its physical and biotic components. They are likely to have an open-ended, humanistic interest in any fact that must be weighed in order to understand the complex relationships between human communities and their habitat. Thus, for instance, it is pointed out here that certain ethnic groups may be endowed with hereditary equipment that makes them particularly tolerant to given environmental stresses. On the other hand, some reactions to environment that at first blush might appear to be the result of biological adaptations are in fact cultural. After showing that the imprint of man's presence on the land is to a degree derived from a number of elements not directly visible, such as traditions, beliefs, and taboos, the writer suggests that there is little to be gained by attempting to delineate with sharp contours the field of action of the geographer, since "the study of man, culture and environment forms a continuum."

The binomial "race and class," as such, has received little if any explicit attention from geographers, and this is not surprising, since the issues implied by the coupling of these two approaches to the classification of mankind do not lie within the area of professional interest—or competence—of most workers in the field of geography.

[279]

In fact, several geographic studies, whose titles indicate an awareness of the ethnic component in a given cultural landscape, do little more than use the racial factor as a convenient criterion for delimiting a region or topic, and hardly attempt to bring into relief specific characteristics resulting from the action of this or that ethnic group. But such treatment is a matter of the individual researcher's approach rather than of barriers resulting from the nature of the discipline. Any fact that must be weighed in order to comprehend fully the origin and functioning of a given cultural landscape, whether rural or urban, is automatically a "geographic" fact. And this statement certainly holds true for the racial component—commonly examined in conjunction with and as a support for culture.

If the horizontal distribution of ethnic communities, living in distinct territories or in the same area as separate groups, can be of concern to geographers, it is obvious that the racial factor does not abruptly cease to be of interest when considered along a vertical or "class" axis. In some cases, indeed, one might speak literally of a geographic or, more precisely, topographic basis for the upended racial spectrum for example, the hillside shantytowns of Caracas or Rio de Janeiro[1] and the layered agricultural settlement pattern of Peru or Ecuador, where no small percentage of the Indian element is contained in the bleakness of the Andean highlands.[2]

Although the theme of this book lies outside the central focus of

[1] The population that finds shelter in the *favelas* of Rio de Janeiro is comprised of the less privileged classes, with a predominance of *Pardos* and Negroes. If these two groups are considered jointly they represent 67 per cent of the favelas' population, but only 29 per cent of the total population living in the former Federal District. SAGMAGS (Sociedade de Análises Gráficas e Mecanográficas Aplicadas aos Complexos Sociais), "Aspectos Humanos da Favela Carioca," *O Estado de São Paulo*, Suplemento Especial I, 13 de abril de 1960, 8.

[2] See, for instance, with respect to Ecuador, Wolf-Dieter Sick, *Wirtschaftsgeographie von Ecuador*, Stuttgarter Geographische Studien Band 73, Stuttgart, Geographisches Institut der T. H. (Stuttgart, 1963), especially pp. 43 and 45. In the case of Peru, Donald R. Dyer has made studies of the altitudinal distribution of population by provinces; see "Population and Elevation in Peru," *Northwestern University Studies in Geography*, No. 6 (Evanston, Ill., 1962), pp. 13–27; and "Population of the Quechua Region of Peru," *The Geographical Review*, LII (1962), 337–45.

geographic research,[3] I feel sure that in an age of interdisciplinary effort which has condemned the "intellectual ghettos where problems are uselessly fractionated" [4] geography has a part to play in the common effort that is being made to understand the problem of race and class. And, in this article, which is far from exhaustive and certainly more suggestive than conclusive, I have attempted to collect a few thoughts on the subject and bring together some examples of questions that are of interest to and that have been or might be touched upon by geographers. I have limited myself largely to examples from Portuguese America, the area with which I am most familiar.

In attempting to understand the individuality of regions that produce the rich pattern of spatial differentiation over the surface of the earth, the geographer is led to examine the relationship obtaining between human groups and their habitat. Even if geography is primarily concerned with the visible expression of man's presence in a given landscape, it is impossible to understand the imprint of his culture without due consideration of those not directly visible elements such as traditions, beliefs, and taboos, which to a greater or lesser degree control the actions that actually result in the material modification of the environment. True, cultural geography does not attempt to explain the "inner workings of Culture," but man, agent of transformation, man, bearer of an accepted and congenial hereditary cultural patrimony, man, who "thinks with his hands," occupies an important place in the structure of the discipline.

Consider now man, the vehicle of biological heredity. Are there circumstances in which the matter of "race" may bear upon geographical problems? The answer is in the affirmative. Human "subspeciation" is basically geographical—continental—in origin. And the different areas with which the various ethnic groups are traditionally associated are endowed, of course, with quite different ecological conditions. In studying the relation of man to environment,

[3] *The Science of Geography* (Washington, D.C., 1965), a report published by the *Ad hoc* Committee on Geography, Division of Earth Sciences, National Research Council, contains a recent statement regarding concepts and methods of geography in general and of cultural geography in particular.

[4] Pierre Chaunu, "Une histoire hispano-américaniste pilote. En marge de l'oeuvre de l'école de Berkeley," *Révue Historique*, Vol. 223 (1960).

the geographer may well inquire whether certain communities are more, others less tolerant of the adverse conditions a given milieu may offer, and to what extent such tolerances have been genetically established or constitute responses "learned" during the life span of the individual.

The matter of lung capacity, blood volume, and blood composition in relation to acclimatization of the Andean people has been the object of a series of studies that, at least, supply the basis for an informed discussion.[5] However, practically no investigation exists concerning possible adaptation of different men to the humid tropical lowlands, which make up such a large portion of Latin America. There is much need for field-studies made with acclimatized individuals. As far as I know, the situation is essentially the same as that described more than a decade ago, when our knowledge of the acclimatization process in hot environments was that obtained from studies of "unacclimatized men abruptly exposed to heat"—partly under controlled laboratory conditions.[6] The kind of information that may be obtained from such experiments is limited in scope and if applied to, say, an assessment of the potentialities of development of Latin American lowlands by local native groups, may be worse than no information at all. It merely furnishes a pseudoscientific basis for a number of hard-dying ethnocentric prejudices.

Evidence points to the existence of a link between certain genetic endowments and enhanced resistance to diseases typical of particular environmental conditions. One of many possible illustrations is supplied by R. C. West in his study of the hot humid Pacific lowlands of western Colombia, northwestern Ecuador, and southeastern Panama; the majority of the population is Negro and Negroid, and the

[5] See, for example, Carlos Monge M., *Acclimatization in the Andes* (Baltimore, 1948). In a volume of abstracts of materials relative to this subject, Monge M. (who founded and for many years directed the Institute of Andean Biology) listed 538 items: Carlos Monge M., *Aclimatación en los Andes: Extractos de investigaciones sobre biología de altitud* (Lima, 1960). A recent study is Alfredo Sachetti's "Capacidad respiratoria y aclimatación en las razas andinas," *Journal de la Société des Américanistes,* LIII (Paris, 1964), 6–83.

[6] Quartermaster Climatic Research Laboratory, Environmental Protection Branch, *Acclimatization to Heat in Man,* Report 214 (1953), 3.

author observed Negroes to be partially immune to malaria.[7] According to a study of another group of Negroes, the Bonis, settled along the Maroni River, these descendants of slaves who escaped from Surinam and found refuge in French Guiana also show relative resistance to malaria, whereas neighboring Creole villages were observed to be severely smitten by the disease. One cause suggested by the investigator, A. Sausse, for the low endemicity is racial resistance to malaria on the part of the adult Negroes.[8] In the course of field work in Mato Grosso State, Brazil, conducted during summer, 1965, the fact was brought to my attention that more than 90 per cent of the residents of the town of Mato Grosso, also known by its primitive name, Vila Bela, are Negroid, including the *prefeito* and other officials. The town (1960 population: 520), located on the right bank of the Guaporé River, was at one time the capital of the Province and could even boast the rare privilege of a gold mint, established by the Portuguese government.[9] A census made in 1816 gave the town more than 5,000 inhabitants and, what is more important, it did not suggest anything like the present racial composition: 3,347 free men were counted as against 2,475 slaves.[10] Apparently due to the ravages of malaria, the seat of the provincial government was moved in 1820 to Cuiabá, which at the time had only about half the population of the former capital. Following the transfer of the administration, there was a general exodus of the

[7] Robert C. West, *Colonial Placer Mining in Colombia* (Baton Rouge, La., 1952), p. 87. Recognition of greater resistance to malaria on the part of Negroes is by no means new in geographic and anthropological literature. See, for instance, Georg Buschan, "Einfluss der Rasse auf die Form und Häufigkeit pathologischer Veränderungen," *Globus*, LXVII (1895), 21–24, 43–47, 60–63, and 76–80. Buschan referred to the "almost complete immunity" to yellow fever and malaria enjoyed by the African Negro and noted that he carried it with him "to other tropical areas (for example, South America)" albeit in a "somewhat weakened degree."

[8] André Sausse, *Populations primitives du Maroni* (*Guyane Française*) (Paris, 1951), quoted in Guy Lasserre's "Noirs et Indiens des Pays du Maroni (Guyane Française)," *Les Cahiers d'Outre Mer*, XVII (1952), 84–89.

[9] João Severiano da Fonseca and Pires de Almeida, *Voyage autour du Brésil* (Rio de Janeiro, 1899), p. 195.

[10] Karl von den Steinen, *Durch Central-Brasilien: Expedition zur Erforschung des Schingú im Jahre 1884* (Leipzig, 1886), p. 42.

[283]

white population from Vila Bela. Fonseca and Almeida, who visited the place in the late 1870s, were much struck by the observation that not a single Portuguese merchant was then established there, "a fact which is probably unique in all Brazil." [11] By the time Anibal Amorim traveled through the state of Mato Grosso in the first decade of this century, the total population of Vila Bela was said to consist of some 300 Guinea Negroes.[12] The predominance of a Negroid population in this remote frontier town is generally attributed in northern Mato Grosso State to a greater resistance to malaria possessed by this ethnic group. Increased resistance to the disease might be enjoyed by the Negroid population of the Mato Grosso town in connection with the presence of the sickle cell anemia gene,[13] which confers a greater than normal resistance to malaria, and occurs mainly in Negroes; in some areas of Africa 40 per cent of the population are carriers of the sickling trait. Considerable genetic resistance to malaria also is said to be conferred by hemolytic anemia produced by a deficiency in glucose-6-phosphate hydrogenase, an enzyme found in the red blood cells.[14] This deficiency occurs almost exclusively in Negroes.

Many components of the hereditary equipment with which different peoples are endowed may prove to be as yet unsuspected assets in the efforts made by the various ethnic groups to live in and obtain the mastery over given environments. It is worth bearing in mind, however, that differential rates of endemicity in some cases may be culturally induced. To return to the Bonis of French Guiana, Sausse has added to his thoughts on a possible racial resistance to malaria the observation that these Negroid people do not leave

[11] Fonseca and Almeida, *Voyage autour du Brésil*, pp. 192 and 199.

[12] Annibal Amorim, *Viagens pelo Brasil* (Rio de Janeiro, n.d.), p. 464.

[13] A. C. Allison, "Genetic Factors in Resistance to Malaria" in *Genetic Perspectives in Disease Resistance and Susceptibility* (Annals of the New York Academy of Sciences, XCI, 1961), 710–29.

[14] Arno G. Motulsky, "Hereditary Red Cell Traits and Malaria," *American Journal of Tropical Medicine and Hygiene*, XIII: 1, part 2 (1964), 147–58. See also A. C. Allison, "Genetic Factors. . . ." Grateful acknowledgment is made here to Dr. J. Fernando Carneiro of the Faculdade de Medicina de Porto Alegre and to Dr. Frank W. Lowenstein of the World Health Organization with whom the writer has corresponded on the subject of genetic endowment and resistance to malaria.

vessels containing stagnant water lying around and, furthermore, that they "live in the continuous smoke of fires, which they keep burning in their huts." [15]

Assuming that their habits afforded the Bonis some measure of protection in their malaria-infested habitat, the opposite appears to have occurred during one phase of Japanese settlement in São Paulo. According to H. Saito, there was a heavier malaria incidence among the farmers who immigrated from Japan during the twenties than among other inhabitants of the same rural areas. The sociologist suggests that certain features of their cultural heritage laid the Japanese open to the onslaught of the disease. Their habits required generous consumption of water for daily baths, the maintenance of truck gardens adjoining the dwellings, and the cultivation of floodplain rice. This led the pioneers to build their houses in bottomlands closer to the sources of water—and to the swampy breeding places of the disease-carrying mosquito.[16] A decade later, P. Monbeig was to observe the effective results of a vigorous campaign waged by the doctors assisting the colonists to get them to build their houses several hundred meters from the streams,[17] an objective reflected in the layout of roads and farm lots in Japanese rural developments.[18]

Here, then, is one more illustration of responses to natural environment that at first blush appear to be entirely ethnic although, in effect, cultural traits play a significant role.

Responses called forth on another plane—that of social and economic interactions—are also liable to over-simplified interpretations. Take the fascinating problem of why certain communities come to be generally recognized as possessing an exceptional degree of industriousness, business acumen, and other qualities, which are held responsible for the success of their many ventures. Perhaps the best known example of such groups, which generally play an important economic role as entrepreneurs, is that of the Antioqueños, described by Parsons in what has become a classic in cultural geog-

---

[15] Sausse, *Populations primitives*. . . .

[16] Hiroshi Saito, *O Japonês no Brasil: Estudo de Mobilidade e Fixação* (São Paulo, 1961), p. 81.

[17] Pierre Monbeig, *Pionniers et Planteurs de São Paulo* (Paris, 1952), pp. 298-99.

[18] *Ibid.*, p. 210.

raphy.[19] When a surge of economic activity got underway in an Andean region of western Colombia cut off from the world by rugged mountain ranges, and spread from there in multipronged thrusts to an ever-widening territory, the usual textbook premises for economic growth were far from having been met. The isolated province seemed to have no particular advantage capable of justifying its rapidly mounting national preeminence in farming, trade, and industry. Except its people. It was almost inevitable that members of a cultural group that became so outstanding should begin to think of themselves and be thought of by their neighbors as constituting a "race" apart. And so, the thrifty, sober, hard-working farmers, businessmen, and industrialists, evolved from miscegenation of essentially Spanish and Indian stock, refer proudly to themselves as "la raza antioqueña." [20] In trying to account for the greater effectiveness of the Antioqueños, whose entrepreneurial vigor is reflected so favorably in the economic position of their country,[21] and of which they now represent close to one-third of the population, some have favored the legend that early Antioquia was settled by Sephardic Jews. Others have attributed the personality of the Antioqueños to a strong dose of Basque blood. That cultural rather than racial cohesion is paramount in the case of the Antioqueños has been shown by Parsons in his geographic study, but the precise way in which this cultural group evolved and acquired its dominant characteristics is still a matter of speculation and a potential subject for several disciplines.[22]

The fact that the Antioqueño revolution evolved in the cool highlands of Colombia would certainly suggest to some students a clear-cut case of environmentalism. They might even expect to find support for this thesis within the camp of geography. Since geographers concern themselves with the study of environment, there are

[19] James J. Parsons, *Antioqueño Colonization in Western Colombia* (Ibero-Americana: 32; Berkeley, Calif., 1949).

[20] *Ibid.*, p. 3.

[21] Albert O. Hirschman, *Journeys Toward Progress: Studies of Economic Policy-making in Latin America* (New York, 1963).

[22] An interesting discussion of the reasons for the economic success of the Antioqueños may be found in Chapter 15 of Everett E. Hagen's *On the Theory of Social Change* (Homewood, Ill., 1962).

two surprisingly widespread and persistent misconceptions regarding this discipline: (a) that the sole environment with which geography is concerned is the *natural* environment; and (b) that a person who cultivates this field is, *ipso facto*, a believer in so-called geographic determinism. In point of fact, of course, there are several rather recent instances where geographers have aligned themselves against excessive appeals to environmental controls by colleagues in other man-centered fields.[23] This is very different from denying the role of natural environment. Such a denial is ill-suited to a discipline that rests or should rest largely upon field observations, leaving to other researchers the dematerialized environments of regional "models."

Human groups living in diverse ecological situations are subject to influences that, in the course of time, may be reflected in heredity, although not all of these influences are known. But the challenge to man's ingenuity posed by different geographic areas also is varied. In this way, peoples gird themselves with different cultures, that is, the cultural heritage varies from place to place. This should not be understood in terms of a "necessary and predictable" response to environment. There is more than one way to grapple with the problems posed by a specific natural region, but the group living there for a long time does gradually evolve, among the variety of possibilities and choices, patterns of conduct that reflect their particular way of making a living in that area. Not necessarily the "best" way, not necessarily the most profitable way, but their way.

The modern redistribution, across the length and breadth of the New World, of the various newly arrived ethnic groups with their individual cultural-historical backgrounds followed paths that were motivated to some extent by economic considerations. But since these took into account the different resource opportunities, the natural environment in many cases comes through clearly in the present distribution patterns of ethnic communities and cultures. And, of course, in the social implications of such patterns. Consider the introduction of "luxury" crops for the European market in a

---

[23] See, for example, James M. Blaut, "The Ecology of Tropical Farming Systems" in *Plantation Systems of the New World* (Washington, Pan American Union, 1959), pp. 83–97; and Betty Megger's "Comments," pp. 98–103.

plantation system of agriculture, which occurred in several humid tropical lowlands of Latin America. A case in point: the predominance of sugar cane, to the practical exclusion of any other crop, along the littoral of Pernambuco, Alagoas, part of Paraíba, Sergipe, and the Recôncavo of Bahia. This economic cycle was favored by the warm moist climate, the excellent *massapê* soils, the supply of firewood offered by the coastal rain forest, and the navigability of a number of the small rivers. All these natural factors, as well as many others, cultural and historical, are woven into the contemporary ethnic tissue of the Nordeste, whose dark hem reflects the massive contribution of African slaves to the coastal population. According to a study conducted by Jacqueline Beaujeu-Garnier during the months of September and October 1961, migrants arriving in Salvador showed the following ethnic breakdown: 36.3 per cent Negro, 26.5 per cent mulatto, and 37.2 per cent white. That the proportion of non-whites should be greater in the migratory streams than in the source areas is explained by the author in terms of an economic stratification that corresponds more or less to racial classification: the most humble tasks and the most precarious economic situations frequently are the lot of individuals of darker skin, who are more prone to pick up and go, in search of a better deal.[24]

The so-called Zona da Mata, with its sugar cane tradition, is not set off from the interior merely by an ethnic contrast. Not only are there fewer Negroes in the semi-arid backlands,[25] but also one gains the impression that social stratification is less sharp, if not less persistent. I venture to suggest two of many possible factors that might contribute to such a situation. First, the *sertão*, by and large, is cattle country, and the easy camaraderie of men in the saddle, the shared excitement of the *vaquejada*, or rodeo, are bound to soften some of the harshness of class contrasts. Second, this is an area subject to recurrent, catastrophic droughts. From the year 1603 to our day, more than 30 severe *sêcas* have been recorded in the Northeast; that of 1877–1879 alone, is said to have "caused the death of 500,000 inhabitants of Ceará and adjacent areas, that is to say, about 50 per

[24] Jacqueline Beaujeu-Garnier, "Les migrations vers Salvador (Brésil)," *Les Cahiers d'Outre Mer*, LIX (1962), 291–300.

[25] See Djacir Menezes, *O outro Nordeste* (Rio de Janeiro, 1937), pp. 63–90.

cent of the population." [26] One has but to read some of the dramatic accounts of sêcas and ensuing famines to realize their leveling effect, especially in the past when lack of transportation aggravated the impact of the natural calamity. At the height of such a disaster, there were no rich, no poor sertanejos—only hungry flagelados,[27] stumbling and falling as they dragged themselves to the coast.

In the Nordeste, the redistribution of ethnic groups was influenced by spatial variations in the natural environment. There are other instances, however, where historical factors clearly overshadow the role of environment. The geographic study of settlement dynamics in São Paulo State alone—the theme of Pierre Monbeig's outstanding monograph[28]—furnishes a number of illustrations. The desirability of agricultural land is determined by such factors as initial soil fertility, real or imagined opportunity for economic and social advancement, and so on; it is obvious that in the case of an advancing pioneer front this attractiveness is constantly shifting from "older" to "newer" areas. Now, if the flow of immigrants shows a change in its ethnic composition over a certain period, the resultant of these two variations—one in space, the other in time—is a geographic segregation of ethnic groups. Thus, in São Paulo State the percentage of Italian and Spanish settlers decreases westward, for the bulk of these contingents arrived before the opening of the new lands. The Japanese, coming late, moved into the pioneering front, which at the time of their arrival lay considerably farther west (although many subsequently were to reflow to the city of São Paulo or the truck-farming belt around it).

Due to the breath-taking rapidity with which many regions of Latin America are changing, groups of immigrants disembarking at different times may end up not only in different areas, but, so to speak, in different sets of opportunities.

Furthermore, even though they belong to the same ethnic stock, come from the same country, and speak the same language, there

[26] Miguel Arrojado Lisboa, "O Problema das Sêcas," *Anais da Biblioteca Nacional do Rio de Janeiro*, XXXV (1913).

[27] Name given in the Brazilian Northeast to refugees driven from their homes by the recurrent droughts.

[28] Monbeig, *Pionniers et Planteurs de São Paulo*.

still is room for significant differences among the incoming groups. Some of these differences may be quite simple and have to do with their experience in the old country (for example, rural or urban background). Some may be more difficult to discern, as, for instance, the decision to become a permanent resident of the host country as opposed to the ambition to get rich and get out. But all such differences may find expression in the landscapes they create, a prime object of the geographer's concern. Obviously, they will also contribute to the image they create of themselves in the minds of the people around them. This image, nebulous matrix of so many prejudices, may vary considerably in time and space.

The ability of the Japanese or Nisei farmer today is generally recognized in Brazil, and the expression *"terra para japonês"* indicates a soil so poor that only the stubbornness of the Japanese can make it productive. And yet, at one time the Japanese immigrants were held by Brazilian public opinion to be "nomads," due to the rapid turnover observed in the *fazendas* as they moved on in search of better opportunities. In this respect, a report made during the 1920s by the Commission of Agriculture and Industries of the Chamber of Deputies viewed this ethnic group with disfavor for, among others, the following alleged reasons: (a) although the Japanese is an excellent worker, he does not set down roots on the coffee fazenda, and this is not advantageous to the country: (b) he is liable to run away in order to get out of complying with contracts; and (c) he prefers to live in a segregated group.[29]

An interesting area of research, indeed, is the influence upon the mobility of immigrants of such factors as the nature and fertility of soils, kind of crops (for example, perennial coffee, as opposed to annual cotton), and tenure framework (owners, as compared to renters). The "footloose," land-destroying Japanese of one area is blood brother to the careful, soil-conserving, terrace-building, manure-applying husbandman of another region.

An instructive comparison can also be made between the Italian "colono" of São Paulo and the Italian "colono" of Rio Grande do Sul: the same designation characterizes two entirely different

[29] Saito, *O Japonês no Brasil . . .* , p. 128.

situations. In Rio Grande do Sul, destination of the smaller and older stream of Italian immigrants, the colono is a freeholder. The Italians, who had been mainly renters back home, settled down in family-sized holdings, not far from German "colonies" in the same state. Although they did not seclude themselves as much as did the Germans, they nonetheless maintained their identity as a national group. Wheat farming had been initiated many years before but became important only after the arrival of the Italians; vineyards also came to be recognized as another typical feature of the Italian cultural landscape in Rio Grande do Sul. In view of the poor reputation of the farm cooperative movement in Brazil, the unusual number and vigor of cooperatives in the Italian zone—mostly related to the production of wine—is significant.[30]

In São Paulo, the Italian colonos were swept in by a second and larger current: bewildered and penniless immigrants, recruited in Italy by the large *fazendeiros* to pick up the hoe and other rudimentary farm implements which the Negroes dropped as, emancipated, they left the coffee *fazendas* and streamed toward the cities. In São Paulo the Italians did not constitute homogeneous and isolated groups; they were not regarded as settlers but merely as *braços*, arms without bodies, which could cultivate, plant, and harvest. Yet, by dint of much saving, a class of small landowners did emerge and, thanks to the value of the coffee crop, several erstwhile colonos were to make remarkable fortunes and contribute to the economic development of Brazil. One Italian-descended writer from Rio Grande do Sul feels, however, that these feats do not stand up to the solid middle-class achievements of the Italian colonos in his state, where "they conquered the land and attained a general prosperity which certainly is worth a lot more than the great accidental fortunes of the Crespis and Matarazzos" of São Paulo.[31]

Be that as it may, there are considerable differences in the results of Italian settlements in Rio Grande do Sul and São Paulo, and the

[30] Mem de Sá, "Aspectos Econômicos da Colonização Italiana no Rio Grande do Sul," in *Album Comemorativo do 75° Aniversário da Colonização Italiana no Rio Grande do Sul* (Porto Alegre, 1950).

[31] Ernesto Pellanda, "Aspectos Gerais da Colonização Italiana no Rio Grande do Sul," *Ibid.*, p. 42.

question remains regarding the extent to which several possible influences are responsible: differences in the Italian background of the immigrants; differences in the institutional slots into which they slipped in Rio Grande do Sul and in São Paulo, differences in time of coming and of opportunity, differences in crops, in markets, and so on.

Monbeig has pointed out how the precarious situation of the colono contributed to advancing the pioneering front across São Paulo and into Paraná State. One consequence of this advance was the partial disruption of existing social stratification. A considerable number of immigrants or their children, as we have seen, managed to acquire *fazendas*. On the other hand, every coffee crisis brought ruin to some *fazendeiros*, who became managers of somebody else's property or resigned themselves to the ownership of a small *sítio*. The cast of the frontier drama, as described by Monbeig, is complete: there is also the land surveyor who has become rich, has changed into a *fazendeiro*, and now owns automobiles and an airplane. And, of course, there is the small freeholder who is about to sell the parcel of land which he has toiled to develop and is destined to become a renter or sharecropper. Fortunes are unstable, for with the prevalent agricultural practices land quickly loses its value; as a matter of fact, it is not so much the land which represents wealth, but what the land produces: coffee or cotton, crops subject to the vagaries of world markets.[32]

In another frontier of settlement, the social evolution of a community free from Old World class stratification was observed by Jean Roche in his monumental study of the Germans in Rio Grande do Sul.[33] The struggle for survival, the poverty of the majority of the immigrants, and the magnitude of the task to be performed wiped out former social distances and developed a feeling of solidarity among the colonists, at least during the early days of their installation in the virgin forest. But, in the course of time, a new hierarchy was to emerge, based on the settlers' economic success in their new habitat.

[32] Monbeig, *Pionniers et Planteurs de São Paulo*, p. 145.
[33] Jean Roche, *La colonisation allemande et le Rio Grande do Sul* (Paris, 1959).

To conclude with Monbeig: the pioneer society is above all a dynamic society. This characteristic is intimately related to geographic dynamism, for fortunes are made and lost as new land is broken and brought into production.[34]

Possibly the fault is mine, but I find it rather difficult to delineate with sharp and orthodox contours the contribution geography can make to an interdisciplinary effort aiming at the study of race and class. By its nature, geography lies at the crossroads of many disciplines, and geographers risk the accusation of trying to be interdisciplinary in themselves, as it were. Nevertheless, I cannot help feeling that the study of man, culture, and environment forms a continuum. I suppose that I have been somewhat spoiled by the teaching of one "accustomed to attach very little importance to the boundaries which separate the sciences of man from each other more than is necessary." [35]

[34] Monbeig, *Pionniers et Planteurs de São Paulo*, p. 146.

[35] A reference to Carl O. Sauer by the eminent Latin-American historian, Tulio Halperín Donghi, "Storia e Storiografia dell'America Coloniale Spaniola," *Rivista Storica Italiana*, LXXVI (1964), 28.

Index

INDEX

INDEX

British:
 in Brazil, 58–63
 in Peru, 73, 79, 81, 83, 88–89, 93
British West Indies, 108
Brito Figueroa, Federico, 216
Buarque de Holanda, Sérgio, 277
Buenos Aires, Argentina, 30, 32, 34, 37, 39, 42, 84
Bunge, Carlos Octavio, 224
Burks, David, 239, 246
Busey, James, 240
Bustamente, Anastasio, 148

Caboclo, 260, 262, 264–67, 272, 275–76
Cabrera, Lucio, 189
Cadiz constitution, 207
Caja de Negroes, 17
Cajamarca, Peru, 74
Callao, Peru, 81, 83–85, 88, 94, 190
Calleja, Don Félix, 19
Cámara Barbachano, Fernando, 3
Campas, 92
Campinas, Brazil, 55
Campos, Brazil, 64–66
Canary Islands, 108, 113, 120
Canas, Peru, 192
Cândido, Antonio, 272
Candomblé, 49, 258, 262
Canelones, Uruguay, 48
Cañete Valley, Peru, 88
Capital investments, foreign, 174, 182, 239
Capitalism, 29, 43, 46–47, 122, 265, 270–71
Caracas, Venezuela, 280
Cardal, Battle of, 37
Cárdenas, Lázaro, 154
Cardoso, Fernando Henrique, 214, 268
Cardoso de Oliveira, Roberto, 264
Cargos, 177, 179
Carhuaz, Peru, 90, 93
Caribbean, 7, 217, 218, 221, 223, 227
Carneiro, Edison, 213
Carracedo, Orlando, 206–7
Carrera Damas, Germán, 204
Casa Grace y Cia, 81
Casa Grande Senzala, 215
Casasus, Joaquín, 150

Caso, Alfonso, 196
Castaldi, Carlo, 272
"Castas," 4, 22, 27, 145, 185, 201, 202, 205
Caste society, 4, 13–15, 18, 21–22, 25–27, 28–50, 150, 206–7
Caste War, 147, 181, 210
Castizos, 160, 165
Castro Pozo, Hildebrando, 189, 190, 191, 194
Catalans, 106
Catholicism, see Roman Catholic Church
Cattle farms, 102–3, 108, 172, 174, 193, 288
Caudillismo, 240
Ceará, Brazil, 64, 288
Censuses, 78, 83–84, 92, 128, 150–51, 201, 202, 283
Cerro de Pasco, Peru, 87
Cerro Largo, Uruguay, 49
Chacabuco, Argentina, 206
Chamberlain, Houston, 224
Chancal Valley, Peru, 90
Chanchamayo Valley, Peru, 88, 89
Charles III, 43
Chevalier, François, 6, 184–96
Chiapas, Mexico, 152, 155, 175, 180
Chiclayo, Peru, 89
Chihuahua, Mexico, 147, 151, 152
Chilapa, Mexico, 155
Chile, 30, 32, 80, 84, 192, 211, 214, 219, 224, 249, 250
 war with Peru, 76, 79, 85, 187
Chileans in Peru, 84–85, 91
Chinese:
 in Dominican Republic, 109
 in Peru, 82–83, 88–90, 93–95
Cholas, 90, 92
Chong Co., 89
Christensen, Asher N., 239
Christie, William Dougal, 60–61, 62
Christophe, Henri, 98
Cibao Valley, Dominican Republic, 104–6, 108, 117–18
Cimarrones, 20, 21, 33
Class and race, 231–55, 279–93
Class society, 3–4, 204, 272
 in Uruguay, 28–50

[297]

INDEX

INDEX

INDEX

[303]

INDEX